Real Estate Evolution:

The Ten Step Guide to (C.P.I.) - Consistent and Predictable Income for Real Estate Agents

By: Dan Rochon

REAL ESTATE EVOLUTION

Dan Rochon

Real Estate Evolution: The Ten Step Guide to (C.P.I.) – Consistent and Predictable Income for Real Estate Agents
Copyright 2020 © Dan Rochon
All Rights Reserved

Although the author and publisher have made every effort to ensure that the information in this book was correct at press time, the author and publisher do not assume and hereby disclaim any liability to any party for any loss, damage, or disruption caused by errors or omissions, whether such errors or omissions result from negligence, accident, or any other cause. This book is not intended as a substitute for legal or investment advice of lawyers, investment advisors, or accountants. The reader should regularly consult professionals in matters relating to the operating their stores, filing taxes, and investments. This book is intended as an educational resource and does not supplant legal or financial advice. All rights reserved. No part of this publication may be reproduced, distributed, or transmitted in any form or by any means without the written consent of the author.

Publisher: Absolute Author Publishing House
Editor: Brian Gawley
Interior Format Design: Dr. Melissa Caudle
Cover Design: Dan Rochon, Denzel Ramos, Frazier O'Leary, and Facebook friends of Dan. Thanks for your feedback!
Front cover photo: Paul Pavot
Back cover photo: Wilfredo Martinez
Illustrations: Monika Wnęk
IN-LIBRARY-OF-CONGRESS-PUBLICATION DATA

Real Estate Evolution: The Ten Step Guide to (C.P.I.)/Dan Rochon

   c. pm.

ISBN: 978-1-951028-63-3

    1. **REAL ESTATE**   **2. SELF-HELP**

PRINTED IN THE UNITED STATES OF AMERICA

REAL ESTATE EVOLUTION

Dan Rochon

Warning! If you do not want to improve, DO NOT read this book.

REAL ESTATE EVOLUTION

"Real Estate Evolution provides real estate agents new and old with valuable insight that will help you make more money. I wish I had this book when I started"

- Paul Pavot, Veteran Real Estate Agent

REAL ESTATE EVOLUTION

Dan Rochon

Table of Contents

Acknowledgment	xiv
Dedication	xviii
Preface	xx
Introduction	xxiv
Step 1: Flourish	1
Wherever You Are, Make a Start	2
Fighting your Demons	4
Be a Professional	7
Take Ultimate Responsibility	7
Master Communication	9
Persuade	10
The Pareto Paradox	13
Active Listening	14
If Yes, then How?	16
Deletion, Distortion, and Generalization	17
Develop Rapport	23
Hierarchy of Communication	26
The Pathway to Success	28
The Self Coaching Model	30

REAL ESTATE EVOLUTION

Reading 36
Your Big Why? 40
    Why do I do What I do? 41
Blind Faith vs. Absolute Faith 41
Study a Person of Excellence 41
Step 2: Look for Leads 43
    Gain Momentum 45
    Discipline Leads to Habit, Which Leads to Success 46
    Lead Generation is Your Priority 47
    Teach a Man to Fish, and You Feed Him for a Lifetime 48
    The Seven Habits of the Top Salespeople 50
        Habit 1 – Lead Generate Each Day 51
        Habit 2 – Time Block 51
        Habit 3 – Provide Massive Value to Others 56
        Habit 4 – Ask for Referrals Consistently 57
        Habit 5 – Start Early 57
        Habit 6 – Have the Right Mindset 57
        Habit 7 – Take Planned Breaks 60
    Where Do Leads Come From? 61
        Transactional vs. Relationship Marketing 61
        Prospecting Versus Marketing 62
        How Often are You Saying it? 63
        What are You Saying? 63
        Who are You Saying it to? 64
    Lead Generation Conclusion 97
Step 3: Focus on Conversion 98
    Proper Procedures for Intake and Conversion 99

Pipeline 100

Tracking Results 101

    Outcomes 102

Step 4: Nail Your Presentation 104

    The 80/20 Buyer Consultation 105

        The Pareto Paradox of the 80/20 Buyer Consultation 105

    Selling 360° – Listing Process 126

    The Shock and Awe Pre-Listing Consultation 127

    Prepare the Agreements 134

Step 5: Get Hired 136

    Procure the Buyer's Listing 138

    Take the Seller's Listing 140

Step 6: Connect the Buyer with the Seller 156

    Be a Fiduciary 157

    Buyers - Write an Offer that Gets Accepted 159

    Sellers – Get the Listing Ready for the Market 166

    Sellers – Officially on the Market 167

    Sellers – Accepting Offers 170

Step 7: Clear the Path for Closing 171

    Buyers 172

    Sellers 173

Step 8: Have Others Sing Your Praises 174

    Get Referrals 174

    Get Reviews 175

Step 9: Build, Support, and Guide Your Team 176

    Should I Build a Team? 176

    Understand Purposeful Leadership 177

- Build a Foundation 178
    - Gain Clarity About Your Values 179
    - Set the Vision 182
    - Understand Culture 183
    - Define the People 184
    - Create the Mission 184
    - Find and Hire the Right Talent 184
- Build Your Team 186
    - Assess. Gain Clarity. Move Forward. 186
    - ALWAYS Look for Talented People 186
    - Attract the Right People to You 187
    - Build a Bench 191
    - How do you Hire the Right Person? 192
    - Know the Traits of Success 192
    - Identify what Level of Talent you Seek 193
    - The Steps to Follow to Hire Talented People 194
    - Go Virtual 205
    - Acknowledge Your People 213
- Lead Your Team 214
    - About Working Together 215
    - Tips and Tricks 215
    - Retain Talented People 218
    - Leadership vs. Management 218
    - Standards and Accountability 220
    - About Training/ Coaching 221
    - Feedback Loop 225
- Step 10: Choose Profit 226

Next Step: The Evolution	230
The Speed of Change	230
Commoditization	240
What can you Control?	241
Conclusion	243
The Real Estate Agent's Hack	248
For Agents in Virginia, and the Mid-Atlantic Region	250
Mastermind Together on Social Media	259
Bonus Resources	262
Bibliography	264
About the Author	273

Acknowledgment

Writing a book is more complicated than I imagined and more fulfilling than I ever could have believed. None of this would have been possible without the help of my wife, Traci Rochon. You were the first person that I gathered the courage to ask to read the initial draft of the book. Not only did you offer specific advice on how I could best communicate the intended message, but you were also patient with me during those many late nights and early mornings that it took me to write. You have unwaveringly stood by me during every struggle and success.

I am eternally grateful to my mentor. You asked me to write this book so that real estate agents can have a guide to a predictable future. You are a role model of accomplishment. You care for the achievement and growth of others more than anyone could imagine. While I promised you that I would not use your name in the book -- I never promised not to thank you.

Thank you to my coaches, Luis Alpizar, John Vander Gheynst, and Tara Smith. Luis, you taught me how to build a foundation of a business and helped me define my vision. John, you helped me to understand that I already have everything I need to get whatever I want; thanks for helping me move the roadblocks that were in my way. Tara, you held me accountable for reaching my goals. I appreciate the partnership that you provided.

A very special thank you to Juleene Dela Cruz. You supported me in almost every area where I am flawed. You have been my right hand, left hand, right foot, and left foot. Without you, I would only be a torso and a head.

Thank you to Lee Beaver for the opportunity that you provided to me. Although the period of my life that followed had many ups and downs, I always have appreciated and supported you and followed your lead. Through the part of my life that I reported to you, I learned more about business and leadership than I thought was possible. Thanks to Mike Coffey for bailing me out when I screwed up the opportunity given to me by Lee. And thanks to Sheila Cuadros for helping to lead me on my newest adventure.

To Frazier O'Leary, I appreciate the many conversations we had during the time that I wrote. You helped me to formulate my thoughts in the best way possible. I also value that you told me the truth when I needed to hear critical feedback. You were a voice of reason to talk me out of using my mugshot photo on the cover of the book.

To Rich Peterson, Paul Pavot, Jonas Mitchell, and John Vilamill, your help in reviewing the early versions of the book helped me to view the content from perspectives that I previously did not consider.

To my Chief Marketing Officer, Nilesh Makhija, I am grateful that you relentlessly chased me down to offer me help to improve my online presence and get more real estate business using Social Media. I was initially reluctant to meet you because I fiercely guard my time and already had an active social media marketing plan in place. Somehow, you convinced me to meet, and when we did, I immediately understood that you have a much higher skill than just knowing how to manage Facebook ads effectively. You are an elite marketer. Thank you for your work in leading the promotion of this book. I am blessed to have met you.

I look forward to the future projects that we will work on together.

REAL ESTATE EVOLUTION

To my publisher, Dr. Mel Caudle, I am confident that you never expected that I would be such a difficult client. Your support and guidance to me as a first-time book author has been vital. I have learned a lot about the process from you.

Thank you to ALL from the Greetings Virginia Sales Network. You enable me to be the best version of myself in business that I can be. It is an honor to serve you. I am grateful that you are a part of our fantastic company, and that every day you give your best.

Finally, to my family, you are a part of my D.N.A., and I am who I am because of you.

Myrna Rochon (Mom), I imagine that as a single working mom, you must have been overwhelmed at times. I applaud your courage, and I am grateful for your dedication to raising Mike and me.

Mike Rochon (Brother), you are one of the few people that I know that works harder than me. You and I are more alike than not.

Frank Rochon (Dad), I am grateful that, as an adult, I have become closer to you. A lot of the qualities that you possess are inherent in me.

Dan Rochon

Dedication

To Traci,

You have believed in me since the first day of the 'Hello Kitty' toaster. Thank you for joining me on our journey.

Love,
Dan

To Maggie,

Always remember to,
Thank someone today.
Be grateful today.
Help someone today.
Have the best day of your life today.

Love,
Dad

Dan Rochon

Preface

Dear Reader,

If you're SERIOUS about growing your sales, specifically, if you're someone who's actively working to grow your real estate sales business, then this may be the most important book you'll ever read.

I say that because, in *Real Estate Evolution*, I'm going to teach you the specific steps for creating C.P.I. (Consistent and Predictable Income) in real estate sales, and I'm going to show you how to apply it to your own business.

I'm guessing that you bought this book because you are a real estate agent struggling to figure out where your next paycheck will come from, or you're currently at a standstill in your business and don't know what to do next.

You might have a deep fear of not being able to pay your bills -- including mortgage/rent, car payment, food, or taking care of your family's needs. You might dread having to go back to a 9-to-5 job or being an Uber driver part-time (or full-time!).

If you feel like you spend too many hours of your day trying to "figure out" how to make sales, instead of selling, then this book is for you. This book will help you whether you are new or experienced.

What you are about to read is a comprehensive guide to becoming a successful real estate agent. You will receive everything you will need to be a successful real estate agent and create C.P.I. in your business.

I have sold real estate since 2007 and have developed an immense amount of experience. During my journey, I witnessed hundreds (and maybe thousands) of agents fail in this business -- which I firmly believe is a shame.

A few years ago, I experienced a significant setback in my career. I had to sell the brokerage I had owned for more than ten years.

At the time, I was a little confused about the journey ahead of me. So, I contacted the most significant real estate mentor in the world and asked for his guidance. I decided that if he agreed to help me, I would follow every suggestion he shared.

He agreed to mentor me based on one condition. He told me to document all the steps I learned and share them with others.

So, after more than a decade of learning the real estate sales business, I wrote what I learned in the manual that you now hold in your hands.

I will show you the exact steps that I have used as a real estate agent, to sell one to 15 homes every month for the past 129 consecutive months during three shifting markets.

It took me more than two decades to learn the sales and persuasion techniques and more than one decade of mastering them in real estate sales to produce the content that makes up this book. It took more than a year to write (at the pace of three hours each day).

During my career, I have traveled the country attending hundreds of seminars and workshops seeking knowledge. I have paid more than $144,000 for coaches and much more than that on other curricula. I condensed much of what I know into the pages that follow in this book. When you study this guide, you will learn what I learned (without investing the time and money that I did).

To write the book, I first reviewed the numerous notebooks in which I had taken notes during the hundreds of classes I attended during my career. I sorted out the most vital pieces that I believed were relevant to every real estate agent, and then I wrote a lesson plan to teach the fundamentals.

I taught the course several times and recorded it after I felt it was well developed. I had the video transcribed, and then I took about three hours a day over the next thirteen months organizing the information in a manner that would be most useful for real estate agents.

REAL ESTATE EVOLUTION

This book offers you a clear path to follow and will result in you having absolute faith in your future. You will receive a game plan that you can replicate to have incredible success.

When you study and implement the program shared here, you will get clarity on how to achieve a consistent income. Becoming a successful real estate sales agent will no longer feel like an illusion or an unreachable goal.

When you have C.P.I., opportunities will start appearing for you. Best of all, you will have CERTAINTY.

When you follow the plan described in this book, you will...

> 1. No longer worry about how you will earn your next paycheck.
>
> You will have certainty in your business, which means you will have confidence that you can pay your bills. Your social status will increase. Your friends and family will see you as a success, and your children will see you as a good role model for business success. Other business people will value you and want to connect with you.
>
> 2. No longer wonder where you will find your next buyer or seller. This means that you will eliminate the anxiety that you feel about not knowing how you can provide for you and your family. You can embrace peace and confidence.
>
> 3. No longer worry about where the industry will go in the future.
>
> This means that you can comfortably move forward while the business evolves so that you can stay ahead of the already changed real estate sales landscape.

When you read this book, you'll notice that it is pretty comprehensive. (After all, didn't you find real estate sales to be harder and more complicated than you imagined before you got your license?)

I recommend that as you read, you push through to the end so that you obtain a broad knowledge of how to succeed.

After you finish, keep it on your bookshelf so that you can refer to it as a reference. (I promise that it will continue to be useful for you when you need help in a specific area of your sales business.)

Dan Rochon

As this book has A LOT to digest, many readers have told me that it is easier to listen to the audio and then take notes in the book. If you have not gotten the audiobook yet, let me help you out. I invite you to do so by visiting www.TheRealEstateEvolutionAudio.com.

While this guide is easy to read and follow, I'm also aware that you're going to need some help to implement the suggestions and strategies.

You do not have to figure out this stuff on your own.

My team and I are here to help you. I've created a free website, www.GetRockSolidCoaching.com, as a resource. You will find an abundant supply of tips, resources, and strategies on that website that are free. You'll also find VERY affordable online classes that you can access to help walk you through the way to C.P.I.

I invested my time, knowledge, and money into writing this book because the real estate business has helped me to live the life I want, and I am passionate about helping you do the same.

To your success!

Dan Rochon

Clifton, VA

February 26, 2020

Introduction

Are you a real estate agent who wants to sell more homes and earn a more consistent income?

Did your broker promise to guide you, and let you down?

You might want to see more results in your business. Perhaps you seek more certainty.

Are you looking for training that teaches you precisely what you need to do to **sell more homes**?

This business can **scare the shit out of you**. It can be frightening.

You already know that you will either spend each night away from your family and friends helping your clients, or worse, you may have few clients. You struggle and wonder, "Where will I get my next prospect?

"How will I pay my mortgage or rent, feed my family, feed myself?

"How will I overcome my struggles?"

You might need your business to grow fast so you can pay your bills, take an extended vacation, provide great things for your kids, or make other things happen in your life.

For many, a career in real estate offers the chance to be your own boss. That goal is often a motivating determinant for those who want to get out from under the confines of a nine-to-five job.
Other people desire to be part of a service that helps others to achieve their dreams or solve their real estate-related problems.

Most agents do not follow a strategy. Seldom do they see a clear pathway. They have no clue where to go, what to do, and require proper guidance and a real plan.

Many **people new to the business will sell fewer than two homes their first year**, and most likely, those will sell to a family member.

The hardest time as a real estate sales agent is during the first six months, because of the lag between our activity and payday. During this period, you work hard to grasp the basics. Simultaneously, you need to shift your energy to find the business so you can pay your bills.

It is tough for most to see their way through month after month after month of effort and notice no wages during the starting phase (trust me, I was there.)

Experienced agents might sell 15 to 36 homes annually and have very little time to do much else. If this is you, you might feel guilty, as you are not available for other activities. Maybe you are glued to the phone most of the time and even sneak in a negotiation while you are supposed to be watching your kid's soccer game (I have been there too).

Have you tried forming a team and realized that building a team takes a different skill than sales? You must learn how to hire, lead, train, and motivate. A few skilled agents can sell 100+ homes with the help of a team.

Right now, **you might be riding the roller coaster of sales.** One month you're up and the next you're down. When you think that you have it all figured out, you find yourself rushing to the bottom of the hill. You hear a big, loud, "BOOM!" as you slam into the ground.

You get up, dust yourself off, and ask yourself, "Now what?"

REAL ESTATE EVOLUTION

You could ask your broker for help. He or she may or may not be able to give you the right plan to lead you to a predictable future. Their advice might be sketchy.

You could attend a seminar and reach deep into your pocket to pay for the education. But that will take time and money, and they very likely will try upselling you on another program that you cannot afford.

There are a million and one things to do when it comes to real estate sales, and sometimes everything outside of your job description can get in your way of creating results and a predictable stream of adequate income.

You might not have the clarity to solve these problems because you're busy paying your bills and trying to do everything yourself. If this problem goes unsolved, you might have no choice but to go back to a nine-to-five job in another industry or continue the pattern of receiving inconsistent, sporadic compensation.

You probably seek a level of convenience and simplicity more than ever and secretly pray for a simpler and more comfortable life.

Eighty-seven percent of all real estate agents fail within their first five years in the business. (1) That's because they run out of money, get too distracted, or don't have the guidance or mentorship they need to succeed.

If you are new to real estate sales, the odds are you will fail.

Why do so many agents fail?

Sometimes people get into the business for the wrong reasons.

They misperceive easy money is to be made – and lots of it. The average real estate agent earns about $40,000 a year, and real estate sales is one of the hardest (not Alaskan crab boat fisherman hard, but emotionally hard) professions in the world. (2)

Selling real estate is not for everybody; in fact, it is not for most.
Another reason so many agents fail is they do not work hard enough. Perhaps they watched one too many HGTV shows that glamorized

the industry. They do not understand that they are operating a business, and just like any business, it takes considerable effort to succeed.

Many agents work real estate part-time. Mostly, this is a bad idea because it takes an extraordinary effort to learn the market and techniques needed for success. If those people who sell real estate full-time probably won't make it, what do you think the odds are that you will succeed as a part-time agent? There are a few exceptions to this rule.

Most do not have their goals defined or a plan of action. And as Hall of Fame baseball catcher, Yogi Berra, said, "If you don't know where you are going, you might wind up someplace else." (3)

Many real estate agents are not qualified to the level that they ought to be. **No significant educational options are available that are designed to raise the standard for real estate agents**.

The lack of agent know-how is a danger that, if not fixed, will be damaging to both the real estate industry and to the home buyers and sellers who rely on guidance from those agents.

The barriers to entry to becoming a real estate sales agent are low.

As a result of the vast gap of knowledge, skillset, and competency needed to succeed, and the number of people who lack the requirements to be successful and pass over the low entrance barriers, many will not triumph

In real estate school, they seldom (unless you were a student of mine) tell you that after you graduate, you will be starting a lead generation business specializing in real estate sales.

Regardless of the industry, **all companies need to generate clients**. If you are not comfortable seeking buyers and sellers to help, you will be disabled; your best option would be to join a brokerage or a team that will feed you the leads – and this hardly would guarantee your success.

REAL ESTATE EVOLUTION

Suppose you don't get a steady pipeline of sellers or buyers, and the cash runs out, causing an entire series of issues. (Yep, I have been there as well.)

You don't want that to happen. That is bad. You need to develop the right plan now, and you don't have time for anything else.

You have discovered this book, which will guide you to tackle these issues and lead you on your way to reliable closings month after month while meeting your own and your client's goals.

Thank you for investing your time in reading this. My name is Dan Rochon. I've been selling real estate for more than a decade.

I have spent years studying sales techniques, business tactics, and persuasion skills so I may help people to solve problems or achieve their goals. I have worked in a sales, coaching, or business leadership role since my first job as a young teenager in 1986.

I am known as the teacher of agents. Throughout the years, I have had the privilege of teaching hundreds of real estate agents to get their license. (This is NOT a case of, "If you can't do, teach" -- it is an "I love what I do, so teach" situation). I have coached new agents, aspiring rainmakers, and the top agents in the business.

I have learned from world-class leaders, such as Gary Keller and others, and my own experience. I have gone from being a waiter to a successful business owner (with many failures along the journey).

I have been a broker, and I owned a large real estate brokerage. I had the opportunity to learn a lot from the agents I served while I was in the role of a brokerage owner.

I'm an associate broker in Virginia, and a full-fledged broker in Maryland and my team also serves Washington DC. I have spent my entire real estate career helping sellers and buyers and assisting agents to be successful, and I can help you be successful too.

For the past 129 consecutive months as a real estate agent, I have had at least one closing (and as many as 15 in a month). My business has been consistent and predictable.

Today, as the owner of the **Greetings Virginia Sales Network,** headquartered in Falls Church, VA, I lead our real estate sales team to be sure our clients receive the best service and that we exceed clients' expectations.

I get the chance to perfect expert knowledge about financing, neighborhoods, schools, and homeownership issues. I profoundly understand topics such as lead generation and lead conversion. Also, I have studied the economics of a real estate agent's actions that lead to results, and, generally, how to be successful in real estate sales.

The knowledge I have gained allows me to guide my team and to provide a group of leaders to help them counsel home buyers and sellers to achieve their goals or solve their problems.

You already have the information you require to succeed; you need to unlock it from your blind spots. This book will help you access what you need to know.

I have trained in the specialty area of neurolinguistic programming and hypnosis. Don't worry – I'm not going to try to make you cluck like a chicken (unless you are into that sort of thing), but I will explain to you strategies about how you can create desire, urgency, and help others to decide.

This book is different from other real estate sales books. It shares the specific systems and processes necessary to succeed. It describes a plan to get the leads in place for you to succeed. It is written by a successful agent who is active in the field, helping buyers and sellers every day. You will learn about each step of the sales process.

This book is a **Step by Step guide about HOW to make real estate sales**. It reveals the secrets that you need to know. It will show you the way to **C.P.I.** (*Consistent, Predictable Income.*)

What you hold in your hands is not based on theory. I have documented decades of learning, failing, and succeeding, and poured the lessons that I have learned into this book. It is a proven guide to how you can achieve excellent results in real estate sales.

REAL ESTATE EVOLUTION

In this book, I will share the lessons I have learned through the years. I will teach you how you can have certainty and predictability as a real estate agent. I will outline strategies to be more productive.

The more you study this guide, the more obvious it will become that you are destined to achieve success. The truth of how to succeed as a real estate sales agent is right in front of you.

During my career, I have learned that to achieve predictable closings each week, there are ten areas of importance. I will share each of these priorities in this book. They are:

- Develop Personally (Flourish)
- Look for Leads
- Convert the Leads to an Appointment (Focus on Conversion)
- Give a Great Presentation (Nail it!)
- Get Hired
- Get Under Contract (Connect the Buyer and Seller)
- Get to a Successful Closing (Clear the Path)
- Get Referrals and Reviews (Have Others Sing Your Praises)
- Build, Support, and Guide Your Team
- Choose Profit

When you read this book, you'll benefit from receiving:

- A guide to having a career track to earn a six-figure income
- Description of a proven system of doing business predictably to allow you to sell more homes and to net more money
- Action plans to follow
- Social media strategies
- Marketing strategies
- Web management strategies
- Prospecting strategies
- Scripts
- Communications techniques that the pros use
- A proven follow-up system
- Facebook advertising strategy to generate a massive amount of leads
- Tools to allow for systematic tracking of client opportunities

- A plan to create constant, continuous, high-quality leads
- How to convert those leads
- What to do to prepare for your appointments
- An explanation of how to use the most effective presentation materials
- Strategies to use pre-listing packages to get hired
- Guide to listing administration
- Systems to help you track your goals and the progress made toward reaching them.
- Database management strategies
- Transaction management strategies
- Client appreciation events suggestions
- A guide on how to use video marketing
- Ideas on how to develop your leadership
- A description of the importance of vendor relationships
- Step-by-step, simple, straightforward strategy
- Blueprint on how to get real, qualified leads
- A plan to increase your reputation
- An approach to have certainty
- Advice from the TOP 1% of 1% agent
- More

When you effectively apply the tools and strategies taught in this book, you will be confident in your future. You will have clarity in your ability to make deals happen and to help your clients.

I will show you EXACTLY what to do. I will divulge to you the way to consistent and predictable income.
You can execute a new approach when you act on the strategies described in this book. I will give you a game plan that you can replicate to have absolute success.

When you study and implement the program shared, you will have clarity on how to achieve a consistent income. Becoming a successful real estate sales agent will no longer be an illusion.

The first eight steps of this curriculum will apply to everybody who sells real estate. During these sections, you will learn a step by step process to implement. You will find a plan that is easy and reliable.

REAL ESTATE EVOLUTION

Step 9: Build, Support, and Guide Your Team will apply to you if you run a team, want to build a team, or if you currently work in a group. The Team Building section will give you a good understanding of how to organize a successful and productive real estate sales team.

During the section on Team Building, you will learn about the first building blocks to create any business. These parts apply to the real estate sales business, and they are:

- Lead generation (which is so important that I devote an entire section to it)
- Organization building
- Leadership

I will share specific directions for each of the business building ingredients mentioned above.

Are you aware that the real estate sales industry is experiencing an evolution? Do you realize how to triumph from this shift?

In the last section of this book, I will discuss the future of our industry and the Fourth Industrial Revolution that is occurring. I will share about Big Data, technology, Artificial Intelligence, and the evolution that is happening, and how you can benefit in this sea of change.
The content given to you is a transcript of many real estate sales classes that I have written and taught and a few stories about my life that I will share with you.

Last year, I met an agent, Sara, who attended one of our live workshops.

Six months after attending, Sara called me to brag that she had **sold 17 homes** during that half-year period. **Before attending the event, she had sold zero homes.** After she came to the class, she maintained an empowering mindset, committed herself 100%, and implemented the actions required.

One agent worked part-time while being the manager of a major retail shopping center, and still closed 21 transactions in a single year as a result of using the strategies described here.

Richard joined the **Greetings Virginia Sales Network** five weeks ago, and he took his fifth listing yesterday. Before Rich joined us, he was a part-time agent who worked as a leader full-time in our industry. Rich has the experience to succeed yet has not been a full-time agent for many years.

Agents who have read this book or attended one of our live coaching courses have given positive feedback.

Here is feedback from students who have attended those courses:

"Dan is a fantastic instructor with a strong knowledge of the topics, reflecting his prior experience as a salesperson and broker. Lessons involved class discussions and stories." -Greg R.

"Dan is a great instructor. He makes the course material easy to understand, with explanations and real-life examples. He is always punctual and professional and is very knowledgeable. I would highly recommend taking any class taught by Dan." - Mike G.

"Dan Rochon is absolutely a fabulous instructor! He was fun, made things easy to remember, and had a knack for making the driest concepts interesting. I hope he continues to be an instructor, so more people can have an experience like I did." - Robert C.

Use this book as a guide to your journey. I guarantee that if you implement the content of this book, it will make a positive difference in your life and business.

When you finish reading this book in its entirety, let me know what you learn and email me at Info@GreetingsVirginia.com with the subject line, 'Aha's.' or hit me up on social media. When you follow me on Facebook and apply to join **Rock Solid Real Estate Agents** by **Greetings Virginia Sales Network** on Facebook, I will be a source for you. I read all my emails, and I promise I will reply (typically in a day or two).

REAL ESTATE EVOLUTION

In this book, I am transparent about challenges and successes I have experienced as a real estate agent and business owner. I hold nothing back, even about tough times, of which there have been many. I describe the systems we've built and share the tools, scripts, and best practices that we employ.

Resources we've used that couldn't fit into the book are available for download at www.GetRockSolidCoaching.com/free-resources.

You will learn the actionable steps that you can execute in your business to get to the next level.

I don't believe there is only one way to succeed; I do think there are best practices that you can replicate. I focus on fundamental truths and the principles of building a business. When you study this book, you no longer will be in the dark.

If you want to improve yourself, make more money, and you feel you can do more, this book is for you. You will have the tools that you need to get into motion.

So, if you're like me and desire to learn more, keep reading, you will learn the latest strategies to:

- Generate qualified seller leads
- Attract qualified buyers
- Convert more leads to appointments
- Get full commission on your listings
- Win listing presentations more often
- Systematize your administrative processes
- Gain more reviews

Here are a couple of FAQs that Agents Ask

I am just getting my license. Does it make sense for me to read this?

I suggest you focus your time and energy on studying to get your license and then read this book. The test is much harder than you think (ask any agent, and they will tell you).

Is this book written for only experienced agents?

No, I wrote this for all agents, and many of the concepts can apply to most any other business. I wrote this for you.

I do not want to build a team. Should I read this book?

Absolutely! There is much information shared that will help you in all areas of sales and business development.

If I want to build a team, will the information in this book guide me?

Yes, it will show you the foundational pieces to properly hire, agree on expectations, and hold each other accountable to those expectations, train, and lead.

Is there help online that can guide me to solve a specific problem?

There is! Imagine having access to the top real estate agents in the world who authentically share concrete strategies with you.

My team and I talk to the top agents in the world, and they divulge what makes them successful. You can view those conversations when you watch our YouTube channel, www.YouTube.com/RockSolidRealEstateCoaching.

In fact, when you **subscribe to our YouTube channel**, the conversations I have with the smartest people in our industry will show up in your activity feed.

You will learn how they achieved their eminence with the least amount of effort. You can implement the strategies that these icons will teach you.

People who read this book often, **SUBSCRIBE TO**:

www.YouTube.com/RockSolidRealEstateCoaching and 'Like' the videos that they value and comment. I invite you to check out the interviews that I host with the most impressive people in the real estate sales world which are posted there.

Apply to join our Facebook Group and join the live conversation with other high-minded real estate agents like you.

You may find us at www.Facebook.com/groups/RockSolidAgents/.

Feel free to ask and answer any questions on the forum. It is a support system for you.

Wouldn't you want to take one short step toward financial freedom now than wonder how you will earn your next commission check? Experience shows that sales agents who engage with the Facebook group and view the conversations on YouTube sell more homes than those who do not.

Is this book hard to comprehend?

This book is easy to read and understand.

I will share information with you that you probably do not know that you do not know. As you read, you will realize that success as a real estate agent is easier than you ever imagined.

The purpose of this book is to guide you to fulfill your potential, reach all your goals, and help you learn to be the best person you can be. I will offer ideas to support you to be able to sell more homes and earn a more consistent income.

My greatest desire is for you to succeed at a massive level. I will help you. Will you help me to help you?

You're not the type of person who would waste their time reading a book and not act. I know this because you would not have gotten even this far in the book if you were. When you take the steps suggested in this book, you will have more certainty and consistency in your career.

When you implement the tactics that you learn, you will join the tribe of evolved agents who had gone before you and obtained predictability and growth in their sales business.

As you sit here reading this, you no doubt already have gained more confidence in what your vision of your future.

Once you read this book and learn the systems and processes, you will be set up to net more money than ever before. You will understand how to profit from your business.

Real estate agents can use the methods described without a doubt. You easily could read this book and recommend it to a friend in real estate sales who you care about.

Will this book change your life as a sales agent? Read on, and you be the judge.

My team and I have sold thousands of homes, and this is how we do it.

To your success!

Dan Rochon

Step 1: Flourish

To distinguish yourself as a successful real estate agent and to obtain **C.P.I.**[*], you will need strong roots.
    First, you must focus on your personal development and chiseling the person you want to become.

Take charge of your success, *across all areas of your life.*

Who you are as an individual will impact every aspect of your business. So, choose to flourish.
    Choose to be the best mom or dad possible, the best niece, nephew, sister, brother, daughter, or son.
    Commit to living the best possible version of your life, and embody that life, every single day.

---

[*] C.P.I. = When I reference (C.P.I.), I will remind you of the meaning so that you remind yourself of why you are taking the steps prescribed in this book, which is to obtain Consistent, Predictable Income.

If you want to be a millionaire, take the very same actions as those who have become self-made millionaires.

Do the work. Dream bigger. Decide who you want to be and *take intense action*.

If your desire is to be a profitable and successful real estate agent, make that decision today!

I stress the importance of acting now because I wish that I had a guide to help me to do this years ago.

When I was in my early 20s, my existence lacked meaning.

I had no solid core to build upon; I was lost and destructive.

I abused alcohol and was a horrible husband to my first wife, Lynsey.

A man will often blame his ex-wife for the demise of their marriage.

With me, I knew that I had screwed up – royally!

If you are young, do not misspend your early years. Use this time to gain a competitive advantage in your life. If you are older, choose to get at it now; you have less time!

Wherever You Are, Make a Start

In my late 20s and early 30s, I worked as a waiter at the highest-end steakhouse in Washington, DC.

Senators, lobbyists, and celebrities would meet there to win over and impress each other, dined on $85 dry-aged porterhouse steaks and drank $350+ bottles of Bordeaux wine.

After 9 p.m., the back-dining area would become congested with the light blue fog of cigar smoke. I would overhear conversations that would be broadcast in the breaking news section of "The Washington Post" the next day.

On those rare slow days, we would glance at the televisions hanging above the giant wrought-iron eagle that guarded the kitchen entryway and watch the talking heads spit insults as if they were main characters in the Hatfield–McCoy conflict. The previous night, those same combatants cordially had dined together at the same table.

I earned a lot of money, but I hated my job.

My vision for the future was clouded; I could see where I wanted to go, yet I had no idea how to get there.

I wanted to be a business owner and to help people.

I was determined to find a way to buy or start a company. I met with business brokers, attended franchise fairs, and had lunch with owners of businesses who intended to sell. My efforts created no real opportunities. **I continued to search.**

The only clear conclusion this amounted to was that I did not have nearly enough money to start a business.

So, I pleaded with relatives to loan me the money that was needed. Their reception was less than warm – they told me to go to a bank.

I went to the bank. They wanted a little thing called "collateral" to lend me a quarter to half a million dollars. Silly banks!

I had no assets to guarantee payment.

I was devastated and confused. I had no real mentors at the time, and I felt alone.

While I was figuring out what to do and how to leave my miserable life of working in restaurants behind me, my girlfriend Traci's brother (who later became my brother-in-law) Dan Adler, invited us to go sailing.

The wind whipped across the bow, and the waves lapped against the craft as we sailed across the deep Chesapeake Bay. I recall that the sun shined brightly.

A couple of hours into the journey, Dan asked me, "Has Traci introduced you to the Landmark Forum?"

I noticed Traci cringe at the question.

"The Landmark, what?" I replied.

Soon after the conversation on the boat, I enrolled in the three-day course that Traci's brother had suggested. I was still unsure of what to expect, but hey, if it was good enough for Dan, it was good enough for me.

At the time, I was a tad bit jealous of Dan. He was just a few years older than me, prosperous, and a person I perceived to be successful in many other respects. I was willing to follow any advice that he offered.

I realized soon after signing up for the class Dan had recommended that some called it a cult. Others called it a personal development curriculum. I found it to be a bit of both and chose to embrace the benefits it offered and leave the rest.

REAL ESTATE EVOLUTION

Traci later shared with me that the recoil I had seen in her face when her brother had mentioned the forum was because she knew that if I took the path that her brother had suggested, I would know to call her on her stuff. Perhaps this was eventually the case, but more importantly, my life changed soon afterward.

Fighting your Demons

As frivolous as it might seem looking back, my greatest fear about taking the Landmark curriculum was they asked me not to drink alcohol during the long weekend session.

I could not dream of abstaining for that long.

At the time, I was what you might call 'a functioning alcoholic.' As I recall, I believe that it would have been best if I was nonfunctioning. At least that way, I would have been forced to make different choices sooner.

Each day, I would wake up dehydrated, with a splitting headache. As the throbbing pain pounded my head, I would weakly utter, "I will not drink today. I will not drink today. I will not drink today."

I half-believed my incantation. I would then chug a cold glass of water, brush my teeth, take a hot shower, and head to the posh steakhouse in DC to attend our 10:30 a.m. shift meeting and then start serving food and drink for the next 14 hours.

Typically, I would lag through most of the day at the restaurant, and then my head would usually clear sometime around 7:00 PM. By 10:00 PM, I would find salvation in my first sip of wine or beer. On most nights, I would drink about a 12-pack of beer and two bottles of wine and then pass out until the next morning.

I managed to not drink during the Landmark class. I didn't know it at the time, but this was my first peek into understanding that I could design my own life.

A few weeks after graduating, I had resumed my daily drinking, yet I knew I was close to making the decision to change.

My last hurrah was epic.

Well, it was epic until I experienced the aftermath.

I woke up balled up on the floor of the master bathroom in our three-bedroom townhome in Alexandria, VA. I had ejected the contents of my stomach long ago and was down to the dry heaves.

My kidneys shrieked with piercing, sharp pain, and my head reverberated with agony. My mouth was parched; no amount of water would hydrate me soon enough.

I waited for hours for a small reprieve. The fetal position was the only arrangement that I could provide a bit of rest.
It was a time for a change.

That day, I got sober. I choose to create my destiny. I went to rehab.

The withdrawal I experienced during the first few months without a drink was so painful that I never wanted to experience those days again.

Early in sobriety, I understood that I would spend the rest of my life free of alcohol. And this time, my pronouncement never to drink again was real.

Today, I consider the most critical decision that I ever made was to stop drinking. I cherish my sobriety more than any other asset that I have. I place it in front of all else. Because I realize that if I ever drink again, I will lose every other gift I possess.

When I attended rehab, I learned many things about myself and addiction. I learned that my emotional age did not match my physical age. Emotionally, I was not very mature, and in many ways, I had acted like a rebellious teen rather than a grown man.

> **Everything that you want is on the other side of fear.** – Jack Canfield

It took me more than a third of a century to grow up, but I was now rapidly evolving.

I started to understand that I could step outside of my comfort zone.

I realized I could be motivated by "Choose to" rather than "Have to."

Now that I had experienced a new relationship with my health through sobriety, I knew I could conquer whatever obstacle was set in front of me and achieve any worthy goal.

I revisited my desire to be a business owner and began to consider real estate sales as an option.

I found out that to get started in real estate, I would have to take and pass a 60-hour licensing course. I would need about $2,000 –

which was far less than the money required for any other business. And the amount of money I could earn in return as a real estate sales agent was unlimited. I liked the idea that I would get compensated for my efforts.

Yet, I still was scared.

It was late 2007, and "foreclosures," "credit crisis," "worst economy ever," "government bailout," were the buzz words on everyone's lips. With little thought about the economy and with ample faith that I would flourish, I enrolled in a pre-licensing school.

In November of 2007, I got my real estate sales license.

I had many fears at the time. I dreaded failure. I was entering a new venture in which I had no experience, and I shrank at the thought of being judged by others.

While I was scared, I knew I was destined to be an entrepreneur. I had now found a way.

During this phase, I started to blossom.

My emotional growth began to accelerate.

I learned that self-actualization is the basis for success in any area of life.

I understood that personal development is the foundation of success.

For you to achieve success as a real estate agent, you will have to grow.

Growth is crucial because your business will only grow to the extent that you do.

As a real estate agent, your number one resource is your mind; this is your toolbox.

You deliver your wisdom through communication using the words that you say, the tonality, inflection, and volume of your voice as well as with your physiology, and the rapport that you create with potential clients.

As you begin to flourish, these will all evolve.

But first, you must start.

Be a Professional

Being a real estate sales agent is easily comparable to being an athlete.

Some are weekend amateurs that seldom play. Some people are professionals that get paid millions of dollars to perform.

Compare yourself to a racing car driver.

When an expert racing car driver has the intuition to pinpoint what makes their car screech or notices that it is too loose when entering a corner or too tight coming off the turn, they help the crew make better decisions so that they win more often.

If you want to win in real estate sales, you must be a professional.

Take the time to study your craft deeply and become an expert.

Agents who master the techniques described in this book have noticed that they live an exceedingly abundant life, sell more homes, and earn a more consistent income.

> "You either allow or create everything that happens to you."
>
> -Jack Canfield

Take Ultimate Responsibility

Have you ever been in the office and overheard a water cooler conversation about the thousands of reasons an agent is struggling?

They always say things like:

"The other agent didn't return my call."

"The home inspector asked for a roof replacement."

"My broker doesn't care about me."

"It's the loan officer/ escrow agent/ cooperating broker/ client's fault."

REAL ESTATE EVOLUTION

"The other agent cut their commission to get the listing."

"Zillow is dominating the search."

The complaints go on and on.

Take Responsibility.

I'd encourage you to consider that 100% of what occurs to you is a result of your thoughts and actions, even when the outcome seems entirely outside of your control.

You can either take charge of your existence or continue to believe that life 'happens' to you.

My suggestion is to accept **Personal Responsibility** for your life and if you want to live the very best existence, take **Ultimate Responsibility**.

Personal Responsibility means that you are accountable for your actions. You design your life. **Ultimate Responsibility** means that you accept that **EVERYTHING** that occurs in your life is your creation.

When you shift your responsibility for all, you will have **Ultimate Responsibility**.

I understand that it might be hard to accept that we are responsible for **EVERYTHING** in our lives.

Envision driving in circles around the Wal-Mart parking lot seeking a space that does not exist. You are responsible for the fact that there are no spaces.

"What?!?! How could that be? How can I possibly be responsible for no parking space being available?" you may ask.

Could you have left your previous destination earlier to arrive at a time when parking slots were readily available?

You will be amazed at the results you witness when you accept that you are 100% responsible for anything that happens to you in your life.

When you take **Ultimate Responsibility**, you will seek solutions to all scenarios.

When you approach life as if you are accountable for all, you will have more control over your destiny and create better results.

If you're still doubtful, try it on for a week and consider the results. How many of the events that occur in your life are direct or indirect results of actions you took?

Which actions can you personally take to gain a different outcome next time?

Other actions you could take

These are actions you could take immediately to enhance your life:

- Be honest with yourself and with others. When you make a mistake, admit it emphatically.
- Be genuine. Be empathetic and place yourself in the other person's shoes.
- Praise others for what they do well and refrain from criticism. If you do have to mention critical feedback to another person, remember that a barber lathers a man before he shaves him. Seek first to find positive input and then share vital and specific strategies they could implement in order to improve.

Master Communication

Life coach Tony Robbins says, "To effectively communicate, we must realize that we are all different in the way we perceive the world and use this understanding as a guide to our communication with others." (1)

The keys to a great connection with another person are:

1. Be in rapport.
2. Ask adept questions.
3. Listen. Listen. Listen.

To reach a high level of communication, give your undivided attention to the other person. Make communication central to the interaction. Eliminate opportunities for distractions from your phone, text, and email, as well as intrusions from co-workers or other people. If you are making phone calls, stand up to increase your energy levels. Use earbuds so you can use your hands to write notes. Remove yourself from loud environments.

The way you speak is often more important than the words that you say.

Mastering communication will take you far in engaging with and securing clients and prospects.

Persuade

The foundation of sales is communication. **When you can persuade, you will be most effective.**
Dr. Robert Cialdini is an author, Regents' Professor Emeritus of Psychology and Marketing at Arizona State University and a keynote speaker on influence (2). He wrote the books, *Influence*, and *Pre-suasion*, where he documents how to best influence others.

In his work, Cialdini explains seven methodologies that you can use to persuade others which are:

- Reciprocation
- Commitment and consistency
- Social proof
- Liking
- Authority
- Scarcity
- Unity

Reciprocation

When was the last time that someone held the door open for you? What did you do when you got to the next doorway? Did you keep it free for the person who held yours open? If you did, you were fulfilling the law of reciprocity.

When a person does you a favor, you often will feel obligated to help them in return.

I go on a lot of listing appointments. From time to time, a prospective seller will miss an interview. When this happens, I know that if the seller genuinely missed the meeting rather than is taking action to avoid me, I will most likely get hired because they will feel the obligation to reciprocate an affirmative response to negate the negative.

You can use reciprocation to help your negotiations. When you ask for a significant concession and the other person turns you down, you can then ask for a smaller courtesy. It is much more likely that the other person will comply with the more modest request.

It is natural for people to want to return a favor.

Commitment and Consistency

Think of climbing a staircase from a small request to a larger one.

Later today, I am scheduled to meet a buyer who is an older lady. She is not comfortable with technology and has had challenges getting documents to her lender so that she may qualify to get a loan. I offered to meet her and help her scan the materials. She has not yet hired me, yet it will be a natural progression for her to do so after we get her qualified to buy through the lender.

Often in online sales, the concept of commitment and consistency is paired with reciprocation. A marketer will offer you something for free and then, in return, ask for you to buy a small upsell. The seller will then make a higher and higher request as you, 'walk-up' the sales ladder. You will often walk-up the stairs to be consistent in your behavior.

A way that you could use this in real estate sales is to ask for a consumer to leave a positive review for you and your services. When they do this, they are then committing to you being their agent and will likely remain consistent in their relationship with you. Often, they will find evidence to suggest that you are their person and fight with others to claim the connection.

Social Proof

Getting testimonials from your clients is a critical component to other people deciding to do business with you. When others say that you are a good guy or gal, then you must be right.

Prospective clients will always look at your reviews and online presence.

Take time to build your reputation by posting informational videos and content that will demonstrate your expertise.

Liking

Mark Zuckerberg understood the concept of liking so well that he became a billionaire as a result of implementing it. When people like you or you are like them, they will more likely agree with you.

REAL ESTATE EVOLUTION

A script that you could use when facing an objection is, "I understand your concern. You are LIKE ME. I would feel the same way. Others in your position have felt these challenges. I had found that when they implemented this solution..."

Authority

When people view you as an authority, they will more likely follow your advice. Having knowledge and experience and being able to competently communicate what you know to another is a great way that you can use an authority in your relationships and have more influence.

I have two friends who are doctors. I very much respect the time that they invested to earn the academic degrees that allow them to use the title Doctor. When I introduce them to others, I always do so while including their titles. As a result, my doctor friends gain instant credibility to those introductions.

Scarcity

"Limited time offer," "only five left," are examples of the concept of using scarcity in sales. Having few opportunities or options is a compelling way to influence because it appeals to the fear of loss in another.

When you show a home for sale to a buyer, and you have knowledge that there are multiple buyers interested in the house, you can influence your buyer to present a better offer because your buyer will be afraid to lose the deal. People will tend to pay a higher price for a service or product when they perceive a limited supply.

Unity

Everybody wants to belong to a tribe. We tend to take pride in our nationality, peer groups, affiliations, sports teams, and friends. When we relate to a group, we feel something bigger than ourselves.

Being unified with others allow us to take pride in our identities — online businesses such as Nextdoor gain so many participants as a result of appealing to our neighborhood identity.

People naturally want to belong. It is also why **Facebook groups** such as **Lab Coat Agents**, **Rock Solid Real Estate Agents,** and others gain so many people to participate.

When working with a buyer, you could emphasize the sense of unity by highlighting the charm of unique neighborhoods, cities, or other locales.

When you are working with a client or prospective client, take the time to find commonalities of identity? Did you go to school together? Were you both in the military? Are you both a swimmer or a runner? When you find these commonalities, you will create a natural rapport and connection.

Seek areas of unity when connecting with others, and you will find better sales results.

The Pareto Paradox

Vilfredo Pareto was an Italian economist who noticed that twenty percent of the pods in his garden produced eighty percent of the peas.

Pareto went on to observe his local economy. He recognized that twenty percent of the people owned eighty percent of the land and wealth in Italy. He noticed these ratios of effort to outcome time and time again, across various circumstances.

Vilfredo's recognition later became known as the **Pareto Principle** or the **80/20 Rule**, which recognizes that it is typical that twenty percent of your activities result in eighty percent of your results. (3)

Communication is the only instance I have witnessed that betrays **Pareto's Principle**.

Of all the actions you take, eighty percent of listening is the most vital.

When I wrote this book, I discussed the **Pareto Paradox** with those who understand the **Pareto Principle** well. We considered if there is indeed a paradox.

Some argued that the 20% that leads to 80% of your success comes from asking questions. If this assumption is true, it would in alignment with the **Pareto Principle**.

Those that I debated with suggested that while initially, the **Pareto Paradox** was a seemingly insightful and exciting 'discovery,' it might not hold up to proper scrutiny.

REAL ESTATE EVOLUTION

I carefully considered other's input on this subject. I asked myself, "Is it more important to ask questions or to listen? Which of these actions generate greater results?"

My answer was that listening is the most vital to communication.

I remain convinced that there is a paradox. People who communicate at a high-level understand that listening is the most important component.

Active Listening

This tends to follow a common pattern: asking questions, listening to the answers, repeating what you heard back to the other person, stopping, allowing for your silence to do the heavy lifting, and hearing what the other person has to say. You can then ask strategic questions to guide him/ her in the direction that you intend to drive the conversation.

Asking strategic questions and listening will allow you to control a conversation. Controlling a conversation will lead to far better results than dominating the communication.

To dominate, you talk, talk, talk, which will not allow you to listen and will inhibit your ability to create rapport with the other person.

When you observe your conversations, you will see commonalities. Pay attention to common objections that you encounter. Listen to the feedback from others.

| It is an inside job. | Often, we assign meaning to an experience that happens "in our heads" when we recall the past or anticipate the future. The way you feel about these thoughts manipulates your actions, which creates your reality. |

We seldom appreciate these models of thought as they occur, yet they are possible to identify. When you observe how these patterns affect your life, you will be able to motivate others and, more importantly, prompt yourself to be happy or anything else you choose.

The founders of Neuro-Linguistic Programming (NLP), Drs. John Grinder and Richard Bandler state that excellence through understanding the subjective experience of ourselves and others leads to our beliefs. (4)

NLP is the combination of the understandings, encounters, expectations, and ideas that are particular to a person. (4) When you recognize your ability to think in this manner, you will learn how you can use it to live a better life and to become a better real estate sales agent.

It is good to know about what impacts us as much as a prospective or current client that we intend to lead, persuade, or motivate.

We experience subjective representations of experience in terms of our five senses and language (4).

- See
- Touch
- Feel
- Taste
- Smell
- The language that we use

You best can understand NLP in terms of The Three Principles (5) of:

- Mind = The infinite wisdom that we possess
- Consciousness = How we create our experience in the world.
- Thought = Our awareness of our Mind and our Consciousness.

Nobody can "make" us feel a particular way. We are 100% responsible for our lives and for how we proclaim our existence. When you recognize this as a reality, you will understand that anything is possible, and you have the power to design your own life.

The great news is that anything is achievable. The not so great news is, when you recognize your limitless power, you never again can blame outside events for your circumstances.

Professional football quarterback, Tom Brady (Sorry to mention him, Patriots haters) summed up the sentiment regarding personal responsibility as follows: "Too often in life, something happens, and we blame other people for us not being happy or satisfied or fulfilled. So the point is, we all have choices, and we make the choice to accept people or situations or to not accept situations." (6)

Brady did not always take personal responsibility for his actions. When Brady was a young man, he would blame others, such as his coach, his teammates, the weather, and anything else to justify any struggles. (6) As Brady matured as a football player, he began to take full responsibility for his actions and results. He became "Tom Brady.

If Yes, then How?

Often, people have fantastic excuses to rationalize the obstacles that get in their way. You might have exceptional reasons.

> You can get stuff done or you can have excuses. You cannot do both.

I respect your rationale, and I encourage you to take a step back and ask, "Is there another way? How can this be done?"

Sometimes life presents us with scenarios that appear give us make one choice. When this happens, challenge the situation.

Ask yourself, "Is it possible to be a **world-class mom AND a highly successful real estate agent**?" and if your answer is, "Yes," then ask, "How?"

Moreover, if you cannot see the way to "How?" ask the most crucial question, "Why?"

Maybe you are selling real estate to pay your bills. Perhaps you are in real estate sales to pay for your kid to go to private school or build a home for your mother (Yes, this is possible as I just am finishing a two-year project to build my mother's house.)

Yes, I said, "TWO YEARS!" While my choice of contractors was wrong, I am responsible for having selected the vendor.

When your "Why?" is big enough, you will find the way, "How?"
If you seek greatness in your life and your real estate sales career, Tom Brady's strategies can provide ample direction. As he stated about his early life, "Until I understood that I'm the reason why I'm in this position, I couldn't fight my way out of it." (6)

To be the "Tom Brady" of real estate sales, and other areas of your life, consider taking 100% complete responsibility for your circumstances. Own your actions and results.

Understanding how communication works will allow you to connect better with others. The more thoroughly you understand the ins and outs of this, the more exceptional you will be in persuasion.

Communication is composed of (7):

- 7% - The words that you use.
- 38% - Your tonality, which includes voice, tone, tempo, volume, and pitch.
- 55% - Your physiology, which provides for posture, physical gestures, breathing, and facial expression.

Most real estate sales trainers will give you a script and teach you what to say.

It is startling how few coaches take the time (and many do not know) to explain why the script you use works (or doesn't work).

When you study communication, you will become a better qualified professional, which will, in turn, allow you to be more persuasive and compelling.

Communication is the response that you get.

Have you ever said something to someone, and what you said was interpreted entirely differently than you intended?

Did you say or think: "That is not what I said."

Take responsibility that their perception is as valid as yours.

If you request something of someone and do not get it, then maybe you asked the wrong question.

Deletion, Distortion, and Generalization

The language you use unintentionally could generate uncertainty, confusion, and other difficulties that hinder your clients from pursuing their goals. When we speak with another person or ourselves, we often filter through, **Deletion**, **Distortion**, and **Generalization**. (8) We screen the words and sounds that we hear, the pictures that we see, our feelings, self-talk, tastes, and smells through these omissions.

Deletion is when we perceive a part of what someone says as not relevant. **Distortion** occurs when our bias pressures us to believe something that we do not intend to believe. **Generalization** is when we associate an experience as representative of all future experiences. (8)

Deletions, Distortions, and Generalizations can work for you when they are used strategically and can hurt your communication if you do not pay attention.

<u>When you realize how your self-talk influences yourself and others, you can choose how you use your words, and to what effect.</u>

Deletion

Deletions are notable by their absence of clarity (8), such as in the following statement "People know they want a real estate agent to help them." A declaration like this can guide someone to agree with you because it is hard to disagree with imprecision.

Let's parse the above statement,

- What people?
- What do they know?
- What real estate agent?
- What help do they want?

A deletion occurs when a portion of the meaning is left out or missed. Sentences with the words "it," "this," and "that" often will allow for misinterpretation.

A sentence such as, "This is much better." can leave a large gap for interpretation. What is much better? How much better? Compared to what?

The environment offers 11 million bits per second for our subconscious to process, yet we can be consciously aware of fewer than 50 bits of information per second. (9) We filter many millions of bits of information in a short period.

The fact that we can perceive a minuscule amount of info offered at any given moment means we can almost always find evidence to support our point of view. Two or more people can have the same experience or be a part of the same environment and perceive knowledge to validate opposite opinions or experiences.

We frequently delete nouns and verbs. We selectively omit words in our communication and leave other words to permeate the gaps. Often when we omit words from our conversations, it leads to misunderstanding.
Look at the statement, "It can be hard to be a successful real estate sales agent."

- What specifically makes being a successful real estate agent hard?
- How do you define "hard"?
- How would you accurately describe "successful"?

Asking questions will allow you to gain clarity.

In your self-talk, you may be saying something such as, "I'm not the kind of person who can succeed."
If you believe a statement like this, it could be damaging to you.
By exercising a more conscious form of communication, you might combat this by asking a question such as, "How is it useful to identify with being this 'kind of person'?"

Terms to observe that might lead to unintentional Deletion include:

- Can't, not able, not likely
- Need, have to, must
- Everybody, somebody, nobody
- Every, always, never

Even though it can be difficult to provide every important detail through the words you use, sometimes the details are crucial to convey accurately. From time to time, you will incorrectly fill in blanks of what is missing or not said.

While Deletion can lead to confusion, it also can be used to your advantage. Vague comparisons can help in sales. Words and phrases that you could use to affect another through using Deletion include:

- Better
- Worst

- Most helpful
- Harder
- Quicker
- More influential
- Less
- More

These terms can add believability to your communication.

Phrases such as, "Our sales team works harder" or, "I work harder" leaves an opportunity for the recipient to fill in the blanks of understanding. They can relate their interpretation of what it means to work and what harder means.

In sales, you could use Deletion by assuming an outcome. For example, you might screen a prospective seller while setting up the appointment, by asking, "As your real estate agent, what do you expect of me?"

When you ask the question above, you infer the other person already has decided to hire you. In addition to moving the conversation toward getting hired, you also have the chance to gather data that you can then repeat back when you attend the listing appointment.

If the prospect answers, "I expect for you not to be a slimy salesman," then when you meet to obtain the listing, you could restate the seller's words to her and say, "Unlike those slimy salesmen, I intend to consult." When you use her exact words with her in a later conversation, you will be speaking her language; thus, you will create better rapport.

Strategic Deletion can be useful.

The United States, Secretary of State Alexander Haig once brilliantly said, "The warning message we sent ... was a calculated ambiguity that would be clearly understood" (10) as he used Strategic Deletion to his advantage while talking about the Soviets.

Distortion

Distortion is when you understand communication to mean something that it was not intended to convey. (8) When you make a statement in which one thing causes another, or your conjecture suggests mind-reading, or when one purposefully assigns meaning stated in the second part of a sentence on purpose from the first part, then you are demonstrating Distortion.

I once taught an NLP seminar on Deletions, Distortions, and Generalizations to a group of real estate agents.

After the course, a student approached me and asked for clarification about the concept. As we spoke, we reflected on another idea discussed during the class. It was the Three Phases of Human Development, which are Imprinting, Modeling, and Socialization.

During ages one to seven, the beliefs that will guide the rest of your life are Imprinted; you could consider this the programming stage. If you are a parent of a child of this age, it would be helpful to know that your kid is designing his/her neural pathway at this time. You might favor reinforcing positive thoughts. Let him/her know that anything is possible in their lives.

> All generalizations are false, including this one.
>
> - Mark Twain

From about eight to twelve years of age, we experience Modeling and interpret what the world will mean to us. We watch others and learn from their actions. If you do not want your future teenager to text and drive, you had better place your phone in the glove box – and we all shall appreciate that you do not check your Facebook feed at the next stoplight!

Between the ages of twelve to twenty-one for girls and women and twelve to twenty-five for boys and men (because we are knuckleheads and slower to learn), the impact over us begins to shift from family to friends as we experience Socialization.

As I explained to the student about Deletions, Distortions, and Generalizations and related it to the example about the Three Phases of Human Development we discussed earlier, I used my eight-year-old daughter, Margaret, as an example. I said, "Maggie is now Modeling."

What I meant to communicate was that she is entering the stage where she emulates the actions of others whom she observes. What the student understood was that Maggie was spending her days and nights strutting down the catwalk.

I laughed and pointed out the irony of what we were experiencing in our communication. The conversation we were engaging in was a perfect example of Distortion.

Generalization

Favorite phrases of President Donald Trump include:

> "Everybody thinks this."
> "Our party always does that..."
> "Many people are saying this..."

Trump once Tweeted, "Many people are saying that the Iranians killed the scientist who helped the U.S. because of Hillary Clinton's hacked emails." (11)

Donald Trump is a master at using Generalization in his communication. To avoid alienating half of my readers with the mention of Trump's name, I'd like to emphasize that Presidents Bill Clinton, Barack Obama, and almost any other successful politician are all masters of persuasion. After all, how else could you inspire half of the country to support you?

The most successful politicians are highly skilled in their ability to persuade others. Politicians and other influential people often use Generalization to achieve consensus, such as when they say, "Everybody agrees that we should implement this program."
Generalizations are comments that you may want to challenge by asking, "Who says?" or "What evidence do you have for that statement?"

The essential words to pay attention to are:

- All
- Never
- Always
- Very

The above words simplify our worldview and restrain us in our interpretation.

For example:

- I never will be able to get ten listings a month.
- No one cares if I succeed.
- I can't see myself as a rainmaker.

To challenge these Generalizations, ask for the counterexample such as:

- Will you NEVER be able to get ten listings in a month?
- Is there ANYONE who cares for your success?
- What's stopping you?

Develop Rapport

Rapport is a friendly and cooperative relationship in which the people interacting with each other strive to understand each other's opinions, thoughts, and feelings, and communicate well. Rapport is a process of responsiveness - it does not necessarily mean that you like each other, but instead that you are like each other.

If you want to be most successful in sales, understanding how to develop rapport will help. Rapport is when you connect with a person at a deep level when you listen to their ideas and can communicate your thoughts to them in a manner that they hear.

> You know that you are in rapport when you experience a physical feeling.

You know that you have reached this state of rapport when you physically can feel it. Create a harmonious relationship with another person, and you will be in a state to best influence.

If you were to learn only one strategy from reading this book, I would suggest learning how to develop rapport and connection with others effectively and quickly.

To develop rapport, you must communicate in the other person's "language." Listen to their words, tonality, inflection, and the pitch of their voice.

Pay attention to their physiology. How do they sit? Is their body moving into yours or away from yours? When you identify the clues of their demeanor, you can connect with them in several ways.

When you have strong rapport with one another, it allows for them to be at ease. When another person feels comfortable with you, they more likely will trust you. In this rapport, you can convince them to take action that will best benefit them.

Two people or a group can experience rapport. Waiters and waitresses often glide across the restaurant floor during a dinner rush and move their bodies in unison. Those servers barely look at each and never collide because they have extreme rapport as they move.

There are several ways to gain rapport rapidly. They include **Mirror**, **Matching**, and **Cross-Over Mirror and Matching**, which all involve being in synch with someone's movements to gain rapport with them and more.

To effectively **Mirror**, imagine you are looking in a mirror. If another person raises their left fist, you will lift your right hand as though you or she were reflecting each other's image.

Matching is when you follow another's movements as if you were looking into a mirror. If they raise their left hand, you raise your left hand. From each other's perspective, you will be raising opposite arms.

Cross Over Mirror and Matching is when you match another person's body language with a different type of action, such as tapping your pen onto a table in time to their rhythm of speech.

Sometimes it makes sense to increase the level of rapport, but not to an extreme degree. An example is when you want to keep a person of the opposite sex at bay from you the reader's handsome or prettiness. Mirroring will develop a more significant connection than Matching will.

Things to mirror and match to develop rapport:

- Breathing pattern
- Posture
- Gestures
- Language
- Voice tone

Breathing is the most significant element of physiology for Match and Mirror because it is unconscious in the other person and easy for you to notice. Follow the breathing pattern displayed in the shoulders, chest, and stomach.

What are other techniques to develop rapport quickly?

- If you are sitting, you can use your body language by leaning toward the person you are talking to, with your hands free and arms and legs uncrossed. When you are open, the person you are speaking with will feel more comfortable.
- Maintain eye contact with the other person for a little more than half of the time. Be careful not to lock eyes for too long because that may make them uncomfortable.
- Nod and encourage gestures and sounds when talking with the other person.
- Smile! (I shamelessly mention this for my own benefit as it appears that sometimes I forget to let my face know how amazingly happy I am.)
- Use the other person's name. When you use their name, it will be viewed as polite and it will reinforce their name in your mind. The most important word to any person is our name.
- Ask open-ended questions. These questions avoid putting the other person on the spot to give a definite opinion.
- Avoid controversial subjects of discussion. Stick to the weather rather than risk falling out over politics.
- Use feedback to review, display, and interpret to the other person what you believe they have said. Feedback gives a chance for any mistakes to be corrected promptly.
- Speak about something that refers back to what the other person has said. Find links between shared experiences.
- Show understanding. Display that you can understand how the other person feels and can perceive things from their point of view.

When you develop rapport with another person, you have a much better opportunity to guide them. If you are an agent who enjoys holding open houses and a seller who you work for says to you, "Holding open houses never work." you could reply to the Generalization presented to you with skepticism, "Never? Is that true? Is that 100% true?" to challenge the seller's thinking, for example.

REAL ESTATE EVOLUTION

Hierarchy of Communication

The hierarchy of communication from most impactful to least impactful is as follows:

1. Face to face
2. Video chat (Google Hangouts, Facetime, Skype, etc.)
3. Phone conversation
4. Text
5. Facebook message
6. Email
7. Carrier pigeon - just joking :)

> Lack of communication is the key to any successful relationship going wrong.

Communication includes verbal, nonverbal, and physical characteristics. The energy we give off, the quality of our voice, tonality, pitch, rate of speech, body language, posture, eye contact, and touch are all ways we communicate. **Face to face is the highest form of communication because it accounts for all manner of connection**.

To be most effective, you would use the communication methods that are highest in the list for a more meaningful conversation. For example, a price adjustment or presenting an offer would need a higher form of communication than informing a seller that there was a showing on their home. When you interact with a seller, buyer prospect, or client, you should connect in the highest form possible.

So, what's the challenge when you're communicating via text or email? The challenge with text is that you will not convey tonality, inflection, nor body language. If the recipient is having a bad day or has a preconceived notion of the situation, they will often read it based on their reception - not the intention of you, the sender.

Consider implementing a strategy of over-communication; my sales team embraces this approach.

With help from our support staff, we communicate with each client at least five times per week. We guarantee our clients in writing that we will interact with them systematically.

We communicate with each other excessively. There is no boundary of too much communication.

When our daughter Maggie was younger, she attended a Montessori Preschool located in Arlington, VA. A very involved Head of School directed the school. I received a phone call from her every two weeks, two emails each week, and a text every few days. All these communications updated me on my child's progress.

After two years of Maggie attending the school, our family found our dream home located in Clifton, VA, and we moved. My daughter had to start at a new school.

A few months later, I grew concerned. I felt the new school was not doing a good job, compared to the first school, which I thought did a fabulous job.

I spoke with my wife Traci and said, "You know what? I don't think this is a good school compared to the other one."

So, we went to the school to observe the students and shadow the teachers. My wife and I both were pleasantly surprised to learn that the second school appeared equal to the first.

At first, I was bewildered about the events; over the next weekend, I contemplated our experience. Then I realized the difference. The school in Arlington communicated in a manner that was over the top, and the other school updated me very little.

My daughter's Preschool encounters taught me a valuable lesson that applies to my business today. I learned that over communication is the key to success in caring for your client.

The standard across my sales team is that our client care specialists communicate with clients four days each week, and our agents do so two days a week. Monday to Friday each week, our clients hear from us a total of six times.

This excessive communication allows us to avoid being a punching bag for our clients when things do not go well, and it also enables us to take time off.

All communications are done Monday to Friday, leaving time for us to enjoy our families on weekends (or for agents to host open houses or to take buyers on tour when appropriate).

In your relationship with your client, you either will be proactive or reactive. It's not fun to react, but if you communicate five days a week, you will seldom have to respond to a client's unexpected needs.

It doesn't matter how you reach them. It could be a phone call. It could be an email. It could be a text. The only caveat I'd suggest here is to ask your clients how they want to be communicated with and then reach out in the manner that best suits them.

If you are presenting an offer, asking for a price reduction, or need to convey any other vital information, you should do so via telephone or in a face to face meeting.

If you get so busy that it is tough to touch base with your clients, you can use a phone broadcast system such as www.SlyDial.com to leave a message without the client answering the phone. This should not be used as a substitute for two voice to voice connections weekly.

The best way you can show the people you serve you care is ALWAYS to be in touch with them. When you do this, you will build a great business through the referrals and reputation you earn.

The Pathway to Success

I once hosted a group of agents to attend Family Reunion, which is the Keller Williams Realty annual convention. On stage in front of 15,000 real estate agents, Gary Keller interviewed real estate icon Ben Kinney. Kinney is a professional speaker, real estate agent, entrepreneur, and owner of multiple real estate franchises. (12)

An agent who was attending the event with me leaned over and whispered how impressive it was that Ben Kinney had experienced so much success. I countered that I believed Ben had experienced more failure than almost anyone else in the convention hall.

> Little Life = Little Possible Setbacks and Little Possible Achievement.

Perplexed, the agent that I was speaking with asked me to explain. I shared with her that to have great success; you will likely also have to experience significant failures.

Someone with the significant achievements of Ben Kinney is indeed massively impressive. He likely can progress quicker and further than most. Yet, it is also true that he takes far more shots than almost anyone else. Ben fails often and fails fast, learns, adjusts, and then retakes colossal action.

Success is subjective and personal. Our perception of others does not serve us except in studying the models of how other people achieve.

Don't judge your self-worth based on another person's highlight reel. Instead, try to define success based on your compass in the areas of life that are important to you and then determine success from those metrics.

Take a moment to consider how you define success.

What is success?

What does success look like to you?

Is success about winning or money?

From 1948 to 1975, John Wooden coached the UCLA basketball team. During that time, his program won a fantastic ten national championships. His team's record was 664 wins - 162 losses during his time as the coach. (13)

If you are a sports fan, you undoubtedly would agree that Coach Wooden is one of the most successful coaches ever.

But, what did Wooden believe about success?

Coach Wooden said, "True success is attained only through the satisfaction of knowing you did everything within the limits of your ability to become the very best that you are capable of being." (14)

I understand the words of John Wooden to mean that when you focus on achieving your highest potential doing something that brings you joy, then the wins will follow.

A way that I define success is to do what brings you the most joy in life.

I have found that instead of chasing money, that when you do what you LOVE to do, the fortune and success will pursue you.

Another way that I define success in life as the obtainment of abundant love.

I completely acknowledge that you can't know if you have achieved 'abundant love' or not, because it cannot be measured.

REAL ESTATE EVOLUTION

I am still considering my definition of success in life; this continues to be a work in progress.

I define success in business as building an organization that is profitable and can exist through time, with or without you.

To this date, I have taken many chances, and I currently consider two of the five businesses that I own or have been an investor in a success. I consider the two a success because, in both companies, I am a minority owner, and neither company relies on me.

There is another entity that I founded years ago which also meets my definition of business success. It is a networking organization called **BNI Positive Power**.

I have been attending this networking event most every Wednesday morning from 7:30 a.m. to 9:00 a.m. for the past dozen years.

I do contribute to this organization at a high level. Yet, it has been well over a decade since they relied on me for us to stay in business. If I were to leave this organization today, another high achieving real estate agent would replace me, and the organization would continue thriving.

In some cases, I outright have failed in my efforts. Of course, failure is as subjective as success. In no situation do I allow failure to define me. **And neither should YOU!**

With those businesses where I perceive I failed, I learned more than I believe I could have if I earned three MBAs from the most prestigious business schools – for this I am grateful.

Years ago, I had the honor of seeing Zig Ziglar at an event in Washington, DC. When I think of failure, I agree with Ziglar when he said, "A failure is an event, not a person."

Other areas of life that are important to assess success include Spirituality, Family, Health, Fitness, Knowledge, Relationship, and Money.

I encourage you to come up with your own set of priorities and then define what success means for each. When you do this, you should be able to measure accurately whether you achieve your goal.

The Self Coaching Model

Programming >> Thoughts >> Feelings >> Actions >> Results

There is a level of the brain that dictates our outcome more than the conscious; this is the subconscious.

> Your potential is unlimited.

The pathway from the subconscious to the conscious allows for our thoughts to manifest in results. Our programming leads to our thoughts; our thoughts lead to our feelings; our feelings lead to our actions; our actions lead to our results, and our results reinforce our programming.

If you intend to change your results, then you will need to do so through hacking the programming that feeds your subconscious. When we get things done, we do so subconsciously, not consciously.

Here is how to change your programming. You may do so through:

1. Meditation
2. Affirmations
3. Visualization
4. Exercise
5. Reading

Typically, I do these activities first thing in the morning. Realistically if I complete three out of five of these activities each day, I consider my day a success.

Meditate

Meditation allows us to access our subconscious directly. It does this by the transference of our brain waves from the highest level of awareness to the deepest level of relaxation. When we are in a deep level of relaxation, we access the part of our mind that retains memories and feelings; this is our subconscious.

The benefits of meditation are vast. Meditation reduces anxiety and depression and helps us to alter how we think, allowing us to cultivate clarity and happiness. **When we have a calm mind, remarkable things can happen**.

If you are new to meditation, consider using an app such as https://www.headspace.com/ to get started. This app will make the process easy.

Affirm

Whether you realize it or not you are affirming all the time. So, you might as well choose what to you're telling yourself.

Some people claim a negative affirmation when they make a mistake. They might say to themselves, "I'm just clumsy" or "That was dumb." These negative statements often become a reality.

Positive statements about yourself also become a reality. You can program yourself by using positive declarations each morning. To see the most favorable results, you must exercise these positive statements frequently.

When you carry out affirmations regularly, **they reinforce the connections between the neurons in your brain, which allows you to deliberately influence the message that your mind hears, strengthening the relationship between the neurons**.

> Affirm that your Mind, Body, and Spirit are always calm.

To be most effective, affirmations should be:

1. Stated in the present tense
2. Share a positive statement
3. Believed by you
4. Short and specific
5. Honest

To supercharge your affirmations, consider writing them with pen and paper at least ten times a day. When you write, it will stimulate your Reticular Activating System (RAS), which is the part of the brain that controls its consciousness. (15)

You could choose to select a broader affirmation that you dwell on for an extended period and add a few others each day.

I write a few affirmations each day to embrace other areas of my life which I intend to improve.

Some examples of affirmations that you could use include:

- I am a leader
- I am a loving father/mother
- I am worthy of reaching my goals
- I step up
- I believe in myself
- I embrace lead generation
- I easily help ___ families buy a home, sell a home, or invest in real estate each year

Visualize

Visualization works because our brains interpret it as real life. When you form a mental image of what you intend to happen, you create a new pathway in the nervous system that strengthens your mind to act in a way that aligns with what you imagine.

> Consistently work to elevate your self-image.

A couple of times a week, I'll sit in a hot tub or steam room after a gym workout. I'll sit there and visualize my family living in the home of my dreams.

Fifteen years ago, I started visualizing living in the home of my dreams. I imagined that the house would sit on at least five acres of rolling hills in horse country.

I believed that it would have an upscale swimming pool with a hot tub and a bathhouse that included a gym, steam room, and sauna. I saw that massive trees would flank the long driveway leading to the house, and the landscaped grounds would have an attractive curb appeal.

Because I live in congested Northern Virginia, which overflows with people, traffic, and urban sprawl, at first, this seemed like a tall order. Very few communities in our area offer large lots.

REAL ESTATE EVOLUTION

At the time, my wife and I lived in a cramped townhome in Alexandria, VA. We rented our basement to a professional personal driver named Mark who was in his late 50s.

At the time, I still worked at the restaurant, and could not see the pathway that would lead me to my dream home. Yet, I could see the destination. I knew where I would arrive; I visualized living in that home for years.

About six years ago, I was working with a great agent, Oscar Rodriguez. I asked him to accompany me and meet a seller who had contacted me to sell their distressed home located on a five-acre lot in Clifton, VA.

We arrived at the location to find a big, overgrown mess of a lawn. A mud lane had replaced what once was a driveway. I later learned the homeowners had hired someone to remove their existing driveway and install a new one. The owners ran out of money and did not complete the job.

When Oscar and I approached the property, I realized the concrete pad behind the house in the spot that a deck once had existed was the intended parking spot. On the right side of the rear entrance, exposed cinder blocks held up the ground, and on the left was the house. We got out of my car, and I recognized the first boarded window.

As we entered the house, I noticed a distinctive scent of dog feces and urine that more than wafted to our noses. In addition to this property's distress, it was also a refuge for seventeen rescue dogs (I believed it was more than seventeen, but that is what the owners told me).

I met with the owners and learned that they had retired thirty years earlier and did not have the health or money to maintain the home.

The inside of the house was worse than the outside. The ceilings were caving in, and few lights worked. It was an absolute disaster; **imagine the Addam's Family's** house, if you are old enough to know the TV show.

I listened to the owners' story, and then I did what I was supposed to do. With no idea of how, I promised the sellers that I could help them, and I took the listing.

As we drove back to the office, I expressed my thoughts to Oscar out loud, "I have no idea how we will sell that property."

Oscar answered, "You know, Dan, that is your dream home."

It took me some vision to see that Oscar was right. The property was a wreck, but it had a fantastic lot that overlooked about 15 acres of cleared rolling land in front of the house, which sat on top of a hill. The house was an eyesore, but upscale homes surrounded it. It had potential.

I thought about it for a day, and then I approached my wife. I would consider that talk one of my most exceptional sales conversations of all time. I convinced my wife that this was our dream home.

It has been six years since we bought that home, and we still are transforming it. Today, it is fantastic. We have most of what I envisioned except for the pool for my daughter. I intend to build the swimming pool and the bathhouse next year.

I am convinced that if I did not visualize this home for nine years and share it with the world, I would not have acknowledged the opportunity. I am grateful that Oscar was with me that day.

If you are reading this next year, and we encounter each other, feel free to hold me accountable. Ask me, "Did you create that pool for your daughter yet?"

As a real estate sales agent, I consistently envision closing ten transactions each month with relative ease. My intention is always to exceed my client's expectations and help them achieve their goals and dreams or overcome their obstacles. I have met these outcomes.

What does it look when you visualize taking significant and strategic actions? What kind of results will you have?

> Intend success.

As you begin to visualize, the subconscious mind will take those thoughts and process them for us to act. We deliver this to our conscious mind in the form of feedback that we interpret as our thoughts. These thoughts also direct our emotions.

Exercise

Physical exercise helps the entire body, including your mind.

When you exercise, endorphins from your central nervous system are released. Endorphins help you to be happier, less stressed, and experience greater levels of peace.

If you do not currently exercise, consider taking a walk each day. Even if you go for a short 15-minute walk, you will feel better and improve your mood. You also could join a gym with a friend or attend a fitness class.

Reading

If you aren't "learning-based," then you're "ignorance-based."

Now, I am NOT calling you ignorant – because if you were, you would not be reading these words. I am suggesting that high-caliber real estate agents seek knowledge and act on what they learn.

Ask yourself, "What would be different if I were to read ten pages of a book each morning instead of watching the news or listening to Howard Stern?"

High achievers read regularly. When you read you learn, and often get inspired to make great choices. People have lived before us and have left clues about success and failure.

I encourage you to read these books that will guide you:

Millionaire Real Estate Agent by Gary Keller and Jay Papasan and Dave Jenks

In this book, Gary Keller and crew study some of the most successful real estate agents of the early 2000s and finds what each has in common. **The authors demonstrate that you can model the behaviors of others, and if you choose to model the behaviors of the most successful, then you likely will achieve the same results.**

Four primary models are outlined in this book:

1. Lead generation model
2. Budget model
3. Organization model
4. Economic model

This book can be considered an operator's manual for building a real estate sales business and should be read by any real estate agent who desires success.

Open by Andre Agassi

Andre Agassi is a retired Grand Slam Champion tennis player (16). In this autobiography, he describes his struggles in tennis and life.

Open is a book that I recommend you listen to instead of reading. When you hear it, it will draw you into Andre's life of hating tennis, doing drugs, and fighting horrible pain, as well as the relationships that helped him.

My favorite part is when Andre identifies his, "Why." Then he transforms from a top tennis player to the very best in the world.

Consider www.Audible.com to listen to this.

Think and Grow Rich by Napoleon Hill

Think and Grow Rich is an essential book about success and self-help written in 1937. In it, Hill states that **desire, belief, and tenacity can allow you to achieve any desired outcome if you can prevent any weak thoughts about those goals and continue to focus on those objectives.**

Just as Gary Keller identified the 'clues' of the most successful real estate agents, Napoleon Hill identifies characteristics of success by studying many of the multi-millionaires and ultra-successful people of the time. The people he studies include Thomas Edison, Alexander Graham Bell, Henry Ford, John Rockefeller, Charles Schwab, Theodore Roosevelt, William Taft, Woodrow Wilson, and others.

The steps to success that Hill describes in his book are:

1. Desire
2. Faith
3. Autosuggestion
4. Specialized Knowledge
5. Imagination
6. Organized Planning
7. Decision
8. Persistence
9. Power of the Master Mind
10. Transmutation
11. The Subconscious Mind
12. The Brain

One of the most useful concepts that I learned in the book is one that Napoleon Hill learned from Andrew Carnegie, which is, **"If you can conceive it and believe it, you can achieve it."**

REAL ESTATE EVOLUTION

Instant Rapport by Michael Brooks

This book is a favorite of mine. In *Instant Rapport*, M. Brooks describes how to create a bond with anyone at any time.

To have a rapport means that you must enter the world of another person. When you do this, you can actively listen to them and understand their point of view. In this state, you will be able to impact the other person more effectively, which is a skill set that will serve you very well as a real estate agent.

Instant Rapport teaches the shortcuts to create this connection rapidly and states that you know that you have developed a rapport when you can physically feel it. One of the many ways the author suggests you develop rapport is a technique called "mirroring," where a person subconsciously imitates a pattern of speech, physiology, or attitude of another.

Four Disciplines of Execution by Sean Covey

This book will teach you that to be an active leader; you must know your goal, how to achieve it, how to lead others to achieve it, and how to hold others accountable in an effective manner.

Indeed, as a real estate agent, you may have experienced a whirlwind of activity. A "whirlwind" is when a million things are vying for your attention. **This book explains that to stay out of the whirlwind it is advisable to understand the one to two things that you should do today that would make the most significant impact on achieving your goal. They suggest that you focus your efforts on those activities first.**

Benjamin Franklin: An American Life by Walter Isaacson

So, what does Benjamin Franklin have to do with real estate sales? Probably absolutely nothing, yet when we study history, it can help us understand how to create our future. Franklin is one of the most successful people who ever lived. When I read this book, I learned dozens of exciting stories about his life.

Ben Franklin was somebody who had a lot of essential qualities that I suggest you study. He was an entrepreneur, an inventor, a scientist, a diplomat, a negotiator, an investor, a

business strategist, and one of our country's most genius political leaders.

He identified his 13 virtues, which he described in his autobiography and are outlined in *Benjamin Franklin: An American Life*. They are:

1. *Temperance. Eat not to dullness, drink not to elevation.*
2. *Silence. Speak not, but what may benefit others or yourself; avoid trifling conversation.*
3. *Order. Let all your things have their places; let each part of your business have its time.*
4. *Resolution. Resolve to perform what you ought; perform without fail what you resolve.*
5. *Frugality. Make no expense but to do good to others or yourself, i.e., waste nothing.*
6. *Industry. Lose no time; be always employed in something useful; cut off all unnecessary actions.*
7. *Sincerity. Use no hurtful deceit; think innocently and justly, and, if you speak, speak accordingly.*
8. *Justice. Wrong none by doing injuries or omitting the benefits that are your duty.*
9. *Moderation. Avoid extremes; forbear resenting injuries so much as you think they deserve.*
10. *Cleanliness. Tolerate no uncleanliness in body, clothes, or habitation.*
11. *Tranquility. Be not disturbed at trifles, or at accidents common or unavoidable.*
12. *Chastity. Rarely use venery, but for health or offspring, never to dullness, weakness, or the injury of your own or another's peace or reputation.*
13. *Humility. Imitate Jesus and Socrates.*

Consider selecting one of the above practices of meditation, affirmations, visualization, exercise, or reading and carry out this activity each day for the next two months. After you master the first habit, try the following practice, master that pattern, and then create the next habit, etc.

Your Big Why?

Do you know why you are doing what you're doing? Why do you sell real estate?

When your 'Why' is big enough, you never will have to worry about, 'How.'

I encourage you to take some time and ask yourself:

- "Why am I a real estate agent?"

- Whatever your answer to that question, ask yourself:

- "What is important to me about that?"

and then ask again,

- "What is important to me about that?"

Keep doing this until you get to the most basic reason – this will be your, 'Why.' You will know when you get to the most exact version of 'Why.' And when you do so, keep your focus on that.

Go ahead and take a break from reading and do the exercise above. Take ten to fifteen minutes and contemplate the questions asked. Write your answers on a piece of paper and revisit the practice tomorrow after your subconscious has taken some time to process and provide you the solutions. Keep visiting this exercise each day until your answer rings true to you.

I believe that the 'Why' of a business (any business) is to add value to the world.

How this occurs is different for each business and business owner. For some, it is in supporting others, allowing people to have better choices, or contributing to make the planet a better place.

Why do I do What I do?

I do what I do to open doorways for others. That's part of the reason I wrote this book. I want to help you have clarity and predictability in your business so you can see that pathway forward for yourself. When I help you chart this course, I have fulfilled my purpose to open doorways for someone else, YOU!

Another reason I do what I am doing is my mother is 72 years old. I am building a house for her on my property. I figure that she looked out for me for my first 20 years or so, so now I will help her. **Without financial success, I would not have had the opportunity to help Mom. This is a huge, 'Why' for me.**

Blind Faith vs. Absolute Faith

To have faith is to have trust or confidence that something will occur. When your belief becomes determined, it will alter your being and activities.

When I started in real estate sales, I studied models of success and derived a **Blind Faith** from those who were successful before me.

Today, I have **Absolute Faith** that there is a pathway for success.

For me, **Absolute Faith** comes from the result of having achieved many of the goals that I set.

I have found that to study others carefully and then replicate their behavior as closely as possible gets higher and quicker results leading in fast obtainment of **Absolute Faith**.

When you follow the plan described in this book, you will sell more homes and earn a consistent income. I intend that you embrace this plan in a manner that you obtain **Absolute Faith** in yourself as rapidly as possible.

Study a Person of Excellence

Who do you admire the most?

Who do you view as successful?

Who are your heroes?

REAL ESTATE EVOLUTION

To model any person, you must first understand the beliefs, physiology, and the way that person thinks.

Here is an exercise that will allow you to model another person's behavior accurately.

1. Identify a Person of Excellence who is either:
    a. A Rainmaker (the real estate leader who makes it, 'rain' with opportunities) with a High Performing Team.
    b. A High Performing Real Estate agent.
2. Identify their strategy.
    a. What is their mindset? Define this in writing.
    b. What are their behaviors?
        i. How do they time block?
        ii. How do they focus on their 20%?
        iii. What is their environment?
        iv. Define this in writing.
3. Prove that you have installed behaviors of the Person of Excellence in yourself.

When you entirely take on the above exercise, you will be able to model your Person of Excellence. You do not need to create a relationship with this person, yet you can choose to do so. If this person is not living or if you do not establish a relationship with this individual, then imagine the answers to the questions.

Your mind is infinite, and you will find the answers. Choose to flourish.

Step 2: Look for Leads

My first few months as a real estate agent were tough. Very tough! I remember feeling the stinging pain of frustration as my initial efforts produced few results.

As a professional waiter, I would go to the restaurant, hustle hard, make a few hundred dollars, and then go home (or at that time of my life, more likely go to the bar). The reward for my efforts came immediately with cash in my pocket.

As a new real estate agent, I would go to the office, work challenging and endless hours, and then wonder, "When will I get paid?"

I quickly realized that I was not going to receive fast gratification. For me to obtain **C.P.I.**[*] seemed to be a challenge.

My efforts as an agent were sporadic, and I was uncertain of which ventures to pursue. Data was coming at me so quickly that it seemed as if I was drinking through a straw from a fire hose.

---

[*] C.P.I. = Consistent, Predictable Income.

REAL ESTATE EVOLUTION

It was hard for me to understand what to do. It seemed that everyone else had an idea about what I should be doing; everybody supposedly grasped what I should do except for me.

I had no real direction or plan. Without focus, I dove all in.

I called expired listings and For Sale by Owners.

I started a BNI networking group.

I hung ugly yellow signs in the median of the street and marked the signs with thick, black Magic Marker declaring, 'Free list of Foreclosures - Call 1-800-555-1212' to solicit phone calls from potential buyers.

I dropped 5" by 7" postcards printed on the dot-matrix suggesting that a renter could afford to be a buyer. I slid those cards into every apartment guide newspaper box in front of every local grocery store.

I knocked on doors.

I attempted every nearly every action presented to me.

I was confused as to my priority about setting up my website, CRM, etc. And I certainly had no clue about how to write an offer or complete a contract.

Amazingly, after a few short days, I booked my first appointment with an expired listing.

I had no idea how to take a listing. I had little idea of anything I was doing. Looking back now, I realize I should have sought out a mentor.

I prepared the best that I could for the interview with the seller. I arrived promptly, walked the outside entry stairs, knocked on the door, took a step back, smiled, met the sellers, and then wholly blundered.

This might have been the only time in my career that a prospect asked me how long I had been a real estate agent. As the answer was less than a week, I avoided the question.

The second time she asked, I pivoted the conversation.

On the third time that the seller inquired, I finally let out a big sigh and answered, "It seems like forever!"

I did not get hired.

My short career as an expired listing specialist ended on that day. Fortunately, I resurrected contacting expired listings years later.

I worked hard yet remained unfocused. Ambitions were abundant, and I mistakenly thought the actions that I took were relevant. My efforts did not produce the sought after returns.

A few months later, I had a few listings, yet I still had not closed my first deal. Frustrated, I asked my broker, Karen, to meet. She was gracious to meet and guide me.

Karen said, "Dan, you are on the right track. You are doing everything right. Just keep doing what you are doing, and you will be successful."

I remember scoffing at the suggestions. I thought, "If I am doing everything right, then why am I about to have to pay my mortgage with my credit card?"

Karen reassured me that I would be OK, and I took a deep breath. I listened to her suggestions. She suggested I develop new habits, stop getting distracted, and stay consistent in my efforts.

I vowed to concentrate my energy. I understood that I needed a better strategy, and I had to find clients. I would lead generate each day consistently, and I would stay focused. I would build upon my efforts.

Gain Momentum

I compare the start of my real estate sales career to the operation of a flywheel.

Picture a giant, steel flywheel that sits idle on a shaft. Pretend that the apparatus is almost immovable, and your job is to thrust the wheel so that it may physically rotate on its conventional bearings.

The flywheel is so dense that when you push it, you get practically zero change.

> **Daily habits result in momentum.**

You keep driving. A bead of sweat breaks across your brow, and you continue struggling with immense effort.

The flywheel begins to make small increments forward in rotation. Eventually, you observe sluggish movements.

Finally, the mechanical device makes one turn. Two turns. Three rotations. On and on. You push until the wheel rotates with enormous momentum and becomes almost unstoppable.

What push created the momentum? Was it the first shove or the thrust most immediately before the energy began? It is impossible to know.

If you stop pushing the wheel at any time before achieving momentum, it would have stopped completely, and you would have had to start the efforts all over again. You would have lost all previous energy and returned to inertia.

Consistency is the answer; **compound actions over time create results**. Daily activities are the key to propel us to achieve our goals.

Your business is much like that flywheel. In the beginning, any effort you exert will produce little return. However, as you continue to work bit by bit, you will see small results. The modest results will build momentum, and at a point, you will maintain force.

Small steps make a big difference. The efforts that you exert today will produce results in 90 days or more from now.

Discipline Leads to Habit, Which Leads to Success

Here's a secret I never shared. **Success is not a sign of intelligence; it is a result of implementing habits one small step at a time**.

I currently sit in a Dunkin' Donuts as I write this. That in of itself is not a problem.

The challenge that I have experienced is that when I allow myself to visit the donut shop each day, I tend to get fat.

Luckily, I also enjoy the habit of working out each day. As a result of my paradoxical relationship between exercise and pastries, I teeter between fitness and fatness.

When I embrace the discipline to say, "No" to sweets, then avoiding donuts, cakes, and pies become a habit. When I develop the practice consistently, I will have the success that I so desire.

Author, podcaster, entrepreneur, and retired Navy Seal Jocko Willink (17) once stated, "While Discipline and Freedom seem like they sit on opposite sides of the spectrum, they are actually very connected.

"Freedom is what everyone wants — to be able to act and live with freedom. But the only way to get to a place of freedom is through discipline.

"If you want financial freedom, you must have financial discipline. If you want more free time, you must follow a more disciplined time management system.

"You also have to have the discipline to say 'No' to things that eat up your time with no payback—things like random YouTube videos, click-bait on the internet, and even events that you agree to attend when you know you won't want to be there.

> "Success is actually a short race – a sprint fueled by discipline just long enough for habit to kick in and take over." -Gary Keller

"Discipline equals freedom applies to every aspect of life: if you want more freedom, get more discipline." (17)

The hardest part of any habit is in the beginning. I recommend you take small steps at a time.

Lead Generation is Your Priority

You derive the advantage that you supply to your clients from doing other activities first. **Do you believe that servicing a client is more important than generating business?**

It is my firm belief that the highest priority of a real estate agent is to find more business. I have this opinion because when you have an abundance of opportunities, then you get to focus on your client's needs. If your mortgage payment, car payment, or school tuition is dependent on closing a transaction, then you will not be equipped to best help your client.

When you got your real estate license, they taught you that as a fiduciary, you act on behalf of another. When you are a fiduciary, you place another person's interest in front of all the others, including your own. When your pipeline of buyers and sellers is full, and you know that you will meet your individual goals, then you will be free to help your clients at the highest level.

If you intend to have a consistent and predictable career, you will have to seek new opportunities each day. The most successful real estate agents embrace the philosophy that finding the business is their priority. Until you drive leads each day, you should do nothing else.

REAL ESTATE EVOLUTION

Your primary intention should be to focus on generating leads for listings. When you get listings, you will control the market and attract buyers. You will feel safer for your future.

With listings, you will have more time available and be able to control your time better. You will be able to attract more business through the marketing that you employ. You can place signs that you have in the yards, advertise digitally, host open houses, and receive referrals from your sellers.

When you work with a buyer, the only opportunities you will have to gain more business will be limited to obtaining a referral or repeat business.

Your craft is to help a consumer to solve a problem or achieve a goal through helping them to buy or sell real estate. When you lead generate each day, you're in a place of power to help those consumers.

You are in the lead generation business, specializing in real estate sales. You should spend at least three hours in the morning every day and an hour to an hour and a half in the evening a few nights a week to accomplish your goals.

The best time to connect with others will be between **8:30 a.m.** to **noon** and between **7:00 p.m.** to **9:00 p.m.**

What does consistently lead generating do for you?

Picture yourself having the option to choose what type of clients you take on and how you get to spend your time. By creating an abundance of business, choices become available.

You could hire an assistant with the extra money you earn. When you hire the right person, you can enjoy more time with your family or spend time with your friends or do any other of infinite possibilities.

Teach a Man to Fish, and You Feed Him for a Lifetime

When my father turned 65 years old, we went on a salmon fishing trip to Alaska. Before our trek, I never had fished for salmon. I now was trolling for king salmon on the world-famous Kenai River.

As a novice fisherman, I understood I would need help. I hired a guide and asked the captain every question that I could contemplate.

In the early morning of our first outing, **we prepared**. We made sure we had our bait, rods, rigs, and other gear.

Next, **we made sure that our hooks were sharp**. Salmon have very thick jaws, and a dull hook would not do.

Then we wisely **choose our strategy**. There were many choices.

We could troll with a lure.

Flossing was an option. Flossing is a method to cast the line with bait less hook upstream. Then you allow the line to float downstream to catch the line in the salmon's mouth, which then will place the hook in their mouth.)

We could have selected drift fishing, which is like flossing. The difference is you use bait.

Plunking, where you allow the bait to anchor in the likely pathway of the fish, could have been an option.

And, of course, when all else fails, we could have used a bobber.

There was a variety of bait that we could have used, and we found that roe (fish eggs) was the most useful.

Finally, we **selected the best moments** to fish. Salmon run at specific times of the year. King salmon typically migrate from the ocean and swim up the rivers to spawn in early June to early July. I learned that an hour or so before or after high or low tide was ideal. (18)

In many ways, lead generating is much like fishing. To have the best opportunity to catch salmon, we used patience, the right tools, and the right gear; you will need the same to have the greatest success in lead generation.

Just like an angler, you will catch the most fish (buyers and sellers) when you:

- Hire a guide
    - Get a coach or mentor

- Ask your coach, mentors, and guides every question you can consider

- Prepare
    - Block your time
    - Know who you will contact
    - Eliminate distraction

- Sharpen your hooks (skills)
    - Practice scripts
    - Understand communication
    - Prepare to overcome objections
- Choose your strategy
    - Will you knock on doors, network, provide value to your sphere, or choose a different method to find buyers and sellers?
- Select the times when the fish will bite
    - When are your prospects home? If you choose to door knock, people more likely will be home on Saturday mornings than Monday afternoons.

My real estate agent friend, Paul Pavot, once shared with me, "In the first grade, my math teacher embedded in my head that math was a class on how to solve puzzles. That change in viewpoint made math fun. Years later, I heard several classmates say it was work and was something they HAD to do."

Paul told me that when we choose to make lead generation fun, it reminded him of how he enjoyed solving the math riddles in school. I agree.

Have some fun with your lead generation and view it as an enjoyable sport. You could elect to think of it as a game. When you do, you will be full of energy and joy and have much greater success.

The Seven Habits of the Top Salespeople

A habit is something that you do repetitively. When done through time, it often becomes unconscious. While real estate sales practices are diverse, there are everyday habits that the highest achieving real estate agents follow.

The habits of success create success, and the patterns of failure create failure. There are no unsuccessful people. There are only ineffective habits.

People who struggle in real estate sales have the habits of:

- Inability to prioritize the most critical activities
- Allowing people, tasks, email, or other distractions to get in the way
- Waiting until later to act
- Looking at life from a negative perspective
- Resistant to help or to seeking solutions
- Allowing chaos in their environment
- Not taking ownership of their actions or life

The habits of those who succeed include:

Habit 1 – Lead Generate Each Day

If you spent three hours every day looking for business, do you think that you would consistently have clients?

Even if you generated leads for one hour a day, you still would create results. If you did this for years, can you see what your results would be?

Each business day, the most successful real estate agents seek new buyers and sellers. The results of their efforts compound and lead to momentum. Besides developing personally, exploring business opportunities is the foundation for success in real estate sales and any other business.

My suggestion is to get real about the time you are willing to commit to lead generation and then take the actions -- no matter what. Be brutally non-negotiable with yourself about this time.

Habit 2 – Time Block

You probably have heard of the concept of time blocking and understand its benefits, yet you might grapple with the implementation. You can be busy and produce no results, or you can be focused and create positive outcomes.

Blocking time for your priorities will allow you to reduce chaos and be more productive. Consider scheduling for the activities of the highest importance. If you intend to be successful in real estate sales, you will have to devote time to finding business.

Time Blocking

To be successful at generating business, you will have to allocate time for it. It must go onto your calendar.

Top achievers block their time so they can lead generate effectively. Block your time for your most important activities first. These should include time for spirituality, health, fitness, family, vacation, personal development, and education, followed by the time scheduled for lead generation, going on listing appointments, and client care.

On the days that you plan lead generation, you should consider doing so first thing in the morning when you will have the highest energy.

Place appointments you intend to attend onto your calendar now -- even if you have not yet scheduled for them. That allows you to have the time available and remain focused on your highest priority. If you are unable to fill in a time slot with a listing appointment, then choose to spend that time lead generating instead. After all, if you have no planned meetings with a buyer or seller, you have no future income.

The most successful agents time block each week and follow their schedule.

A Typical Schedule

A high producing agent's schedule would be:
- **8:30 a.m.** to **8:45 a.m.** -- Participate in Power-up (Inspirational Conversation) Call
- **8:45 a.m.** to **9:00 a.m.** -- Scripts and Roleplay
- **9:00 a.m.** to **Noon** -- Generate leads
- **12:00 p.m.** to **1:00 p.m.** -- Lunch
- **1:00 p.m.** to **6:00 p.m.** -- Show properties, prepare for showings, attend education, or continue to generate leads

Other parts of your life are worthy of committing your time. Sections of your life that you might apply focused time could include:

- Spirituality
- Family
- Business
- Health
- Fitness
- Relationships
- Finances
- Rest

You also could schedule a time for anything else that is important to you. You will increase the chances of achieving your goals when you arrange devoted time to the tasks that will create the outcome that is essential to you.

> **Distractions cause failure.**
>
> **Good habits and focus cause winners.**

How do you time block?

To be effective, you first will have to prepare. These tips will guide you.

Do your best to eliminate the possible distractions that have become a part of present-day life. Eliminate the social media alerts from your phone and turn off the ringer as well as the text notifications.

If you can, respond to your emails at the end of each day or early in the morning so you have a clear inbox that will not get in your way.

Tell those around you that it is essential for you to stay focused and ask for their support. Let those people know when you are available so they will be less inclined to interrupt you.

REAL ESTATE EVOLUTION

Follow these steps to be successful.

Step 1 for Time Blocking: Identify your goals.

What goals could you create that would create the most amazing life you could imagine?
What is vital for you to achieve?
How will you feel when you achieve your goals?
There is a story about Warren Buffet and his long-time pilot, Mike Flint. Flint had an established career as a pilot, which included flying Air Force One and medivac for the Air Force as well as working as Buffet's private pilot. (19)
One day, in jest, Buffett said to Flint,
"The fact that you're still working for me tells me I'm not doing my job. You should be out going after more of your goals and dreams."
So, Flint asked Buffet for help. Buffet obliged and asked his pilot to write his top 25 goals in life, and Flint did.
Next, Buffet said, "Now circle your top five goals," and Flint did.
Buffet then told him to cross off the other 20 goals that remained on his list and avoid those at all costs until he had achieved one of the five goals intended. (20)
To summarize Warren Buffet's suggestion on goals:

1. Write your top 25 goals.
2. Circle the top 5 goals.
3. Avoid working on any other purpose than what is circled AT ALL COSTS until you achieve a goal.

Compare Buffet's strategy of focusing on less to that of digging a trench.
When you dig an inch wide and a mile deep, you will remove as much dirt as when you dig a mile wide and an inch deep. Both will require an equal removal of dirt.
Digging deep with focus will create better results.
I suggest that you take the time to do the above exercise now, so you have clarity on your intentions in life and in business. When you choose to pursue fewer goals, you will have greater focus, get better at the tasks and activities required, and more effectively achieve your destiny.

Step 2 for Time Blocking: Identify your highest priorities.

After you have identified your top goals, ask yourself what three priorities most will help you to achieve your goals.

In your sales business, this probably will be lead generation. It also could be managing your money or planning. Other priorities may include recruiting, hiring, leading, training, or anything else that will drive the best result, but lead generation always comes first.

Remember to **focus ONLY on the priorities that will drive the highest return.** To again quote Warren Buffet, he once said, "The difference between successful people and very successful people is that very successful people say, 'No' to almost everything."

Buffet is in good company about his relationship with the words, 'Yes' and 'No.'

Apple's former CEO, Steve Jobs, once said, "People think focus means saying yes to the thing you've got to focus on. But that's not what it means at all. It means saying no to the hundred other good ideas that there are. You have to pick carefully." (21)

I encourage you to take the advice from Warren Buffet and Steve Jobs. Be very selective regarding how you spend your time. Pick your priorities very carefully.

Step 3 for Time Blocking: Select how much time you will invest in the activity.

The more time you allocate to a task, the better results you will have. You might have to counterbalance your time. For example, one week, you might emphasize finding business, and the next, you might focus on recruiting.

Step 4 for Time Blocking: Schedule your priorities.

If you select lead generation as your task, then schedule this on your calendar as a recurring event. You also could block time for family, going to the gym, or anything else that is important to you.

Step 5 for Time Blocking: Add buffer time between events.

It is essential to schedule 'white space' between events. Because if something unexpected comes up, you will be challenged to handle it if you do not have extra time scheduled.

If you are like many people, you might struggle to commit sections of your day to only one task. If this is you, then start by booking an hour a day first thing in the morning for your most important job. After you master one hour blocking each day, consider adding another and continue to do this until you are your most productive.

You should do the most critical things in the morning when you have the most energy. After you complete the highest priorities, you can handle other less important matters.

Step 6 for Time Blocking: Remove the less essential tasks from your schedule.

You will have to rely on others to help you with the less important things. You could hire someone to mow your lawn or clean your house. You also could hire an assistant to complete your business's clerical tasks.

There is a plan for the best leverage in the **Build, Support, and Guide Your Team** section of this book.

Habit 3 – Provide Massive Value to Others

There are many ways to provide value to our clients. We help our clients by sharing our wisdom and knowledge. We reassure others and guide them.

We help our buyers to understand what the best communities have to offer. We help them to stay out of trouble by using the correct forms and helping with the paperwork, as well as using the proper disclosures.

We market the homes for sale in ways to get the best offers.

Our intention should be to exceed our client's expectations. This entire book outlines the value that we share with our clients.

Habit 4 – Ask for Referrals Consistently

When should you ask for a referral? **ANYTIME that someone thanks you for fulfilling your service.**

You should endeavor to ingrain response to a thank you as if you were Pavlov's dog.

When they say, "Thank you," you automatically should respond,

"You are welcome. By the way, who do you know who also is seeking a high level of care and service that has a real estate need?

"Perhaps they desire to buy a home, sell a home, or invest in real estate? Maybe someone in your family, or your work, or perhaps someone you go to church with?"

Habit 5 – Start Early

Knock out the essential stuff early. You will have more energy and be able to remain more focused.

I have watched agents come into the office late in the day. They like to sleep late. Those agents say that they operate better later in the day. I respect this, yet I encourage them to see if they can implement a different way.

If you enjoy snoozing late in the morning, what results do you see in your business? In your view, could you improve the outcome?

Habit 6 – Have the Right Mindset

Tony Robbins suggests, "The most painful mistake I see in entrepreneurs is thinking that just having a good plan or a great product is enough to guarantee success. It's not. Business success is 80% psychology and 20% mechanics. And, frankly, most people's psychology is not meant for building a business." (22)

How do you prepare for success?

You first must understand that if you intend to be successful, you will receive A LOT of, 'No's.' **When you prepare yourself to know that a 'No!' means NOTHING about you, you will achieve greater success.**

That is the reality of being a salesperson. You will make many more requests for business than you will receive affirmative answers.

REAL ESTATE EVOLUTION

I have coached hundreds of agents in a one on one capacity. During this time, I have observed that a mindset of resilience is the most significant predictor of their success in real estate sales.

Embrace the Fear

What scares you? What will hold you back? Don't worry. Fears are standard; the good news is you can **embrace the fear and TAKE ACTION** anyway.

I assure you that **you CAN succeed**.

Take a moment to consider your existence. You consist of 37.2 trillion cells! (23) When you understand that our reality expands beyond our comprehension, it becomes easier to approach the things that scare you.

You are a spiritual being in a physical manifestation. Your mind is infinite, and you can assign meaning to anything.

You can create lead generation to be a thing to fear, or you can create lead generation as something to embrace. The choice is yours.

For the last several years, my wife Traci, daughter Maggie, and I have joined our extended family each March on vacation at a lovely resort in Punta Cana. The performers from Cirque de Solei practice at the retreat that we visit, and they offer shows and events for the guests.

When Maggie was about five years old, and we were visiting the resort, she was working with a trainer who was encouraging her to do the flying trapeze.

Of course, Maggie was wearing a harness and was very safe. She started to climb the giant ladder upward step by step until fear overcame her, and she descended the steps back down.

When she touched the ground, I whispered a few words of encouragement to her. She harnessed every bit of strength she could and climbed the ladder again.

This time she got to the top of the steps jumped forward and gleefully soared through the air on the swing that was high above the safety net.

It was amazing. When Maggie returned to Earth, I asked her, "Sweetie, how did that feel?"

She replied, "Daddy, I was scared."

I asked, "And you pushed through it and did it anyway. How do you feel now?"

Maggie said, proudly and with excitement, "I feel great, Daddy!"

I recognized a parenting opportunity, and I shared with her that we all experience fear. I explained that joyfulness and success often reside on the other side of fear.

Rejection is Expected

The most productive agents will have 20 conversations about real estate each day. They will ask another person if they intend to, "Buy a home, sell a home, or invest in real estate."

Daily lead generation is the foundation to become a successful real estate agent.

The most significant cause of agents avoid prospecting is they fear rejection. They often are anxious that a prospect might be offensive or pass judgment about them or say no.

When generating leads, you must realize that rejection is never about you. Getting declined is what will occur most of the time. If you cannot overcome the fear of rejection, this is not the right career for you.

Fear is good. It protects us from danger. What you could recognize is that asking to help someone with their real estate needs is not dangerous. When you realize that you are asking to allow you to help them with a vital service, you more readily will embrace the activity.

A few weeks after we returned from Punta Cana, Maggie was practicing flips from the diving board at my in-law's home, and she invited me to join her.

I declined her invitation. She teased me and asked if I was afraid?

I said, "Yes."

"What are you going to do about being scared, Daddy?"

I taught her too well.

There was NO WAY that at the age of 45, I was willing to learn how to flip from the diving board!

REAL ESTATE EVOLUTION

Habit 7 – Take Planned Breaks

To advance your career further, faster, better, you must take the time to think and plan. When I started selling real estate, I almost always worked. I seldom took time off to plan or think.

> Winning happens before the game starts.

Throughout the years, I have learned that if you stay in action most of the time, you cannot be as effective as if you took deliberate time off. When you take breaks to unwind, prepare, and evaluate, then you can return with colossal force.

On the Tim Ferriss Show podcast, Ferriss interviewed Paul Levesque, aka, 13-time WWE wrestling world champion "Triple H." During the conversation, Triple H recalled a story about a professional boxer, Floyd Mayweather. (24)

On September 19, 2009, at the MGM Grand Arena in Las Vegas fight between Mayweather and Juan Manuel Márquez, Triple H visited Mayweather in his locker room before the bout.

Triple H found Mayweather lying on a couch watching a basketball game. Puzzled, Triple H asked Mayweather if he was wound up about the fight would begin in minutes.

"Why would I be wound up?" Mayweather replied.

"I'm either ready, or I'm not. Worrying about it right now ain't gonna change a damn thing. Right? Whatever's gonna happen is gonna happen. So, I've either done everything I can to be ready for this, or I have not." (24)

Triple H thought, "Fair enough," and they continued watching the basketball game on TV before the fight.

Mayweather prepared with passion before the contest and went on to win the event in a unanimous decision. (25)

Today I take planned time off. I block for my time to spend with my family, to rest, think, read, listen to podcasts, go to the gym, and to plan. I place these priorities before anything else on my agenda. I take most Saturdays and Sundays off so I may rejuvenate.

Each Sunday night before I go to sleep, I review the highest priorities of my upcoming week that will receive my focus. I contemplate what actions will I take to drive the business. The answer to this question typically will revolve around:

- Recruiting and attracting highly talented people who seek more than they have.
- Finding sources of business.
- Training, leading, and motivating the people I work with.

Then I decide which things will result in the most significant success and take immense action concentrated on those things.

When you plan with enthusiasm and take regular time off, you will achieve more exceptional results. Like Floyd Mayweather, when it is time to perform, you will be prepared to compete. You've either done everything you can to be ready or not.

Where Do Leads Come From?

There is no wrong way to get a lead (unless it is calling someone from the DO NOT CALL list.) All lead generation techniques work when you do them consistently.

As your business grows, you should consider adding additional sources.

Transactional vs. Relationship Marketing

Transactional Marketing means you work with people you have not yet met. You can do this through radio advertising, Internet advertising, telemarketing, networking, other paid advertising, and other ways.

Relationship Marketing means you work with people you have met -- or at least you had a conversation with the person.

Consider using both methodologies.

Intend to meet a high number of people through **Transactional Marketing** and then use **Relationship Marketing** strategies to provide them excessive value and convert them as an advocate at a high level.

It is a smart strategy to focus on maintaining valuable relationships with those who you know. These people will be the moat around your business that protects outside influences and the evolution of our industry from harming you.

The strength of your database represents the strength of your business. The larger your pool of people is, and the more systematically you contribute high value to those people, the more insulated your business shall be from threats.

To scale your business, you must cultivate those contacts you already know and create new ones through developing transactional connections into meaningful relationships.

Everyone you know today (except your mother) was at once a stranger to you. You met them, established a connection, and cultivated a relationship.

Your intention with **Transactional Marketing** should be to transform those people into your **Relationship Marketing** system.

Prospecting Versus Marketing

Prospecting costs you time and marketing cost you money. Both time and money are precious resources that you should respect and manage well.

If you are new to real estate sales, you probably have more time than money. If this is the case, then you should choose to prospect.

Ways that you could prospect include knocking on your neighbor's doors. You could contact for sale by owners and expired listings. You might also network, host events, and systematically add value to those who know you. You might host open houses, specialize in probate sales or divorces, and more. Your intention should be that others see you as the resource about real estate for your community.

If you have been successful in real estate sales for a while, and if you have money to invest, then you should consider marketing. You should do this because when your time is exhausted on your prospecting efforts, the only way to scale will be to market.

For any marketing activity, I recommend that you have 18 months of expenses set aside to continue your marketing campaign. If you stop short in your marketing campaign, then you will not receive the full benefit of your efforts.

Ways that you could market for business include mailing postcards to a farm or your sphere of influence. You could do video marketing (I suggest you hire **Vyral Marketing** to do this for you). You could advertise on Zillow, radio, television, Facebook, or Google Pay per Click, and more.

As you invest in marketing efforts, do not allow your ego to interfere with your business's mission. Your business is designed to earn a profit so you may fund a perfect life. Be sure to track the return of every dollar that you invest and remember that many marketing efforts will take up to 18 months to bear results.

Ideally, if you intend to do a lot of business, you will have to both prospect and market.

Listings

Your primary intention should be to generate leads for listings. You should seek listings so you will attract buyers. For each listing that you take, you should attract two buyers.

Results

What type of outcomes do you intend to have for when you lead generate?

Your results will depend on:

- How often are you saying it?
- What are you saying?
- Who are you saying it to?

How Often are You Saying it?

Most successful real estate agents generate leads each workday. On average, they consistently speak with ten to twenty people about real estate every day.

Unsuccessful (or at least, 'less successful') agents will prospect sporadically or start and stop and decide that prospecting does not work. They will get rejected by a prospect and then cease the activity.

If you intend to be successful, then select how many people you will speak with each day and do the activity without fail.

What are You Saying?

Most agents who fear lead generation do so because they do not know what to say. If you always knew what to say to an objection, would you ever experience fear of calling an expired listing? To best develop your skill, you should practice your scripts and role play at least 30 minutes each day.

REAL ESTATE EVOLUTION

There are several groups on Facebook where you can find a roleplay partner. I suggest that you type "Real estate role play partner" in the toolbar of your Facebook page, and you will find plenty of groups. Join one or two of them and find several partners. You should consider more than one partner. Because it might take a few before you find someone who will be as committed as you in practice.

You may visit www.GetRockSolidCoaching.com/free-coaching to get access to all scripts my sales team uses.

As a real estate agent your "toolbox" is your knowledge. Delivering what you know is also the value that you provide to your clients. You share your wisdom in many ways, including:

1. Communication Skill
2. Persuasion Skill
3. Time Management Skill
4. Market Knowledge Skill
5. Presentation Skill
6. Consultation Skill
7. Problem Solving Skill
8. Leadership Skill

Your efforts will compound. Your performance will be a result of the time on a task that will allow you to get results, as well as a new business that will come from referrals, sign calls, and Internet advertisement.

Who are You Saying it to?

When I started selling real estate, we ran many Craigslist ads of our listings for sale to attract buyers. The strategy of running these advertisements has been one of the best techniques that I ever have used.

Unfortunately, at the time, many other agents caught onto this plan, and Craigslist had to change what they allowed. So, this successful way of getting business was shut down in a moment.

I share this story with you, so you realize that it is smart to build multiple strategies to gain business. Because you might lose a given plan at any time.

You should develop a single approach or two at a time before you add another.

Pick ONE or TWO of the ideas described below that best fit your personality. Select the things that you will love to do. Avoid the tactics that you dread.

- Sphere of influence
- Networking
- Cold Calling/ Circle Prospecting
- Open Houses
- Facebook touches
- Facebook ads
- Door Knocking
- Marketing to a Farm
- Expired Listings
- For Sale by Owners
- Internet Lead Providers
- Pay per Click
- Zillow/ Trulia/ Realtor.com
- Video

There are many ways to get business, and they all work if you implement and continue the actions. **Choose the one or two that match your behavior and style and then crush it!**

Sphere of Influence

Regardless of which lead generation strategy you employ; **your sphere of influence should be the foundation for your business**. The highest return for your business will be through the people who know, like, and trust you, and this should be your foundation. **No other strategy will trump this resource**.

Your sphere of influence (SOI) includes people who know, trust, and like you. You have authority with these people because of your relationship. Your family, friends, past co-workers, people you went to school with, parents of your kid's friends would all be a part of your SOI. Other people you have a relationship with also can be a part of your sphere.

For individuals you meet face to face, you should use a high touch campaign to gain and maintain mindshare. To get a return, you will

REAL ESTATE EVOLUTION

have to communicate with your sphere in a systematic, predictable manner.

Your sphere of influence is your business. When you routinely communicate with the people who know you and offer them value and contribution, your database becomes technology-proof, recession-proof, and competition-proof.

People will view you as a resource in real estate when you methodically provide value and contribution to a group of people who know and like you. When they have a need or when a friend of theirs has a need, the likelihood is high that they will rely on you.

If you are uncertain of who is in your SOI, stop reading this book, pick up your phone, and search the contacts.

Add anyone you have had a business relationship with.

Go ahead. Take the time to do this exercise now.

Here are some questions to help you identify your sphere of influence.

Who receives payment from you?

Who do you help in their business?

Who are you connected with via social media?

Who are your children's friends' parents?

Who goes to your church?

Who do you see at the gym?

Take time to meet a new person each day and add them to your database.

Which (Customer Relationship Management) CRM should you use?
Use **whichever one that you WILL use**. If you keep track of your people in a shoebox, that is good enough if you use it!

When you add new people to your CRM, you want to gather mindshare, so they see you as the resource for real estate. You can do this by reaching out to them using a systematic method each week for two months. Share something of value with them.

You could send them a handwritten note or add them to your Facebook friends list. You could call them and invite them to attend an event with you. It does not matter what you do to touch your new contacts if you provide value and contribution and do so with a system.

After you have gained mindshare with your people, then you will touch them for a less aggressive campaign. The same rules apply to the long-term nurture campaign regarding adding value and contribution.

Systemized SOI Touches

Each year, our sales team takes the following steps to add value to our sphere of influence in an organized fashion:

- (52) Fifty-two Q & A emails sent
- (12) Twelve Social Media touches
- (4) Four phone calls
- (2) Two teaching events for their kids
- (12) Twelve print newsletters
- (4) Four client appreciation events
- (8 - 13) Eight to thirteen touches for each event

You might not have the resources to do as many activities as my sales team does. Neither did I when I started! Just build up to it through time by adding touches that you enjoy and will do consistently.

You often can partner with vendors to reduce the cost of your events and marketing. Be sure to check with your broker to be certain that any joint ventures or affiliated advertising are RESPA compliant.

After 18 months of doing this, you will get a 10 percent return from your sphere. In other words, if you have 250 people in your sphere who you provide a valuable contribution to, you will do 25 transactions from that database after 18 months of communication.

I outline the specific steps that we take for each of these touches below. **Do not get intimidated by the amount of activity that my sales network employs.** When I started, it was much less organized. Just add one step at a time and build until you have a system to communicate and massively add value to your people.

(52) Fifty-two Q & A emails sent

Every week, we email a **Question and Answer video** to our sphere of influence where we answer the most pressing questions asked of us by our clients. In the videos, we educate our audience instead of selling to them; these position us as the expert and adds value to them. Through this process, we gain trust.

In the hierarchy of communication, a video presentation is high touch. Video allows us to communicate to many on a massive scale.

Video allows us to be found online and to be able to leverage our time since we record it once, and it remains available. Our prospective clients often view the videos before we meet, and they become better educated about the home buying or selling process.

To identify the topics to speak about on your videos, type in a few keywords such as, "Real Estate buyer" "Home Search" or "Sell my Home" in the search bars of Google Trends, Quora, YouTube, or Buzz Sumo and you will find the trending and common topics that people search.

You also should search on YouTube to identify the subjects that get the most viewers. Use those same topics in your videos and share a one- to three-minute video explaining the issue. We track who opens the emails and views the videos. Then we follow up with those people to answer any questions.

If you want to get ideas on how best to implement a video strategy, I invite you to visit www.youtube.com/GreetingsVirginia, and subscribe. We post new videos on that channel each week containing information relevant to the consumer.

We also send a Q & A video to real estate agents where we share **proven** strategies to grow your business that include:

- How to **maximize** your productivity.
- The tactics, dialogues, and best practices to **close more sales!**
- How to **'Get to Yes'** through scripts.

If you would like to view these videos and more, subscribe to our YouTube channel at:

www.youtube.com/RockSolidRealEstateCoaching

When you subscribe, comment on the videos, and give us a 'thumbs up' on the videos that you love. That will help us to get higher-level interviewees that we will interview for you.

(12) Twelve social media touches

We touch our sphere of influence each month via Facebook by adding value. You could "like" a post or comment on a post.

The simplest way to add value on social media is to say, "Congratulations," "How have you been?" or "Cute baby."

This type of interaction always is welcomed and never is intrusive.

Social media is, of course, social. Consider it your digital twin that will allow you to bridge your physical world with the virtual. You can use Facebook to connect with your people systematically.

On Facebook, you should seldom ask for business and, instead, find a way to contribute to others. When you use social media effectively, you can leverage your relationships to benefit your sales business.

(4) Four phone calls

The phone calls are where you make your money; this is the most critical step to your follow-up process and should not be missed.

When you call, ask them how they are and end the call with a request such as:

> "Oh, by the way, we have had a great year because of friends like you that send referrals to us and thank you!
>
> "Can you help me with a problem?
>
> "You know that I am a pretty competitive person, and I always intend to reach my goals.
>
> "We are currently a little behind achieving this quarter's aims to help people, and I was curious. Who do you know that is in the market to buy a home, sell a home, or invest in real estate that I could call today?"

REAL ESTATE EVOLUTION

When you add tremendous value to your people, they will be inclined to think hard about who to refer to you.

(2) Two teaching events for their kids

I am passionate about helping people and specifically young people. The life's mission is to help people achieve their greatness and to open doorways for their success through my writing, teaching, coaching, and mentorship.

Twice a year, I teach a class designed for teenagers called Quantum Leap (QL). We offer this all-day seminar to the 14- to 18-year-old kids of our sphere.

Life at that age can be confusing. Their friends often have considerably more influence over them than their parents do. Sometimes **these teenagers** have no idea where to go, or what to do. They **need REAL direction** and a **REAL plan** that they can see, touch, feel and have confidence that they have faith in their future.

It's a fact that many teenagers are scared. Some mask it well, some act out. Even in the best upbringing, they fear what it will be like when they become an adult. They are finding their way in the world and creating an identity.

Through the class that we teach, students are empowered to achieve what they want in life. We train the attendees to:

- Make more desirable choices
- Develop important habits
- Move past barriers
- Boost productivity
- Create wealth

Sometimes teens ask their parents for guidance and seek mentoring. They could turn to their friends and find answers. They could act out with negative behavior.

If they don't gain clarity, they could get lost as a young adult (Trust me, I have been there).

We don't want that to happen. That is bad. Parents are grateful that we spend the time to help their kids. Kids from across the country often travel to attend. If you know of someone you would like to attend, visit: www.QuantumLeapFallsChurch.com

(12) Twelve print newsletters

Each month a printed newsletter is delivered to the homes in our sphere.

My marketing team transcribes the Q & A videos that we produce. Then they highlight those topics in a printed newsletter and deliver them to our sphere.

(4) Four client appreciation events

An **appreciation event** for your friends and sphere of influence is a great way to let those you care about know that they are meaningful to you. With these events, you can grow your relationships and meet prospective clients.

When you host a client appreciation event, it shows your sphere that you care for them and that you are grateful for the relationship you share.

Each year, my sales network hosts the following events.

1. **Spring Charity Game Night Poker** – This started as a poker night. I was surprised at how few people play poker. So, we changed the night to a game night that includes poker. In our last event, we raised $1,725 for a local hospice center.

2. **Summer Nights at the Movies** – We coordinate with the local movie theater for them to allow us to set up a table in their lobby. We buy a book of tickets and give these to our friends and clients who show up. Often, we partner with other real estate agents to host this event.

3. **Autumn Pig Roast** – This is a fun event that we host at my home each year. We order a pig (and some veggies for those who are anti-hog) and smoke it all day long. We usually will rent a moon bounce for the kids and play horseshoes, cornhole, and other games.

4. **Winter Christmas Tree Giveaway** -- We buy trees for our sphere of influence in exchange for a donation from them to Toys for Tots. The investment for this event is $35 per Christmas tree, plus the cost of some hot chocolate and cookies and the cost to pay Santa and a videographer.

REAL ESTATE EVOLUTION

Many people have good feelings during the holidays and assign those same emotions to us when we buy them a tree. We give friends a gift that stands in their living area for a month or so, during a period when they're most likely to have a party at their own house. Our past clients and friends often tell me about how good they feel about the gift.

Our Christmas tree event is well received, and we collect truckloads of toys that we donate to kids in need. It is a win-win to help our past clients and sphere as well as to help the community.

(8 - 13) Eight to thirteen touches for each event

Each event gives you a chance to touch your people many more times. You may connect in the following ways:

You may invite via:

- (1) Phone call
- (1) Text
- (1) Facebook
- (1) Video email
- (1) Printed postcard mailed to their house
- (1) Sly broadcast
- (1) Eventbrite
- (1) Face to face when available

You will see those who participate in the event.

You may touch your people after the event by:

- (1) Thank you note sent
- (1) Thank you email
- (1) Eventbrite thank you
- (1) Thank you call
- Use of the event video for promotion

You may view the events that we host for our sphere of influence when you visit www.GVAppreciatesYou.com.

You can conveniently view the curriculum of real estate sales and personal development classes that we offer by viewing www.GetRockSolidTraining.com anytime.

I invite you to attend a class if you are in town, or contact me at info@GreetingsVirginia.com if you would like to book me to teach near you.

Some of the classes that I teach include:

- The Seven Steps to Selling 36 homes in 12 months
- How to Sell a Massive Amount of Homes with Facebook
- How to Hire, Lead, Train and Develop a Virtual Assistant
- How to Increase your Profit by $100K by the next 12 months
- Purposeful Leadership
- Using Words That Matter (Neuro Linguistic Programing)

Sphere of Influence = 10 to 1 return per year after 18 months.

Networking

Networking is a strategy that allows you to leverage your time.

Consider this as an approach of **One to Many**. People you meet through networking should be added to your CRM to help you with systematic follow-up.

To thrive in networking is a bit counterintuitive. Many people believe that when you attend an event, you should seek people to help you. Despite logical reasoning, the opposite is true. If you want to be successful at networking, you should focus on helping other people first.

For example, if you go to an event and there is a baker, an auto mechanic, and a carpet installation person in attendance, who do you meet?

I suggest you introduce yourself to the carpet guy because you most likely can support him.

ALWAYS give first. Most people will feel obliged to return the favor. This is called 'Reciprocation' and is a fundamental part of being human. We naturally want to help those that help us.

REAL ESTATE EVOLUTION

When you give to others, be sure to inform them of your intention to create a reciprocal relationship. If they do not help you back, then replace the relationship with another.

As a real estate professional, you can create thousands of contacts. These contacts have tremendous value so anyone that wants to be a part of your 'inner circle' should be committed to helping you.

As a new agent, I had a lean sphere of contacts. I wondered how I could succeed in a business where I had no experience that relied on referrals and relationships when I knew few people.

I remembered that as a part of his print and promotional products sales business located in Prescott, AZ, my father used to belong to a networking club.

I called Dad and asked him to explain to me about the organization of which he was a member. He described to me that the group was a networking organization called Business Network International (BNI), where its members met each week to share referrals.

The association that my father told me about seemed to be a way to create the relationships that I would need.

I wanted to join BNI. So, I found the region's local representative, Juli, and I spoke with her to understand the process.

At the time I met with Juli, I had had my license for less than two weeks. I soon realized there would be challenges.

I learned that joining a club would be near impossible. So, I pressured Juli, "How do I start a group?"

She chuckled and assigned me a series of homework assignments. She sent me on my way.

I was asked to read a book, ***Givers Gain: The BNI Story*** by Dr. Ivan Misner and Jeff Morris about successful networking.

Juli asked me to visit two existing BNI chapters, find a venue to meet, and compile a list of 75 local business owners. She also asked me have a one on one meeting with three regional organization presidents and one local founder.

I perceived that the BNI representative, Juli, thought that I would not complete the tasks assigned to me. I was, however, grateful for her guidance.

Two days after we initially met, I called Juli and let her know her that I had completed all my assignments. I was ready to start.

I founded **BNI Positive Power**. For the first six months of my real estate sales career, I spent about 40 hours a week creating and growing the organization.

The purpose of **BNI Positive Power** is to have a team of extraordinary people committed to helping each other build their business. Those people do so through participating in a group to create opportunities in a structured and professional environment.

Every Wednesday morning for more than a dozen years, I have risen before the sun, showered, and traveled to attend **BNI Positive Power**.

BNI Positive Power has had an average of **32 members** at any given time. Throughout the years, **214 people** have been members, and we have passed **$13,564,708** of **closed business** that has landed in the pockets of the affiliates.

BNI has accounted for an average of **$117,000 gross income** each year that I have been a sales agent and continues to be a strong pillar of my business. I invest about five hours a week participating with the organization, which results in an income of about **$450 per hour** worked; this is one of the most profitable income streams that I have.

When you participate in a regular networking event, consider volunteering for leadership opportunities so you have a better chance to serve others. As a leader, you can be visible and gain credibility.

Cold Calling/ Circle Prospecting

Circle Prospecting involves making phone calls to somebody within a geographic territory and asking them for business. Calling around your listings is an excellent way to solicit new clients.

Typically, for every listing you take, at least one other person in the area is looking to list their home also. This is an excellent way to leverage your ability to take listings and get more signs in more yards.

The massive advantage of circle prospecting is that you will have zero to little competition from other agents. Many other agents are just too scared of rejection to pick up the telephone and start a conversation with a stranger. (Be sure to observe your offices policy on the Do Not Call list.)

REAL ESTATE EVOLUTION

Tools for Circle Prospecting

To find phone numbers of a specific area, you could use:

- Remine - www.Remine.com
- Cole Realty Resource - https://www.colerealtyresource.com/

Most auto-dialers have a "neighborhood search" option that will pull (and scrub do not call members) phone numbers. You could use the following for an auto-dialer:

- Mojo Sells - https://www.mojosells.com/
- Vulcan 7 - https://www.vulcan7.com/

When you are on a phone call, you often will need to identify the value of a home quickly. So, if you are a Realtor, you could use:

- Realtor Property Resource - www.NARRPR.com

Many agents immediately will give up on a prospective client if the seller indicates they will not sell for six months or more. You should realize that when you circle prospect, you will be filling a pipeline of future business.

Follow-up is the key to success with those you call while you circle prospect. Those you identify as candidates to sell in the future should be added to your quarterly phone calls and mailing campaigns as well as monthly valuation email campaigns.

Open Houses

Open houses are the most cost-effective way to get new business. More than half of home buyers will visit an open house during their search. (26)

When you employ the best systems and use the right skills, hosting an open house will yield you a tremendous benefit. Only your sphere of influence (when worked properly) will give you a better return.

Inviting people to an open house is inexpensive. It will cost you paper, ink, (maybe) an envelope, and some well-placed time/sweat equity. Make the most of inviting as many people as you can. Your seller will appreciate it, and you may run into your future client.

Here is the open house system that my team and I use to optimize our conversion rate.

Before the open house

One day before the occasion, post 20 or more directional signs in the area. Ask the neighbors for their permission to place them in front of their lawns and use this opportunity to inquire about any future real estate-related plans.

The signage should be clear to read from a distance and should be visible far enough in advance to give the buyer enough opportunity to stop. Check with your local officials for any laws concerning roadside signs.

Promotion

To get even more opportunities from your open house, you could treat it as an event and promote it excessively. When you approach it as a special occasion, you will get business from sources outside of the actual open house.

Here are the steps to employ:

- Knock on the doors of ten homes to the right, ten homes to the left, and twenty homes in the front and invite the neighbors.
- Place onto the MLS.
- Highlight the open house on your website.
- Create an event on Facebook and invite your sphere of influence to the event.
- Create and post a YouTube video announcing the open house and the features of the home.
- Create an event on Craigslist.

Post onto:

- Instagram
- Twitter

REAL ESTATE EVOLUTION

- Other social media "flavor of the day" sites
- Military by Owner
- Zillow
- Active rain

Post the listing in all local real estate open house groups. A few of the local groups and pages that my team posts our events in and on include:

- OPEN HOUSES -- NORTHERN VIRGINIA
- NOVA Open Houses
- Fairfax County Open Houses
- Open Houses This Weekend
- Listing Exchange of Northern Virginia - brought to you by Ekko Title
- www.facebook.com/GreetingsVirginia/ - Company Facebook Page

If you do video marketing, include the open houses in all video emails to your sphere of influence and real estate agents and add the client to the email.

Consider hosting a canned food drive and include this in all the promotions.

Target market in a 1-mile radius.

More than one-third of people will relocate to the same area where they currently live. (27) The listing agent or the hosting agent of the open house must look at all people who could be the right candidate for their listing. Those who will move from a close radius are good candidates to contact.

Are there apartments nearby, for first-time buyers?

Are there townhomes for people looking to move to a bigger home?

What about people downsizing or potentially retiring?

Is there someone who is paying a rent close to or slightly less than the mortgage?

If you stop and think about it, there is a logical path to people's moves; tap into it.

- Identify any tenants who live in the area.
- Identify smaller homes that are 25 percent less expensive than the house that you will be hosting.

Contact the people identified above and knock on their doors or call to invite them.

- Identify absentee owners who own more than one home within a five-mile radius. These investors might be interested in buying another home in the area.

Other Promotion

- Create and print 20 fliers.

These fliers should showcase any other open houses that your company is hosting on that day. Also, include a few other listings in the marketing that are within one mile of the event. There should be a few homes displayed on the flier that are 20 percent higher in price and some that are 20 percent lower in price.

- Print 40 surveys and bring six clipboards and ten pens with you.

- Print the Mini Property, Market, and Neighborhood reports from Realtors Property Resource® (RPR®). Obtain the real estate statistics from a resource such as Get Smart Charts (if it is available in your marketplace).

You will have these ready at the open house. You should print only one copy of each report so that when a visitor looks at it, you can solicit their contact info. (More on that below in **the open house section.**)

REAL ESTATE EVOLUTION

At the Open House

- Do a Facebook live video from the exterior of the open house. A script that you could use for your video is:

    "Greetings, this is Dan, and I want to invite you to join me today at 123 Main St. for an open house viewing. This home has (mention the features) and is located (mention the benefits of the location). Come by today between 1 p.m. and 3 p.m. for a viewing."

- Use an I-pad to collect the correct information from your visitors.

Our team created a landing page on our website for this purpose. We ask every visitor to complete the online form, which includes a place for them to input their home address if they are thinking of selling. The buyers also can select the option to be emailed homes that meet their guidelines in the area where they are searching to buy a home.

When you greet the prospective buyers, hand the clipboard and survey to them. Share with them,

> "Here is a worksheet that will help you to consider if this is the best home for you.
>
> "Would you mind completing it as you view today, and if it is OK with you, I would like to share your feedback with the seller."

When the visitor is getting ready to leave, you can inquire about the feedback. Ask,

> "Is anything that you rated less than a five out of five on your worksheet?"

If they say it was all a five, encourage them to write an offer that will get accepted. If the buyers rate an area less than a five, then inquire,

> "What is it about the kitchen that makes it less than a five out of five in your view?"

When they answer, you can say,

> "I know of a home with a kitchen that you described that is a five out of five. Would it be useful if I share that with you?"

When they say yes, it allows you to gather the correct contact information from them if you have not already managed to obtain this.

The market data you printed before the open house should be displayed. When the visitor looks at the one copy of the RPR® reports and Real Estate Statistics report, tell the visitor,

> "I'm happy you located the market data information that I prepared.
>
> "That is my last copy. I will not mind sharing a more detailed description of the local market economy with you.
>
> "Would that be useful?"

When the prospect says,

> "Yes."

Reply,

> "Great, what is your best email address? I will share it with you."

Take the time to get to know the people visiting. Seek to grasp what they are looking for and explain the data from the RPR® reports and Real Estate Statistics Report to them. You should help them to interpret the market data.

After the Open House

After you host an open house, you will have a short amount of time to qualify a buyer and understand their eagerness to buy. The sooner you reconnect with them, the more likely you will be able to work with them.

- Follow-up with all visitors and place them into the database.

- Call those buyers you met the same night and solicit an offer or share other homes with them. Remember that the buyers do not care about the service you can provide. They care about the homes. So, lead every conversation with sharing properties that match their criteria and marketplace statistics they should know.

- Send a video update to people who visited the house. You could say something like, "Bob, it was nice to meet you and Jane today at the open house at 123 Main St. I promised to update you about some other homes in the area, and I will email those to you later today. I will follow up with a phone call, as I promised, at 7 p.m. Enjoy your afternoon!"

You want to be thoughtful of the money you spent to buy the signs you have posted in the neighborhood, so you should have a plan to retrieve your signs later.

- Review the mapped-out destination chart and retrieve all the signs.

To best serve the sellers, you should communicate specific feedback that you acquired from the visitors.

- Take a selfie in front of the house and text it to the seller.

- Share a video update to the owner. You may use your smartphone to record a quick video and email the video with the seller. A script that you could use for this is,

"Ms. Owner, we had a great open house today, and x number of groups came by. I will draft a summary of the feedback and email you tomorrow. (Give a brief synopsis of any interest about the property from a buyer.)"

- Email feedback to the owners the day after and call them to discuss the feedback.

There will be times that a buyer will be ready to buy many months after you meet them. You want to ensure that no buyer falls through the cracks. The key to success is to follow up periodically with the visitors. If they do not get into immediate action to buy with you, then you should follow up at least monthly with an email and a phone call to check in.

When you follow up with the buyer, reference the open house's address, because the buyers very likely visited more than one home on the same day.

Conclusion for the Open House System

Hosting open houses can be one of the most productive activities you can do as a real estate agent. They give a home much-needed exposure and bring buyers straight to the doorstep.

The system described above is a comprehensive strategy. As a solo agent, it would be challenging to implement all the steps.

If you are an agent on your own, you could implement as many of the steps as possible. Choose the steps that you will employ and then do them systematically for each open house.

If you are a **Rainmaker** or **Leader of a Team**, you could leverage the steps above to your staff.

If you would like a copy of the checklist that we use that includes the delegation of each step described above, visit www.GetRockSolidCoaching.com/free-resources.

REAL ESTATE EVOLUTION

Facebook Ads

You can post property ads on your Facebook business account Facebook by placing an advertisement with pictures and description of the property being listed to display directly on the news feed of people "likely to move" in your city.

Facebook is a visual platform. As a real estate sale is most often an emotional purchase, you can appeal to the consumer through posting attractive ads. People scrolling Facebook will be encouraged to learn more.

The Facebook platform allows you to target geographically. With the analytics of Facebook ads, you will be able to identify the precise metrics of your advertising efforts.

In the first rendition of this book, I started to describe a **step-by-step process** for you to create an advertisement on Facebook.

Midway through writing, Facebook changed its advertising rules, so I restarted the section.

A week after I completed the second round, Facebook changed the rules again.

I realized that if I were to share a step by step process with you, it would soon be obsolete. So, I will share general guidance. If you desire up-to-date specific instruction, email me at Info@GreetingsVirginia.com with the subject line, 'Share Facebook Strategies,' and I will introduce you to a resource that will help you.

To optimize Facebook ads, you will have to target the right audience. Here is general guidance on how to build the best advertisement for your viewers:

- Narrow the target of your promotion and make it local. Exclude people who are not very probable to be your next buyer.

- Use the most appealing graphics to engage the user. Use the best copywriting. A well-written advertisement should attract someone, describe what you are offering, capture the buyer's desire, and call them to act. Use emojis in the text to allow for your content to better stand out among all other posts.

- Use a landing page. Most website development platforms, such as **WordPress** and **Squarespace**, will allow you to create a landing page quickly. The purpose should be to direct a user to a single page that shares with them the information they are seeking and to gather a way to contact them.

- **Test your ads.** You will never know that you have it right without proper testing. When doing advertising, you should test, test, and test again.

Here's a fundamental way of how you do it.

- Create a Facebook post that will showcase a home for sale.
- Use visually attractive photographs.
- Post onto Facebook and choose the best target audience that you think most likely will be interested in buying the property.
- Use Facebook to collect the contact info.

This approach will require a small financial investment each day. You should expect about a **one percent immediate return** and about a **three percent to five percent return** over **18 months** with your advertisement on Facebook.

Facebook Ads Warning

Years ago, my team and I generated many prospects through advertising on Craigslist. Other real estate agents began using this same approach and saturated Craigslist's pages with ads. Craigslist changed their algorithm so consumers could not directly click through a property advertisement to your agent website; this no-cost approach of advertising on Craigslist went away.

Then we began advertising on Google Pay Per Click, and for a short time on Zillow. As other real estate agents used these same platforms more and more, Google and Zillow increased their prices and became cost prohibitive. The return on the investment no longer made sense, so we stopped advertising on those platforms.

Beware that as other agents advertise on Facebook more, the price for ads probably will rise. When this happens, Facebook likely will become a bad choice for advertising.

REAL ESTATE EVOLUTION

Door Knocking

Knocking on doors is a free, old school technique, and there is no barrier to entry (unless it is a gated community or No Soliciting community). The results for this vary greatly based upon skill, follow-up, and strategy.

Many agents are fearful of knocking on doors, so you will have zero competition, which allows for better conversations that more likely will produce a positive result.

> Knocking on doors is a great way to get some exercise.

A successful strategy takes consistent follow-up and is not an immediate gratification strategy; often, you will find sellers who will be selling in the future. You will have to follow up with these sellers using a system. To get the best results from door knocking, you should do so in the evenings around **5:00 p.m.** or **6:00 p.m.** or on **Saturday morning** between **9:00 a.m.** and **11:15 a.m.** You might consider high-priced townhouses or rowhomes if possible since you will be able to reach more people.

Remember to get their contact information when you speak with a person at their door. You should carry blank greeting cards with you so you can write a thank you card as soon as you leave their house before you knock on the next door. It might be inconvenient to draft a letter while you are walking, yet more effective than if you wait until you return home or to the office.

Immediately after your visit, you will remember more crucial details about the homeowner.

Knowledge such as their kids' and dog's names and other significant factors can be mentioned in your note. And, of course, include your business card. Then add each person that you meet into your database so you may add value to them in the future.

Your best contact while visiting people is the chatty neighbor who is in everyone's business. The gabby person will tell you everyone in the neighborhood who is getting divorced, married, or fired from their job. They will share an array of other reasons that a homeowner might want to sell soon. I have one such person in my database.

I've completed four transactions referred to me from this person generating $2.1 million in sales.

Here is a great script that you could use while knocking on doors.

> "Hi, my name is Dan, your local real estate agent. I just wanted to say hello and introduce myself to you. If I ever can help you with anything, please consider me as a resource.
>
> "Let me know if you ever have any questions about real estate or need any support at all. If you ever would like a professional analysis of your home, I would love to help.
>
> "Here is how you can contact me. Thanks very much."

Marketing to a Farm

Marketing to a farm is conventional for many top-producing agents. **If you were to start a new farm today, in 18 months, you would see the return on your efforts**.

To optimize the farming activity, you should be integrated into your community as much as possible. You should do events, postcard market, and door knock.

To best establish a farm area, you should become integrated within the community as much as possible. You should host local events in the area often. Each quarter you should knock on doors, and you could use other methods, such as mailing postcards to the people who live there, etc.

Consider starting with your own neighborhood and then expand. In the beginning, you might consider limiting the size of your farm to 100 homes (in the supplement to this book, *The Survive and Thrive Game Plan,* which you may find by visiting www.GetRockSolidCoaching.com/Gameplan/ I'll show you how to break down a farm so you can handle over 300 homes!) and increase to more houses as you have success.

Expired Listings

Some of the most successful real estate agents in the business specialize in listing homes that did not sell with another agent the first time; these are expired listings.

REAL ESTATE EVOLUTION

An expired seller has two hands in the air. One hand says, "I want to sell my home." The other says, "and I'm willing to pay a real estate agent to do it!"

Conversion rates for prospecting expired listings are high, and it is a very effective use of your time. People who own a listing that just expired often intend to sell their home quickly. These phone calls are usually short, which allows for more contacts in the same amount of time as other methods.

If you choose this method, you will compete with very few highly skilled agents and many limited experienced agents who will do it for a short period and then cease the activity.

You can call listings that expired yesterday or listings that were on the market and expired six months to three years ago.

For sellers that expired in the past six months or longer, you will approach them with the best script.

If the market has increased in value since they were last on the market, say,

> "Mr./Mrs. Seller, I see that you were intending to sell a few years ago and were not able to do so. Now that the market has increased x percent since you were on the market, would you be interested in selling?"

If the market has decreased in value, say,

> "Mr./Mrs. seller, I see that you were intending to sell a few years ago and were not able to. Would you be interested in selling today?"

Expired Listings = **The results of this will depend on your skill**.

FSBO – For Sale by Owner

If I told you I knew a seller who is 100% going to sell their home and they have not hired an agent yet, would you like to meet them?

If you answered yes, then I can introduce you to dozens or hundreds of them today. Every For Sale by Owner (FSBO) on the market meets the description at the beginning of the previous paragraph.

After you visit with a FSBO, you will have to systematically communicate with the seller in a manner where you offer value and contribution. To do this, you should share with them any of the strategies outlined in the Lead Generation section of this book.

You could take the time to explain to them how to post their property on Facebook. You could offer to host an open house for them. You could provide any other thing that will help them to sell.

As you systematically communicate with the sellers, they will relate to you as a helpful resource in real estate, and for every five that you visit and help through your system, one will hire you.

The key ingredients to listing a FSBO are:

1. Get in front of them.
2. Understand that on most first-time appointments, you are there to create a connection. (There are a few where this is not the case and, in this event, be ready to list them.)
3. You must provide them value.
4. You must follow up with them with purpose.

FSBO sellers have the highest contact to appointment set ratio and lowest appointment held to getting hired ratio. Twenty percent of FSBOs that you contact will list with you when you follow up with them appropriately.

If you want to get one listing per week, then you must have a face-to-face with five FSBOs per week. You get hired at a lower rate (one out of every five meetings) than most other techniques because FSBO sellers often believe that you will have a buyer when you visit them, and they want you to view their home rather than to list it.

FSBO = **1 out of 5** that you meet face-to-face should list with you.

Internet Lead Providers

Several companies will arrange a referral relationship with you in return for a referral fee. The fees charged by these companies range from twenty-five percent to thirty percent. Most of these have requirements for you to have a record of success, and all will hold you highly accountable for your success.

Internet usage has everyone accustomed to fast response times. So, it would help if you thought regarding responding in less than 24 seconds rather than 24 hours. Speed wins this contest almost every

REAL ESTATE EVOLUTION

time. When an Internet lead comes in, your chances of conversion are highest if you call them while they are still on the website. It would help if you strived to have as close to an instant response as possible for incoming Internet leads.

My team and I invest a lot of money in Facebook advertisements. I have spent a large amount of money and time on developing our official company website, .

To hold the money invested accountable for online advertising for results, you must respect that Internet leads can get expensive, and you should respond to them at a high level.

My experience shows that buyers and sellers captured on the Internet often begin their online search as much as 18 months before they intend to buy or sell. To fully optimize the opportunity of the Internet, we must follow up with these prospects for an extended period.

A large part of the high producing agent's business is often derived from direct online lead generation efforts or from relationships they have established with online providers. Here are a few that you could apply to work with:

- Dave Ramsey, ELP - https://elp.daveramsey.com
- Agentology - https://www.agentology.com
- Agent Machine - https://www.agentmachine.com
- Veterans United - https://www.veteransunited.com
- Home Light - https://www.homelight.com

The relationships that you have with your online partners will be vital, and they are at the mercy of your high performance. As a minimum, you should intend to close ten percent of the leads that your online partners introduce to you.

If there is no phone number given with an Internet lead, it is your goal to set up a phone appointment via email. You may accomplish this with a little skillful back and forth communication.

The first reply via email is, "Here is the information you need."

And then you ask a question to generate a conversation, such as,

"What exactly are you looking for in a home?"

When they reply, you can take the next step by emailing,

"That sounds like a very nice home that you described. Let's do this. Let's set up a phone call so I can thoroughly answer your questions."

When they respond affirmatively, you should email them,

"Great, what is the best phone number and when are a few ideal times that I may call you?"

Internet Lead Providers = **Between five to ten percent**, depending on if the leads go directly to you or if you are competing against other agents.

Pay Per Click

I ran an actively managed Google AdWords campaign for one year with poor results. My conclusion was that there was a low return on investment for this method.
If you choose to explore this advertising option, you might consider getting someone to manage it for you. Word Stream -- https://www.wordstream.com/ is a company that does an outstanding job of managing an AdWords campaign.
Google PPC = one **out of ten** = A lead. **One hundred leads** = five **sales over two years**. You must methodically stay in touch with them during those two years.

Zillow/ Trulia/ Realtor.com

Advertising on Zillow/Trulia/Realtor.com is a marketing strategy that supplements some agent's prospecting activities. A few agents in my marketplace invest as much as $25,000 each month to these platforms and they generate a massive amount of sales as a result.
If you consider using a platform such as Zillow, I recommend that you take a comprehensive look at the investment vs return. These lead generation sources are often cost-prohibitive, and if you choose to rely on them, you never will be in control of your business.
There are a few geographic areas that I have found where Zillow provides a good return. I accidentally learned this when I hired an agent for my team. She already was working with Zillow in a very rural area. I soon learned that the return in this area made sense

because there was little competition from other agents in the small town, we were advertising to.

Video

We use video as a large part of our marketing and conversion.
The script to share with those clients is:

> "We share video marketing messages every two weeks that are educational and share value (not selling) with our clients, past clients, and friends."

Here's what to say on a phone call with your acquaintance or prospective lead, for example:

> "Hi, is this Greg?
>
> "Greg, my name is Dan Rochon – I'm with **Greetings Virginia Sales Network** here in Alexandria, VA. I see you subscribe to the real estate videos I publish about what's going on with local home prices.
>
> "Have you seen our latest video on _____? Great! I'm calling with two quick questions,
>
> "First, do you have any questions about where the market is heading or about buying or selling a home, I can answer for you in my next video? If I pick your item, I'll send you a $25 gift card. Great! Happy to answer that.
>
> "Do you also happen to know anyone in your circles who may need to buy or sell a home? Okay, thank you.
>
> "When do you plan on moving, by the way? Thanks for your time, and if I pick your question for a video, I'll let you know."

If you know the person you're calling, soften up the opening line:

> "Hi, this is Dan! I'm calling to check to see how things are going. I also have two quick business questions for you if you have time…"

If you are an inside sales agent making calls on behalf of our agents, the script changes to:

> "Hi, my name is Anthony with **Greetings Virginia Sales Network**. Dan Rochon asked me to call you, and Dan wants to know…"

Converting a lead begins with getting enough information to contact the prospect. Then the process moves to building rapport, credibility, and a relationship and ends with a phone or face-to-face appointment.
At the end of each conversation or meeting, you ALWAYS should schedule the next step or phone call. The maximum time between touches for any prospect should be three months. The script to use to set this up would be:

> "Would you mind if I follow up with you in the (next season -- winter, spring, summer, fall)?"

Other Strategies

Here are a few things that might help you in your lead generation efforts.

- Host a competition.

See who will generate the most converted leads in a set period versus another person from your office. Fierce competition and accountability create results.

- Build a video blog.

Brand yourself on social media.

"Power out? No problem -- You can still dunk in the dark."
That was Oreo cookie's brilliant Tweet when the lights went out for twenty-two minutes at the Superdome during Superbowl XLVII.
It turns out that Oreo had a team of fifteen people monitoring the game, ready to respond with timely and topical updates about what was happening during the game. (28) (29)
You probably do not have a team of fifteen people at the ready to respond to local happenings, but you still can benefit from using social media.

REAL ESTATE EVOLUTION

Smart use of social media allows you to reach a targeted group in a manner that other media does not offer. In 2019, it costs more than $5 million to advertise on television during a Super Bowl. (30) Oreo proved that at a small fraction of the cost compared to other media, social media is powerful. Oreo proved the point that social media can be a terrific tool to promote your business.

You can use social media to your advantage in many ways. You should select a few strategies and then put them into a system.

Interact on a regular schedule

A system you can use to interact on a regular schedule will allow you to be proactive in your efforts while preventing distraction. For example, you could the following:

Each day

- Place one comment on five of your connections' posts.
- Like (or Love) five posts that show up in your feed.
- Message five people.

Mondays

- Post about a local topic (such as the pothole repairs Main Street) or acknowledge a local vendor or business owner for how they have helped a client of yours.
- Share a snippet of a video intended to help consumers on all business platforms.

Tuesday

- Express gratitude.
- Share a snippet of a video intended to help real estate agents on all personal accounts.

Wednesday

- Share about a family-related event.
- Share a snippet of a video intended to help consumers on all business platforms.

- Ask a question on your platforms. You should plan to start a conversation.

Thursday

- Share about something you have learned. Your nugget of knowledge could be about real estate, organizations, leadership or anything else you have learned.
- Share a snippet of a video intended to help consumers on all business platforms.

Friday

- Post something to display an appreciation about a friend, family, or colleague.
- Share a snippet of a video intended to help consumers on all personal platforms.
- Ask a question on your business platforms.

Saturday

- Share a story about something you have done that has helped a real estate client.

Sunday

- Share something about love, appreciation, God, relaxation, or inspiration.

Groups

Facebook and LinkedIn both have groups where you can provide value as a professional. Find a group that you enjoy and then become an active member.

Remember that your job in the groups is to provide value that relates to the group's members. You should not promote yourself or services actively, yet you should be a resource. For example, if you belong to a local mom's group, and a member is seeking a connection to a contractor, you could make the introduction.

REAL ESTATE EVOLUTION

Through time, you will become known as the resource for real estate-related needs. When someone is in the market to buy a home, sell a home, or invest in real estate, you likely will be mentioned by members you have helped in the past.

Use longtail keywords on your website for SEO.

Longtail is the use of hyper-local keywords. Instead of posting content online such as "Virginia Real Estate Agent," you could post, "3 Bedroom townhomes in Alexandria, Kingstowne, VA with a fireplace." You will get fewer visitors and have less competition from other websites, and the visitors you get will be high-quality leads.

Email drip to your people.

Email is a less productive activity that should supplement your other efforts. Email drip alone will produce almost zero opportunity.

Post videos on YouTube.

Google owns YouTube, and this is an area where you have much less competition for eyeballs on the Internet. When you combine this with long-tail keywords, it can be beneficial.

Post blogs.

Become the hyper-local expert by posting content about the neighborhood.

- Obtain testimonials on an iTunes podcast, such as www.greetingsvirginia.com/gv/client-testimonials

Follow up quickly and get permission to add people to your database.

Agents in the **Greetings Virginia Sales Network are** supported by the **Inside Sales Agents** to be sure that our response time is quick and conversion rates are high and that we can follow up effectively over a long time period.

If our office speaks with 100 people a day, then conservatively, thirty percent of those people will provide their email address. That's thirty emails a day for our team that we will add to our company CRM.

Asking for Email Addresses

Each day, you talk with new clients, former clients, current clients, leads, and more. At the end of every conversation, everyone, even the administrative team, should say:

> "By the way, we send out two helpful videos a month, and I'd like you to receive them. What your best email address?
>
> "The emails will come from our team leader, Dan Rochon."

You want every contact to know this when they hand over their email address. When your connections know they will receive valuable emails, your open email rates will increase dramatically since you will build a 100% permission-based email list.

Lead Generation Conclusion

The average real estate agent does not place focus enough on generating leads each day. Every four months or so, many agents will have one to three closings and zero in between.

The sporadic closings happen because the average agent spends most of their time servicing their clients. When the average agent goes to the closing, they must begin all over looking for a new client. You can change this cycle when you focus on the highest priority of lead generating.

Later in the **Evolved Bonus Steps: Build and Lead Your Team** section, I will share strategies on how you can leverage so you can focus on lead generating each day.

Do you want to amplify the strategies described in this section? I share the top scripts that have allowed me to help 1,000s of clients in, *The Survive and Thrive Game Plan.* You may get a copy of this guide by visiting www.GetRockSolidCoaching.com/Gameplan/ I'll show with you the specific tactics that have worked.

Step 3: Focus on Conversion

Some real estate agents do not have a lead generation problem because they have figured out this method of the sales process; these agents have a conversion problem.

The very top performers understand that the gold is within the lead generation, and the platinum is within the lead conversion. To obtain **C.P.I.**[*], as a real estate agent, you will have to be consistent in your follow-up. I have discovered that my sales team receive more sales from people we already know than from the various new people we meet each week.

Conversion usually takes time, and when someone in your database is ready to buy or sell and they contact you, it sometimes appears like a thing that happens all at once. It is most often a result of many actions taken over time.

When you speak with a lead, you should probe, prod, dig deep. Unpeel the onion. Ask many questions, such as:

---

[*] C.P.I. = Consistent, Predictable Income

- Why is that important to you?
- What is significant about that?
- Tell me more.

At the end of every conversation (phone and in-person), you should say,

> "This is what will happen next..." at the end of EACH conversation

Seek always to provide value and contribution. NEVER leave an appointment or phone conversation without setting the next meeting (phone or in-person).

Proper Procedures for Intake and Conversion

A complete intake and needs analysis are essential to set good appointments. When you do a correct intake, there should be a smooth flow in your conversation, and you should ask the right questions. A thorough intake will lead to efficiently conducting business; you will earn a higher income.

This system is proven to be proactive in avoiding complications in the future, instead of being reactive to problems when they arise.

> "The price of inaction is far greater than the cost of making a mistake."

Practice one step each day.
I describe a lot of details in this book. Much of it is probably new to you, and it may seem overwhelming. I promise that when you follow these methodologies, you will have more consistent business and make more money. You do want to make more money, don't you? High-level salespeople understand that sales are a process that you will get better at through education, practice, review and adjustment, and implementation. I highly recommend you select one piece of the process at a time and master it before you move onto the next. Practice a step each day, master it, and start following the methods described above. Do not allow the magnitude of the process to get in your way of implementation. It is better to start, make a mistake, reset and adjust, and start again versus never starting.

Pipeline

Some agents follow up with seller prospects for years before they get hired. When those agents get the job, it sometimes appears as a single event. Most of the time, it is the result of many actions the agent has followed in a systematic process through time.

To convert a prospect most effectively to a client, you should use a plan.

If you lead generate regularly, you will have the opportunity to sell homes. When you have leads, you should follow up with them in a consistent manner. To systematically follow up, keeping track of your people in a pipeline will be helpful.

The more prospects you have, the more business you will do, the more people you will help, and the more money you will earn.

Your intention while generating leads should be to provide value. When you provide value, people want to reciprocate and will nearly always give you their name, phone number, email address, and home address. Your purpose should be to turn your activities into appointments; this will take persistence, systems, skill, and timing.

When you lead generate, it should be your goal to get a date. You should understand where you are in the process.

If you are a single guy and you walked up to a pretty lady at the bar who you never have met before, would you ask her to marry you? I would guess, probably not.

Treat the conversion process like the dating process -- one step at a time that naturally leads to the next level.

Understand where you are and strive to move the process toward the next step. If you receive a lead without a phone number, you should get the phone number.

Consider using a simple pipeline tool to organize your possibilities. In your pipeline, you should track prospective clients from 1 to 10, with a 10 meaning they are ready to roll today.

Here is the way you could arrange your prospects:

Ratings –

10 = Appointment scheduled or Hired (not on the market yet).
Will write an offer to get accepted or list with us in:
9 = Less than 30 days.
8 = Less than 60 days.

7 = Less than 90 days.
6 = Less than 120 days.
5 = Introduced to a lender or referral partner.
4 = Agreed for follow up for next quarter or sooner.
3 = Expressed Interest (Contact).
2 = Expressed Interest (No Contact).
1 = Prospecting

Sort the candidates who will buy or sell in a systematic format; this will allow you more easily to understand who you should follow up with today. You will be less likely to get bogged down, calling people who are not ready to buy or sell now.

The maximum time between touches for any prospect should be three months. The script to use to set up the next follow-up is:

> "Would you mind if I follow up with you in the (next season -- winter, spring, summer, fall)?"

When you call them in the next season say,

> "Hello, this is Dan Rochon. You asked for me to call you in the summer and it is the summer. Are you still considering selling your home?"

You NEVER should leave ANY meeting or conversation without setting up the next step. An appointment for another phone call is acceptable.

Tracking Results

How does a football team know if they are a good team or improving?
They keep score.
Why do they keep score?
They keep score so they can measure performance. Just like any sports team or other business, to increase your effectiveness, you must keep score.
When we focus on a simple scorecard to track the metrics that will lead to achieving our goals, it makes it easier to keep on track. The conversations I recommend that you monitor are:

REAL ESTATE EVOLUTION

1. Appointments attended
2. Clients (buyers or sellers) who have hired you
3. Closings
4. Profit

These are conversations that feed each other.

You should be aware that "Appointments attended" is the leading measure that results in "Clients (buyers or sellers) who have hired you" that leads to "Closings," which results in "Profit."

I suggest you focus your energy on the appointments that you attend, and all else will follow.

When you know your numbers, you will be able to identify gaps.

When you have a lot of conversations and attend a few appointments, then your opportunity is to change the words you use (better scripts) or speak with different people. If you have a few conversations each day about real estate, then your chance to improve is to have more discussions.

What is important is that you have the conversations each day of the week. I recommend having at least ten conversations about real estate each day. But if you choose to do fewer, define your standard, and never have fewer than you want.

A real estate conversation is the following:

A two-way communication about real estate where you are asking a friend, family member, someone else you know, or someone you do not know.

> "Who do you know that needs to buy a home, sell a home, or invest in real estate?"

or,

> "What are your real estate-related plans?"

Outcomes

To understand the expected conversion rates for real estate agents, you should understand the following: (31) (32)

- Contacts per hour range from:
    - 1 per hour for a beginner
    - 17 per hour for an advanced agent

- Contacts to the appointment will range from:
    - 25 to 1
    - 150 to 1

- Appointments to hired will vary from:
    - 4 out of 10
    - 8 out of 10

To obtain the higher numbers, you will have to use an auto dialer such as:

- www.Mojosells.com
- www.Vulcan7.com

Mojo offers a triple line dialer that will allow the highest amount of contacts. Vulcan7 provides a straightforward user interface. Both platforms synch with many of the most popular CRMs.

If your MLS has access to www.remine.com, you can improve your contact to appointment ratio by targeting the sellers most likely to sell.

Step 4: Nail Your Presentation

Although every home sale is different, they all also share certain elements. My team and I have developed many effective systems and strategies to implement the ten steps described in this book.

In this competitive real estate marketplace, people have choices. They have many options. You should communicate your value to others in the most effective way possible so they will hire you.

Sellers and buyers choose to work with me for several reasons. Over the past decade-plus, I have documented the critical details and I share those with you. As you read through this section, you will become confident that you are the best agent to help buyers and sellers.

Your job is to help people **MAKE THE RIGHT CHOICE** with as little stress as possible. An agent's job is to guide a buyer, seller, lender, title company representative, or cooperating agent to an agreement.

Using a defined system and effectively communicating with your clients how you implement your system will lead to **C.P.I.**[*] for you as a real estate agent.

The 80/20 Buyer Consultation

In 2018, Founder, Chairman, and CEO of Keller Williams Realty, Gary Keller, gave his Family Reunion Vision Speech, where he described the evolution of data, search and transaction care.

In the convention hall where Keller spoke, the following was cast onto the giant digital display at the front of the room to accompany his speech:

- Book: YOU owned data + search and transaction
- MLS: WE owned data + search and transaction
- Public Search Portal: WE own inventory data + transaction data; THEY own search data + eyeballs
- What's Next? Depends on YOU

The consumer now has the same access to homes for sale data that the agents have. Many buyers believe an agent's only job is to find them a home. **Those buyers are wrong**. The buyers lack the understanding of the way that, as an agent, you will support and protect them throughout the transaction.

As the transition of access to information has evolved from agent to consumer, it has become more vital that we provide a high level of care to our buyers. We must keep those buyers out of harm's way and effectively communicate how we will help to guide them at a high level.

I have found that it is obvious to follow a proven system.

It is a mistake for you to neglect to appropriately interview, consult, and set expectations for the buyer so you will avoid problems in the future.

The Pareto Paradox of the 80/20 Buyer Consultation

In an earlier chapter, I explained a concept that I coined the **Pareto Paradox**, which is the seemingly self-contradictory idea that is

---

[*] C.P.I. = Consistent, Predictable Income

relevant to all aspects of sales. This principle states that in communication, the highest return on your actions, eighty percent, comes from listening.

The **Pareto Paradox** is at odds with the **Pareto Principle**, which states that twenty percent of your most impactful actions usually will generate eighty percent of your successful outcomes.

With the **Pareto Paradox** in mind, I designed the **80/20 Buyer Consultation.**

Do not get confused by the name of the **80/20 Buyer Consultation,** that twenty percent of your consulting results in eighty percent of your results. The opposite is accurate. This represents the **Pareto Paradox** in effect during the **80/20 Buyer Consultation**.

The **80/20 Buyer Consultation** is designed to show you the needs and means of a home buyer. Experience shows that throughout this consultation, you should **listen eighty percent of the time** and **ask questions and consult twenty percent of the time**.

Choose to overemphasize listening and understanding. Of the actions that you will take, eighty percent of your time spent listening is the most vital.

My team and I use a systematic approach to consult with our buyers, which allows us to have more sales with fewer problems. Be proactive. Follow the steps of the process in order.

Here are step-by-step instructions to follow in the 80/20 Buyer consultation:

1. Call the prospect within 5 minutes or less.
2. Complete the buyer's questionnaire.
3. When they are done speaking, summarize what they have told you.
4. Dig deep.
5. Send a Google Calendar invitation for them to attend the next step of the conversation. This could be for a face to face appointment or for another phone conversation.
6. Film a short video to introduce yourself to the buyer and text it to them.
7. Introduce them to a lender.
    a. Review the buyer's ability to buy.
8. Set up/ host the second phone call.
9. Set up an in-office appointment.

10. Share the obstacles in the market.
    a. Short Sales
    b. REO's
    c. New homes
    d. Underwriting
11. Hitting the bullseye conversation.
12. Two showings or less.
13. Showing homes and using 1 to 5 script.
14. Home inspection conversation.
15. Preparation before the initial appointment.
    a. Prepare
    b. Share market statistics
    c. Ask for transparency
16. Prepare for the buyer tour.
17. Share market statistics.
18. Ask for openness.
19. Get hired.

It is most useful to ask a buyer to meet at the office because it will allow for you to present a higher professionalism. You also should qualify that all buyers should consult with a lender before you show them homes.

Before you meet with the buyer(s), **DO NOT mention the Buyer Listing Agreement**. You will get hired at the end of the consultation process before you show any homes to them.

Correctly following the process makes it easy to get hired. If you mention the paperwork earlier than you should, the buyer often will become uncomfortable and most likely reject you.

Have a minimum of two phone conversations with the buyer (while sharing homes for sale that match their criteria, consulting on the process with the discussions outlined in this section, providing value, and developing rapport).

During the conversion time, you need to connect with the buyer. The more you communicate with them with the highest level of communication possible, the greater the rapport and trust that will be developed. Please take the opportunity to film a short video on your phone and share it with the buyer.

Speed to lead -- Call the prospect within five minutes or less. Seventy-five percent of home buyers interviewed only one real estate agent. (33)

If you have an average ability to sell but you converse with the prospect quickly, you will beat a lazy agent who has superior skills. **Speed to lead always will conquer immense know-how**. You should contact prospective clients as soon as possible; think in terms of minutes (or seconds) rather than days.

When you get a lead, your response time is the most vital thing that will impact your capture and conversion. If you have a moderate skill set, you will beat the other agent with a high skill set due to your quick response.

Many home buyers expect agents to be available to show them homes at any moment. Many agents will accommodate those buyers. If you choose not to consult your clients before working with them or, worse, you embrace not getting hired by your buyers, you will do less business.

Complete the buyer's questionnaire.

When you speak with the buyer, refer to the home as a "Home." Your buyer will experience a greater emotional connection when you say the word "Home" instead of "Property" or "House."

When you complete the buyer questionnaire, you can do so over two phone appointments and one office appointment. You should spend one to two hours consulting with any prospect before showing any homes. That will allow you to be proactive in setting expectations and avoiding future problems.

You might think, "Ouch! Two phone appointments and one office appointment?!?! One to two HOURS consulting a buyer?!?!"

Others have told me that they were genuinely shocked when they read my suggestion to take the proper amount of time to understand your buyer's needs and consult them.

Many 'newer' agents spend less than ten minutes asking questions of a buyer before they take them out to look at homes. Even advanced, 'more successful' agents seldom spend the proper amount of time with a buyer because those agents want to save time.

While I respect the rationale of a real estate agent who intends to reduce the time of consultation to a minimum, I guarantee that the **80/20 Buyer Consultation** will save you time, and you will sell more homes. When you emphasize helping a buyer upfront, you will avoid the problems that are typically associated with a transaction.

You could organize the **80/20 Buyer Consultation** as,

- Initial phone conversation (or video chat) (30 minutes)
- Secondary phone conversation (or video chat) (30 - 45 minutes)
- In-office appointment (30 – 45 minutes)

A proper buyer consultation will allow you to understand the buyer's:

- Needs
- Wants
- Motivations
- Means (ability to purchase)

Complete the intake sheet by asking questions. Listening will let you know if the prospect **wants to buy** and **can buy.** Find out what is essential to the buyer.

If you are embracing Internet lead generation, you often may encounter people who are motivated to buy, yet they are not qualified through a lender to do so. Many times, those buyers will not have the credit and income to get a loan. If this is the case, you will cultivate the prospective buyer through time, when appropriate.

Summarize what they have told you.

Example: "Danny and Karen, this is what I heard. You ideally would like to buy your next home in the next thirty days. You are looking for a five-bedroom home in Alexandria with three baths and a big backyard."

Dig deep.

A real estate sale often is the most significant transaction a person will make in their lifetime. The sales techniques that work for salespeople in smaller sales will not suffice in this substantial situation.

Your clients don't care about you. They care about themselves and their problems.

Don't believe me? The next time you participate in a group photograph, notice you look for when you view the photo. Yep, I thought so.

The deeper that you grasp the issues and fears that they have, the more homes you will sell. Buyers need to feel reassured and that they are making the right decision. Your job is to guide them through the buying process, so they feel excited when they buy.

Most agents never take the time to understand the essential motivation of their clients. You should endeavor to understand their basic needs and then dive deeper to understand their psychological needs.

For example, if you find out that a single man is looking for a three bedroom, and two-bathroom townhouse near his job, you have done a proper intake.

When you continue diving deeper into the conversation, and you learn the man just experienced a bitter divorce, you have done better.

When you learn that he is terrified he will lose his kids and he wants to live close to them, you will be better prepared to help.

What does this mean to him as a man?

Maybe he would view himself as a bad father, a failure.

Perhaps during your first conversation with the gentleman, you will not profoundly appreciate his divorce woes. Yet, as the relationship develops, you should strive to understand his deep desires fully.

Avoiding being a bad dad is a pretty compelling reason for your single man to buy – and much more meaningful than your original understanding of the necessity for the person to buy a 3/2 townhome.

Homebuyers and sellers are often:

- Scared about a relocation
- Nervous
- Anxious
- Eager to get going
- Concerned about the transition
- Worried about their kids' school

- Apprehensive about a new job
- Stressed about a relationship
- Thinking of a potential gain or loss
- Sometimes (often) emotionally attached to the property they are leaving
- Have many memories are associated with the home
- Tense about money

Your job is genuinely understanding the buyer's deep needs. The more extensively you can know a client's obstacles, the better you will be able to help them. When you guide the buyer to recognize their needs, you then can lead them to understand the solution.

Practice good listening skills. Ask questions and listen.

Always repeat what your prospect says. Strive to understand your buyer's genuine desire and needs. The better you know those, the better you will be able to serve them.

Send a Google Calendar invitation.

If you do not know how to use a calendar invitation, consider asking a colleague to guide you on how to use it. Google makes this application relatively intuitive and easy to learn. When you send a calendar invitation, it allows you to do a few things. When they accept the request, they are giving you the first 'Yes' of the sales process.

In many cases, the recipient will have reminders set up on their phone and computer, and Google will send them an event reminder. When Google does this, it will be another touch coming from a third party to remind them of their commitment.

At the end of every conversation of the sales cycle, you should set the next appointment, and when you do this, send them a calendar invitation for the next step (phone call or face to face) via Google.

Film a short video to introduce yourself to the buyer and text it to them.

Most phones will allow you to film a video and text the video to another person. Use this option to begin developing a relationship with the buyer so they get to know you.

A short script that you could say is,

REAL ESTATE EVOLUTION

"Mr. Buyer, this is Dan Rochon with the **Greetings Virginia Sales Network** with **ABC Realty**.

"It was a pleasure speaking with you, and I look forward to helping. I will call you and Jane tomorrow night as we scheduled and share some homes online with you.

"If anything changes between now and then, please let me know."

Introduce to a lender.

You should have an excellent relationship with a couple of lenders. It is a smart plan to introduce your lender to the buyer. Because if you use another lender you have no connection with, you will have no leverage to get things done with the lender if the deal falls apart.

It will benefit your buyers for them to leverage your relationship capital with the lender so the lender will take great care of your clients. If you are new to the business, ask a colleague or your broker for an introduction.

Discuss the difficulty of obtaining financing and highlight why they should use a lender you know. One of the fundamental questions you should ask is if the customer is a cash or finance buyer. If he is a finance buyer, connect him to one of your preferred lenders.

When the buyer uses a lender you know, it will help the buyer in a few critical ways. The buyer more likely will avoid any difficulties, and if a problem does arise, the lender will hustle to fix it. The buyer will be able to leverage your relationship with the lender to get things done.

To connect the lender to the buyer, say,

> "Mrs. Buyer, I have a lender who specializes in helping buyers that (mention their situation -- first time home buyer, veteran, move-up, move-down) and has the best rates and terms in the business.

"I wouldn't mind doing this. I can introduce them to you."

Send this email to <u>both the prospect and the lender</u>,

"Mr. and Mrs. Buyers,

"I want to introduce you to Mr. Lender with the XYZ Mortgage company. Mr. Lender is a top lender and has helped many of our clients to get **the best rates and terms** for their loans. He can do the same for you. Mr. Lender's phone number is 123-456-7890, and his email is Mrlender@xyzmortage.com.

"Mr. Lender,

"I want to introduce Mr. and Mrs. Buyers, who are looking for a single-family home in Arlington and would like to buy in the next three months. They are a lovely couple moving from California. Mr. Buyer's phone number is 703-555-0123, and his email is propectreadytobuy@gmail.com.

"Please let me know if I may further facilitate an introduction."

The key terms to mention in the script above are 'best rates and terms.'

As soon as you send the email or text introduction to your lender, you should verify the receipt with a call.

This phone call accomplishes two outcomes. First, it reminds your lender of the value you provide to him or her, which will benefit your partnership. Second, it will help to get the lender onto the phone promptly with your buyer.

As you can imagine, when you condense every moment of the process, the more likely you will be to get a sale. If your lender calls the buyer within five minutes of you hanging up the telephone, it will bear much more fruit than if the lender calls the next day.

Call the lender to review the buyer's ability to buy.

When you have a well-established relationship with a lender, he/she will guide you to the best options for the buyer. You should seek to be in connection with a lender who seeks solutions. The lender should be a partner with you in your relationship with the buyer.

Call the lender to ask for the buyer's status.

Ask if they can obtain financing now.

Do they need help from the seller for closing costs or a grant program?

Inquire about the best strategy that will allow the buyer to get the home.

Set up/ host a second phone conversation.

At the end of your first conversation with a prospective buyer, you should set up a second phone appointment. If two or more decision-makers will be involved in the purchase, be sure you schedule all buyers for this appointment. The purpose of the second conversation is getting into a relationship with secondary buyers that you did not speak with on the first call. It is also a chance to begin the consultative process.
To set up this call share with the buyer,

> "Thank you for taking the time with me to explain the ideal home you seek. When I have a great client like you take the time to explain to me what is important to them, it allows me to hit the bull's-eye and find the best home for you.
>
> "Let's do this. Let's set up a phone conversation for tomorrow night. When we speak, we can review a few homes that match your criteria so I can be sure I understood you well.
>
> "When is the best time you and your husband can speak on the phone? And can I show you the option for a home?"

To prepare for the second conversation on the telephone or FaceTime, select 10 - 12 homes that fit the criteria you learned from the first part of the intake.
Consider the buyer's needs. For any listings that you share with the buyers, review the history of the listing agents, and understand if the property is a short sale, Real Estate Owned (REO), or other challenging option.
 Your goal should be to choose the best homes that match your buyer's wants and needs that also will be the most likely to get to the closing finish line.
During the conversation, email a list of the homes that you could show to the buyers. Review the selected homes with all home buyers and decision-makers who should be on the call. Consider the houses one at a time with each buyer and reduce the number of options from ten to between four to six.

Do not email the homes before the conversation. Because if you miss the mark with the homes you share, you want to be able to handle the objections.

You should have the following conversations on the second conversation and the first face to face meeting.

Set up an in the office appointment.

At the end of your second call, you will set a date in the office. If you belong to a larger brokerage, you probably can meet them at a different office or location of the same office. If those don't work, meet them at a Starbucks or other public place.

You **DO NOT** want to meet them at a property. Because you will not have the chance to complete the consultation, and it will be awkward to get hired while showing homes.

To set up this time, say,

> "We are going to set up an appointment for you to come to my office so we can **GET THE PROCESS STARTED.** And at the same time, we will review the homes I have found for you that are the closest match.
>
> "I am going to contact your lender to let him know we will work together so he and I can work together to help you with the home buying process."

Share the market's obstacles.

1. Discuss REOs (Real Estate Owned) and the difficulties:

    a. Verbal Acceptance

The bank often will communicate verbally through their listing agent that they accept the offer. There can be a delay between this communication and receiving the documents in writing. The bank has not yet agreed to sell the property because a contract to sell real estate must be in writing. (This rule is called the Statute of Frauds, and an exception to this is for a lease that is less than one year – which would not apply in an REO situation.)

b. As-Is

In most cases, the bank (seller) will not do any repairs or improvements to the property.

c. Bank Addendums protect the bank, not the buyer

You most likely will use an offer on the forms created by your local municipality. You will write the offer on a proposed contract that equally will protect the buyer's and seller's interests. The proposal will go from the buyer's agent to the listing agent to the bank's asset manager.

When the accepted offer returns to the buyer, it will be on an addendum that 100% protects the seller's interest and negates the buyer's benefit. For example, if the buyer is not able to close on time, they will probably have to pay a penalty to the seller. If the bank cannot get to the closing on the date agreed, there will typically be no penalty paid to the buyer.

2. Short Sales Difficulties

Short sales are not short. Many times, they take six or more months to complete, and they do not always get to the finish line. If a seller is seriously delinquent on paying their mortgage, often they will not follow your advice to complete the activity necessary to short sell.

You can advise the buyer that this process will take a long time and seldom get to closing. If a buyer wants to look at a short sale home in the summer, you could say,

> "So, are you ready to wait for the bitterly cold month of December to get a, 'No?'
>
> "My job is not to tell you what to do or what not to do; it is to give you the information so you can make a smart and informed decision."

Change the season in the script above to six months from the time you are speaking. Discuss the difficulty of obtaining financing and highlight why they should use your lenders. Tell your buyer that sometimes they will find a home on the Internet that probably will not be an option because it is a short sale.

There will be a few times when another buyer previously had the short sale property under contract and did not buy it. In this scenario, a negotiation often already has occurred between the seller and the bank. When this happens, the bank usually has verbally approved the sale, and the short sale might be viable.

3. New Home Builders

Buying a new home is an excellent option for some buyers. When the buyer purchases a new home, they will be able to select the floorplan, style, and finishes to suit their taste and be the first to live in the immaculate new home.

Often, a buyer does not understand that they should have representation in a new home sale. Your job is to consult the buyer about the pitfalls of not using an agent.

At the beginning of the sales process, you should tell the buyer,

> "New construction sales are different than resales. When you visit a new home community, you will meet a builder's (seller's) agent. The builder's representative at the new home model will have the seller's interest at heart -- not yours. Their job is to get you to spend the most money possible while receiving the fewest bonuses.
>
> "I will be able to get you the most value for your money. I will proactively negotiate on your behalf to get you the most rewards, discounts, extra perks, and best financing. The builder's agent will seldom even tell you that there are options or incentives. I will look out for you.
>
> "If you buy a new home from a builder, you will have to understand that the contract ultimately will protect the builder's interest and negate yours. I will explain to you all the contract's challenges so you can make an informed decision.
>
> "Take a small stack of my business cards and share these with the builder representative when you meet. I will help you with any challenges along the way. Or better yet, let me know

the communities that you are interested in, and I will schedule the tour."

4. Underwriting challenges

Share with the buyers,

"Mr./Mrs. Buyer, even great buyers with ideal financing like you have challenges from time to time when they go through the loan underwriting process. Underwriting is the final process that the lender takes to approve your loan.

"Do not be surprised if they ask for a bunch of crazy documentation as we get closer to the sale date."

When you share the conversation up-front with the buyer, and if there are underwriting issues, then you appear to be a professional in the buyer's eyes. When you do not consult them in the beginning, and the lender is a hassle, then they think you do not know what you are doing.

Discuss the difficulty of obtaining financing and highlight why they should use your lenders.

Share your mobile app!

If your brokerage provides you with an app you can share that will allow buyers to search for homes, you should share that with the buyer. A good app should enable another to view homes for sale, understand the market performance, and access neighborhood reports.

Your app also should allow an agent to view the history and preferences of a user and prompt you to act when required.

Hitting the bull's-eye conversation.

You do not want a buyer to think they can buy a home that does not exist, and you do not want to show homes to a buyer for the next ten months.

To best manage a buyer's expectations, you should have this conversation with them.

Share with the home buyer,
> Thank you, Mr. Buyer, for taking the time to describe your ideal home. I have found that when this occurs and if the house exists, **we will Hit the Bull's-eye**. If, for some reason, the property does not exist, we should change one of three things:

- Price
    - Perhaps we will need to speak with the lender and see if we can adjust your buying power.

- Location
    - Maybe, instead of buying in Arlington, VA, we might consider Annandale, VA, where the homes are slightly less expensive.

- Type of home
    - We might have to consider a townhome instead of a single-family home or three bedrooms instead of four.

When you have the above conversation with the buyer, you are setting up yourself for success when you cannot find a home for them. You will be able to refer to this conversation and ask them to choose which of the three conditions they would like to change?

This approach allows the buyer to have a perceived control that will allow him/her to make a choice that best will serve them and allow them to make an adjustment that will let them buy a home instead of wasting their (and your) time.

Two or fewer showings.

This technique takes a bit of skill, so you will want to practice it to be sure you deliver it effectively.
Describe to the buyer,

> "Thank you for hiring me to help you find your ideal home.

"According to what you have described to me about your dream home, I took the time to find some homes to show you that meet your criteria, and I can help you find your ideal home in a short time.

"The first time I will show you three to four homes so you can find your dream home. But because it is an emotional decision, we will go to a second showing to reinforce your choice from the first showing, and we can go to a maximum third showing to make the final decision. I am here for you if you need me. I need to help you to get your dream home quickly.

"Seventy-five percent of my clients buy their home on the first trip, and 100% are buying on the second trip. Does this surprise you?

"Each time we are going to see a home, please bring your checkbook and be prepared to buy your dream home."

It is imperative that when you have the above conversation, the buyers understand you will work with them until they find the right home. You do not want them to believe they are limited to two showings; you do want them to expect that while working with you it will take ONLY two showings to look at homes.

Showing homes and using the "1 to 5 script."

Years ago, my wife Traci was working with a young couple, Josh and Gina.

Gina was about eight months pregnant with their first child, and they needed a larger home for their growing family.

Traci showed them every house that met their criteria, and they unsuccessfully wrote offers on seven homes. As we all were spinning our wheels, Traci and I decided to take a new approach, and I took over as the agent.

Shortly after taking over, Josh gave me a call and announced they would like to place a new offer on a home that they previously had written a proposal for that did not get accepted.

I was excited for them because I knew if they already had written an offer that did not work that they now would understand what they needed to do to write one that would get accepted. I was wrong in my assumption.

When I asked Josh what they wanted to offer, he told me that it was **$20,000 LESS** than the previous offer that they had presented on the same home three weeks earlier that was not accepted.

I was confused about what Josh and Gina had hoped to accomplish. I was unable to gain an understanding when I asked questions of Josh. I wrote the new offer, presented it, got laughed at by the listing agent, and eventually fired Josh and Gina as clients.

I was baffled about what had occurred, and I reflected deeply to gain clarity. As I pondered the events, I realized two things that allowed me to adjust our process of serving our buyers that made a positive difference for our future.

Before this experience, I would coach our agents that when they were touring homes with a buyer, their job was to **"Write an offer."** After this experience, I learned to change our intentions. I realized our job when we were taking a buyer out was to **"Write an offer that gets accepted."**

The second thing I learned was that what I believe happened with Josh and Gina was one spouse sabotaged the other.

Often in a healthy relationship, one spouse will be passive, and the other will be dominant. If the dominant person has pulled over the other to move forward when the submissive person is not all in, it likely will cause problems in the deal's future.

As I understood what occurred with Josh and Gina, I devised a system to limit the same outcome of a spouse or partner passively being an obstacle to their success. To prevent a buyer from sabotaging another buyer, you, as I did, could use the "1 to 5" script.

Before showing a home, ask if there is any other decision-maker who will be a part of the home buying process. Perhaps it could be a parent, friend, boyfriend, girlfriend, or anybody else who will have power over the decision.

If there is another person who will have authority, ask your buyer to invite them to look at homes together.

Advise the buyers to use the 1 to 5 worksheet that will allow each of them to make the collective decision independently. To explain how using the 1 to 5 worksheets will benefit the buyer:

Agent to buyer,

> "Thank you, Mr. and Mrs. Buyer, for the opportunity to help you buy a home. You must be excited, and I am eager to

guide you through the process of purchasing the best home for you and avoid or overcome all potential obstacles that can occur.

"As you will both be living in your new home, you must understand that you will be making a collective decision that must work for each of you independently, would you agree?"

Buyer to agent,

"Yes."

Agent to buyer,

"Great. So, then, what I would like for you to do as we tour homes today is to write all your notes on this worksheet about each home that we view. As you complete the form, do not discuss your opinion with each other until you leave the house. During the tour, you will rate each home on a scale of 1 to 5.

"Now, TRUST ME, nobody ever rates it a 5. So, if you do so, we immediately should go back to the office and write an offer that will get accepted.

"Now, if either of you rates it a one or a two, then we will agree that, regardless of what the other rates it, we will take a pass on that property. Does that make sense?"

Notice the language of the dialogue above. By using a 1 to 5 scale when we said, "Nobody ever rates it a 5..." we've eliminated the top twenty percent of the options, which allows for any home above an eighty percent fit to be a top priority to write an offer that gets accepted. If we used a 1 to 10 scale, we only would have removed ten percent of the opportunities.

As we allow each buyer to do an independent review, it will prevent the dominant buyer from influencing the passive person.

Agent to buyer,

> "Give each home a nickname when you view it so you easily can recall your favorites. It can be confusing to remember many."

When you show homes, print two copies of the MLS listing, along with a showing cover sheet rating the property from 1 to 5, and give each one the pad with the papers.

Home inspection conversation.

I have found that for many agents, the home inspection is a critical time that an unreasonable buyer or seller can blow up a deal. To help prevent this, before you show any homes, you should have a conversation with the buyer about what to expect when they complete the home inspection.

A home inspection will ensure the home's safety and protect the purchaser. You want to be sure that your buyer is getting the right house, and you want to be confident that you set them up for success, not getting scared when the inspection happens.

Tell the buyer,

> "You want to buy a home that has no defects. We will protect you by getting a home inspection. 100% of the time, the home inspector will find problems with the home. I NEVER have helped a buyer where that did not happen.
>
> "What we want to be concerned about are the "big rocks," such as the roofing, plumbing, electrical, appliances all being in good working condition. What we DO NOT want to do is ask the seller to fix every minor detail, because that will not be in your best interest."

Often, problems that can occur in a transaction easily can be prevented when you correctly set the expectations for your client. When you have the above conversation with the buyers before they even look at homes, you will set them up to be reasonable for when the home inspection occurs.

REAL ESTATE EVOLUTION

Preparation before the initial appointment.

- Call your client the day before, reminding them of the date.
- Review Showing Instructions for Homes to be Sold.
- Print a copy for each buyer of the "Buyer Synopsis" from the MLS.
- Print a copy of the "Agent Synopsis" for yourself.
- Print a 1 to 5 Script for the Client.

Prepare for the buyer tour.

Do not set more than three to five homes, maximum, to show at a time: the buyer only will be confused and tired and not be able to decide.

Review homes that match your client's criteria and identify ten possibilities. Share these homes via email and have a phone conversation with your buyer — narrow your list to five or fewer homes during this conversation.

Have a minimum of three phone conversations with the buyer (while sharing homes for sale that match their criteria, consulting on the process with the discussions outlined in this worksheet, providing value and developing rapport).

Buyer Tour Preparation - **ALWAYS Remind an Appointment with a buyer 24 Hours Before Meeting and ALWAYS be 100% Ready to Meet with a buyer one Hour Before Meeting**.

Meet the buyers.

Lead them to the conference room. Sit at the head of the table and let them sit facing each other. Ask them if they want to have tea or coffee and make sure they are as comfortable as possible.

Have a copy of the lender letter in hand before your first meeting with a buyer.

The next step is to get the paperwork ready.

To get hired, the buyer or seller needs to sign a representation agreement. You must fill in every blank of the contract; if a part does not apply, input, "N/A."

Share market statistics.

You should be the local real estate economist of choice for your community. Understand that it is your professional duty to provide your clients and prospective clients with perspective.

When you meet with a seller or buyer, share the relevant local market data, and help them to interpret the information so that you know what it means. Keep in mind that buyers will be driven more by emotion, and sellers are more transactional.

As a fiduciary, you have the responsibility to consult your buyers about the local market statistics. When you let them know about the market upfront, it also will allow for you to guide them to make better offers when the time comes.

You will be proactive when you advise your client at the first meeting of the **Original List Price** to **Sold Price ratio**. This will help you later when it is time to write an offer that will get accepted.

Have the market statistics ready and printed for your meeting with the buyer. The most important things to know are how long the houses in the area stay on the market, the price they sell for, and whether it is higher or lower than the listing price.

Show your client that you are the expert, and you know your local market stats. Ask your broker for local resources that will provide the market data for you.

My team uses http://www.getsmartcharts.com/statistics, the local MLS, and Remine.com to obtain information to share with our buyers.

Ask for openness.

The more authentic you can get your buyers to be with you, the better you can help them.

Say to the buyers,

> "Mr. and Mrs. Buyer, when you and I leave a home, you will get into your car, turn your heads to each other and say something.
>
> "I ask that whatever it is that you will say when you turn your heads to each other, that you tell it to me.
>
> "Even if it is, 'What in the hell is this guy doing? Has he not listened to anything that we have said? How could he show us the house that he just did?!?!'

"When you authentically share your thoughts with me, I will be able to serve you best; after all, I work for you, and my job is to guide you."

Notice the presumed closing technique in the last part of the previous sentence.

Selling 360° – Listing Process

You want to get started on the right foot with your seller and obtain the information required to understand their situation. We employ the **Selling 360° -- Listing Process** to gather this data.

I call it the **Selling 360° -- Listing Process** because we take a comprehensive look at our seller's circumstance from all perspectives.

We view the seller as if he or she sits in the middle of the circle, and we strive to scrutinize their situation from all angles around them.

You probably already know that your competitors seldom do their homework before they meet with sellers. Often, they do not ask you the questions required to understand their concerns nor even ask what is important to you in how they help.

You should inquire,

- Where are you moving to when we sell?
- Why are you moving there?
- What challenges could get in your way?
- What is your motivation to sell?
- What improvements have they made to the house?
- On a scale of 1 to 10, how would they rate the condition of the property?
- What do they think their property is worth?
- As your agent, what are your expectations of me?

Your job is to gather as much information as possible to understand best how to help the seller. If you were to consider using a systematic approach to dependably know their goals and problems, you would attain an absolute advantage over your competition.

The Shock and Awe Pre-Listing Consultation

My sales team and I go a bit overboard with our pre-listing campaign. Our great enthusiasm is an intentional method that allows us to share the massive value that we offer to our sellers.

To get a full perspective of the magnitude of the **Shock and Awe Pre-Listing Presentation**, visit www.GetRockSolidCoaching.com/free-resources to access the forms and documents associated with the information described below.

The following steps are taken to prepare for the listing appointment:
Research:

   a. Review social media and Google
   b. Prepare a Comparative Market Analysis (CMA)
   c. Print the tax record
   d. Use the RPR® valuation
   e. Access the Zillow information
   f. Get market statistics
   g. View comparable homes

You should complete your research upfront and thoroughly understand the house. Take the time to examine the community and surroundings.

It also would benefit you to understand as much as possible about the seller(s).

Review social media and Google.

I research each seller before the meeting; this supports me to notice better who they are and best prepare to help.

One time, I was getting ready to meet a seller, and I stalked his Twitter feed before we met.

I found that he recently had traveled the world with no real agenda, going from an airport to an airport, flying in whatever direction the next standby ticket took him.

I viewed photos of him cliff diving, sitting with a tiger, and taking an expedition through safari country.

REAL ESTATE EVOLUTION

I swiftly made a judgment before we met that the seller was a risk-taker. I also perceived that he would be swift to decide to hire me (or not), and likely he would want to protect his time.

Based on my predictions made from viewing the seller's social media, I entered the listing presentation prepared to take the listing quickly.

It may have been my fastest appointment ever. It went something like this,

I said to the seller,

> "Did you receive the information that I shared about our services?"

He replied,

> "Yes."

"Do you have any questions?"

"No."

"Great, are you ready to get the process started?"

"Yes."

"Okay, then here is the paperwork that we need to get started. Sign here, here and here."

And he did.

Another time, I was ill-prepared and attended a listing appointment at a condominium located on the 11th floor of a mid-rise building. I arrived at the seller's condo that overlooked a beautiful lake surrounded by outdated retail shops and restaurants.

As we discussed the local amenities, I made the error of commenting about the convenience that the shops around the water below would offer a buyer for years to come, and I suggested to highlight this benefit in our marketing.

What I did not know but the seller did, was that the stores were slated to close in the next six months. A developer was tearing them down and rebuilding residential condos in their place.

I quickly could have learned that information about the pending redevelopment by completing a simple Google search before we met. I did not do my research, and I failed to get hired.

Prepare a Comparative Market Analysis (CMA).

You can rely on valuation tools to help. Yet, manually reviewing the data always will be best. The best way to estimate the value of a property is through manual research.

When pricing a property, take your time to research and prepare. Listen to what the seller thinks that it is worth, view the automated valuation sites, and complete your independent study.

If the prices in the above methods vary by greater than three percent to five percent, then you know you have a problem that you need to research deeply.

When it is possible, select three homes that are active or pending, and three that recently have sold, and choose properties in the same community.

If you are not able to do this, select properties within eight blocks in an urban area, one mile in a suburban environment, and ten miles in a rural area.

The best CMA will consider homes of the same type and location. In a balanced market, you could choose properties that have sold up to 180 days ago, and in a changing market, you would want to consider homes that have sold 90 days ago or sooner.

Choose like-kind properties. You want to match a townhome to a townhome and not a single-family property. You should compare a three-bedroom to a three-bedroom, and if this is not possible, you will have to adjust the price. Recognize the age of the home that you are comparing and find others in the same range.

Print the tax record.

I share the tax record with the seller so I can get into an automatic 'Yes-set' with them before I review the pricing of the CMA. I explain more about the 'Yes-set' close in the hiring section.

Use the RPR® valuation.

If you belong to the National Association of Realtors®, you can use this tool to provide powerful analytics that you will be able to share with the seller. With this resource, you can display property reports, local market trend reports, and share this data with the seller using our company branding.

You may access the Realtors Property Resource report at www.narrpr.com.

Access the Zillow information.

The seller already looked at his home on Zillow and saw the estimate provided, so you should be aware of how Zillow has manipulated their thoughts. Take the time to review and print this data.

Get market statistics.

If you have access to Smart Charts, you will want to review and print the information about the statistics of the area that you will visit.

View comparable homes.

You want to research the community, and if you have a chance, go inside the other homes that are on your CMA. The more that you know, the better chance you will have of success.

Before you meet with the seller to get hired, there is a series of communications that will help you develop trust and rapport with the seller and ultimately get hired.

By the time you get together, your prospective client should understand that you are a resource who will help them.

In the **Greetings Virginia Sales Network**, we have a well-developed system to introduce ourselves to a seller. Before we meet with a seller, we communicate in a manner that our competitors do not.

Here are the ten touches that we deliver to a prospective client before we meet:

1. Have the initial phone conversation/ do the intake.
2. Send a Google Calendar invitation.
3. Film a short video to introduce yourself to the seller and text it to them.
4. Send a handwritten thank you card.

5. Deliver the Shock and Awe Pre-Listing Package to include our 193-Point, step-by-step plan.
6. Send email 1 -- How we can help you with 123 Main St., Alexandria, VA 22310?
7. Share the webinar -- Top Dollar Secrets -- How to Add up to $30K to $60K to the value of your home.
8. Send email 2 - Our E-Brochures and Other Marketing.
9. Send email 3 -- About Selling Your Property.
10. Call the day of or day before the appointment to remind them of your meeting.

Have the initial phone conversation/do the intake.

On your first phone conversation, you should pre-qualify. The most important things to understand during this discussion are:

1. What price do they want to sell?
2. What is most important to them in a real estate agent?

During your initial conversation, you should confirm that:

- All the decision-makers will be present for your appointment.
- You have enough time booked for your meeting.
- The seller wants to sell (and not "test the market").

Send a Google Calendar invitation.

As previously mentioned, sending an invitation via Google Calendar will increase the likelihood of the person attending the next step and get the other person used to saying, "Yes" to you.
You will increase your professionalism in the process.

Film a short video to introduce yourself to the seller and text it to them.

When the seller views multiple videos of you, they will feel connected. In two of the emails that we send during our process to get hired, we include videos describing why so many people hire us.
You may effortlessly view those videos by visiting our company's YouTube channel anytime at www.youtube.com/GreetingsVirginia. I

suggest that you please subscribe. You will have access to the weekly videos that we share with our sphere and others.

Send a handwritten thank you card.

This old school technique will allow you to stand out.

After all, how often do you receive a written note in the mail? To better make the point, how many emails are currently in your inbox?

Sometimes, especially for older sellers, they appreciate a handwritten note much more than an email. On several occasions, a seller told me that they hired me because I took the time to deliver a personal touch in a short letter written to them.

Deliver the Shock and Awe Pre-Listing Package.

When you deliver a pre-listing packet to the seller, you are separating yourself from much of your competition. An excellent pre-listing presentation sets the foundation for your meeting to get hired, and it should be delivered to the seller before you meet.

In the information you share, you should include the services that you offer and why they should hire you.

Consider ordering a professional folder. You can get one designed quickly on an outsourcing website such as www.fiverr.com. If you cannot afford to invest in a professional folder, see if your brokerage has some available that you could use.

In your folder you deliver before meeting with the seller you should include:

- The questions to ask other agents.

You're going to tell the seller what questions to ask the other agents. Be sure you ask questions that make you look good and that you're prepared to answer.

- A letter to the prospective client. Thank them for the opportunity to apply for the job to help them to sell their home.

- An easy exit listing agreement.

Many agents will lock their clients into lengthy contracts. Some sellers fear getting stuck in a long contract. To alleviate this concern, my team and I offer upfront to let our clients fire us at any time. I do not want to be in a relationship with a client who does not want to be in contact with me.

When a seller lists their home with us through our EASY EXIT Listing Guarantee, they can cancel their listing with us at any time. No hassles. It's easy.

My team and I have strong opinions about real estate services. We believe that if a consumer is unhappy with the service they receive, they should have the power to fire their agent.

It takes a strong belief in the quality of one's service to make this kind of statement, but we never settle for less than the highest professional standards. We are confident you will be happy with our service and results. That's a simple truth. We always stand behind our service.

We ask that if a seller is not happy for any reason that they give us a chance to fix the situation.

Agent to the seller,

> "I'm so passionate about helping others that if you don't like the services that I provide, unlike a lot of my competitors, you could fire me, and there'll be no cost to you at all.
>
> "There will be no termination fee, marketing cost, or other expenses that you will pay."

You can download the details about the following steps of the pre-listing plan at www.GetRockSolidCoaching.com/free-resources.

- **Send email 1** - *How we can help you with 123 Main St., Alexandria, VA 22310?*
- **Share the webinar** - *Top Dollar Secrets -- How to Add up to $30K to $60K to the value of your home.*
- **Send email 2** - *Our E-Brochures and Other Marketing.*
- **Send email 3** - *About Selling Your Property.*

Call the day of, or day before, the appointment to remind them of your meeting.

When you do the steps described in the sections above correctly, you will not have to sell yourself at the listing presentation. That will allow you to listen to them and advise when you meet rather than pitch and sell.

The only time that I must sell myself at an appointment is when the seller is a highly dominant (High "D") who did not take the time to review any of the information that was shared. In this rare event, I only have a few minutes to answer their inquiries anyway before they decide.

Prepare the Agreements

In the middle of the processes described above, you will have to prepare the listing paperwork. You will have to select the correct agreement.

Listing Agreements

You can choose four types of listing agreements.

Exclusive Right to List

Mostly, you will want to do an **Exclusive Right to List** agreement with your sellers. In this agreement, the seller agrees to pay for your service if a buyer buys the home.

Exclusive Listing

The first listing that I took in my career was an **Exclusive Listing**. At the time, I did not understand the difference between an **Exclusive Right to Sell** and an **Exclusive Listing** agreement. An "Exclusive" arrangement sounded right to me, and this is the document that I brought to my appointment.

When I showed the signed contract to my broker Karen, she peered over the top of her glasses, and inquisitively asked me, "Um, Dan, did you mean to this?"

Shortly after I heard that question, my broker schooled me on the difference between the agreements.

In the **Exclusive Listing** agreement, the seller agrees to compensate you if you or anyone else except the seller finds a buyer who goes to closing.

Offering an **Exclusive Agency** agreement could be a solution to provide to a FSBO because it will allow the seller to maintain the control that they seek, and you will get paid if anyone other than the seller finds the buyer.

Open Listing

In an **Open Listing**, the seller can hire multiple agents and only pay the broker who brings them a buyer who writes an offer that is accepted by the owner. In residential sales, it is almost always a bad idea to agree to this type of relationship.

Net listing

In most states, a **Net Listing** is not legal because it can allow an agent to take advantage of a seller. A Net Listing is when a seller agrees to pay the broker any amount of money over an agreed-upon sales price. For example, if the seller wants to sell for $300,000 and tells you that any dollar above $300k will be your compensation, this would be an example of a **Net Listing**.

Other Documents

Other addendums, disclaimers, and disclosures will be needed. Your state will require additional forms to be signed, and your broker can guide you through which are necessary.

Buyer Listings

These agreements mirror the **Listing Agreements,** except a **Net Listing** is not an option.

Many agents are reluctant to ask a buyer to sign a **Buyer Listing**. The hesitation by an agent to request a buyer to hire them has always confused me; I do not know another business where a service provider would offer to provide their service while hoping that they get hired in the future and get paid for their work.

Step 5: Get Hired

As with any of your real estate-related activities, you should consult your broker about the appropriate process to help a buyer or seller. I share the knowledge in this section with you based on my years of experience as a sales agent and broker in Virginia and Maryland.

As each state requires you to use unique documents, this portion offers a general explanation about getting hired.

Congratulations! You did your daily lead generation, converted the prospects, set the expectations, and they are ready to hire you.

Now, what do you do? **You get hired**!

You will notice that the bulk of getting hired happens well before we get to this point in the process. A natural progression of an excellent presentation leads to a prospect hiring you. The next steps should flow smoothly to getting hired.

How often will you get hired?

The factors that will impact your conversion rate of getting hired will be:

1. Your skill.
2. Your prospect's motivation.
3. The relationship you have with the prospective client. Were you introduced to them by a friend or business associate, or are they a FSBO or someone that you have a weak connection with or someone else that you cold-called?

Each agent will get hired at a different rate, and there are average ratios that you might consider.

The most straightforward rule to follow is that if you attend 50/50 seller/buyer appointments, you will have to visit twice as many meetings than what you will close.

On average, seventy-five percent will hire you, and then seventy-five percent of those who employ you will go to closing.

I once participated in a class when we were discussing the percentage of times that we got hired. A well-known top-producing local agent announced that he got hired in more than ninety-eight percent of his appointments.

When he answered in this manner, I thought to myself, "Either he is lying, or he is not attending enough appointments."

While it could be possible to get hired almost 100% of the time if your meetings were all generated from referrals, repeat business, or a good book of contacts, it is unlikely if you are to scale your business.

For those appointments made from contacting FSBOs, expired listings, Internet lead generation sources, etc., your ratio likely will be lower. Also, there may be appointments that you attend where taking the listing would not make sense. Such as when the seller is not motivated to sell, insists on a price that will never sell, or is a jerk.

Do I get hired every time? No way. And in my opinion, neither should you! (However, you should intend to take the listing 100% of the time that you want to.)

If you do get hired every time, you probably only are going on referred appointments or those with past clients. These are the premium appointments that you should continuously seek. Yet, if you only go on these types of meetings, you will be limited.

On average, I get hired on sixty-eight percent of my seller listing appointments and eighty-five percent for the buyers. In the last twelve months, I have attended 133 listing appointments, and ninety-one times I took the listing.

Procure the Buyer's Listing

Meet the buyer at the office.

When meeting a buyer at the office for the first time, follow the steps outlined below.

Say hello to Mr. and Mrs. Buyer. Shake their hands, so you show confidence, while still being friendly and approachable. (Don't have the 'dead fish' handshake and don't crush someone's hand either).

When you sit down with the buyers, review the information that you have gathered and finish any steps you have missed in the consultation outlined in the **80/20 buyer Consultation.** Typically, you should have only the market statistics and specific homes to review at the face-to-face meeting.

Say to the buyers,

> "Hello, you must be Mr. and Mrs. Buyer. It's great to meet you today. Let's sit down for a few minutes; I have just a few quick items to share with you before we go find you a home today!"

Sit at the head of the table with them together on one side of the table or the other. Do not have them split up on either side of you. You need them together to present appropriately.

Ask if they need any water or coffee. Be sure that if there is an office window in the room that their back is to the window. You want to situate them in this manner, so they do not get distracted by anything happening outside.

Review their intentions with the buyers and be sure you are aligned. Say to them,

> "Just so I understand how I will best help you, you said you were looking for a home because of _____.
>
> And you need to have _____ bedrooms and _____ baths, and you'd also like to have _____ in your new home. Is that right?

> And you said the price range your mortgage lender approved is up to $_____. You also stated that you'd like to be moved by _____.
>
> Great, based on that knowledge, I've set up several homes for us to check out today. I can't wait to show you, and they're homes that will be ideal!"

If there are any conversations from the **80/20 Buyer Consultation** that you have not yet had, have those conversations now.

After the **80/20 Buyer Consultation,** the buyer(s) have spent much time with you and should be eager to get started. They almost should be getting a bit irritated with you. they probably are sitting forward in their chair, anticipating beginning the process.

Now is time to let them off the hook. Say,

> "Are you ready to go and look at your homes?"
>
> "Yes!" they will anxiously reply.
>
> "OK, we just need to OK a few pages of this form, and we can get the process started."

Slide the **Buyer Listing Agreement** across the table and point to the first page that needs an initial and hand them a pen. When you do the complete process, you will get hired more than eighty-five percent of the time.

DO NOT make signing the paperwork a big deal.

Signing the paperwork is just a natural step in the process, and before signing, the buyers are probably on edge because they are excited, and you have delayed them.

At this point, you have spent one to two hours consulting the buyer on the phone and in-person, and they should be anxious (and maybe on the verge of a little annoyed with you that you have not shown them any homes yet).

Emotionally, the buyers should be relieved to stop the conversation and start the process, and signing will give them an 'out' of the conversation and allow them to do what they want to do, which is look at homes for sale.

Ask, "Are you ready to start the process?"

When they answer, "Yes!" in an excited manner, you will know that you have correctly followed the process.

Say, "I just need you to OK a few pieces of paper that will position us so that I am looking out for your interests rather than the seller's."

Slide the paperwork across the table and say, "Just initial here, here and here and sign here," and get the process started.

Go through the paperwork and ask them to sign the buyer representation contract. Get a **Buyer Listing Agreement** signed before you show any homes.

Take the Seller's Listing

By now, you have completed the **Shock and Awe Pre-Listing Consultation.** You have identified their intentions, goals, timing, expectations of you, and understand their goals, and you also shared how you will help them. You will have wasted your efforts if you do not get hired.

If you have completed the steps correctly before the listing appointment, you will not have to sell yourself at the interview. The sale of 'you' and your services should happen before, not at the meeting.

When you arrive at the listing appointment, the seller should know that you are a credible expert who will help them achieve their goals or solve their problems. You want your seller prospects to view you as a professional who will help them.

When speaking with the seller, always refer to the property as a "House" or a "Property," which allows the seller to experience a less emotional connection with the property.

When you meet with the seller, you intend to develop rapport as quickly as possible. Remember that rapport is about being synchronized in a manner where you understand each other's feelings and communicate well with each other. It is a physical phenomenon that you will feel. If you don't feel the rapport, slow yourself down, and pay attention.

Follow these steps on the appointment:

- **Be on time**
- **Be ready with a well-prepared presentation**
- **Knock on the door**
- **Take a step back**
- **Smile**

When the seller answers the door, you shake their hand, look at your watch, and state,

"Hello, Mr. Seller, I am Dan Rochon. We had a two-p.m. appointment, and it is two p.m. May I come in?"

Say,

"This is a pretty vital choice that you are about to make, to list your house for sale today."

- **Bring them to the table**.

When you do this, you control the conversation, and you place yourself into a natural position so that you can have a business conversation.

Some people are more social, relationship-driven, and will invite you into their family or living room and offer you milk and cookies. You should resist the urge, accept the cookies (even the warm gooey, double chocolate chip with walnuts, made from scratch cookies), and guide them to the kitchen or dining room table.

- **Preview the coming attractions.**

Let the seller know what to expect at the appointment. Tell him or her,

> "Thank you, Mr. and Mrs. Seller, for taking the time to meet with me today. I respect your investment of time and my intention today is to answer any of your questions, set up a plan to get you the most money, and get the process started.

REAL ESTATE EVOLUTION

"I appreciate the time that we had together on the phone, and I have done a lot of research to prepare for our meeting today.

"Today, we will review your motivation to sell, and I will best understand your situation.

"We will walk through the house together.

"I will show you the market statistics to include the seasonal and historical trends and then share comparable homes so that we may make the best pricing decision.

"I will answer any questions that you may have, and then when you are comfortable and confident that I best can help you, we will get the process started. Sound good?"

While you sit at the table, you will review their motivation to sell their home and let them know what the next steps of the conversation will be before getting started to market and sell their home for the highest profit.

- **Walk through the house and note any improvements needed to sell.**

I have been advised to walk through the house both without the sellers and with them.

The pros of walking alone are that it will let you get through the process more quickly. I have found that in a massive sale such as real estate, the more time spent with the seller allows for a greater connection and trust in the relationship. Even for a speed demon such as myself, spending more time with my clients (or soon to be clients) makes sense.

The downside of having the seller walk the house with you is that it will allow them to "fall in love" with all the significant improvements they have made. They probably will tell you about all the reasons why their property is worth more than the neighbors.' Do not fret; just listen and take notes. You will be able to guide them to reality later in the conversation when you review the comparable homes for sale and those that recently have sold.

They might become nostalgic and focus on good or bad memories that they had while living in the home. If this happens, it would be best that you know upfront so that you can understand what is impacting them profoundly. The more you can understand what is emotionally affecting the sellers, the better you will be able to help.

- **Take notes throughout and listen to all that the seller shares with you.**

You should pay attention to anything that could be repaired or improved. Often, the sellers will not have noticed the home's small defects. Later, when you sit down with them again, you will be able to review these items that need improvement.

- **As you tour the property, ask seven trial closing questions.**
- The **trial close** is a test to check their interest before you enter the closing step. You're 'taking the seller's temperature' to understand how likely they will be to hire you. When you identify their motivation, you will be able to understand better how assertive and quickly that you should act to a **final close**.

Casually ask trial closing questions such as,

"Would it be OK to do an open house on Saturday and Sunday?

"When is the latest that we may show your home?"

"Should the 'For Sale' sign be placed in front of the house or at the corner?"

"Should we hang the lockbox on the railing or the front door?"

"What specific features about your house and community should we include in the marketing?"

As you test the seller with the questions above and listen to their answers, you will understand how likely they will be to hire you.

REAL ESTATE EVOLUTION

- **Have a seat back at the kitchen or dining room table.**

It will be natural for you to advise them while convening at a table. For vacant properties, stand at the kitchen countertop, go to your office, or another venue after your house visit to sit.

- **Review the macro market stats** using www.GetSmartCharts.com. (If you do not have access to Smart Charts, ask your broker for another resource to get this data.)

Share about things such as future infrastructure improvements, companies that might be relocating or downsizing, and other factors that might impact the value. You can use this opportunity to isolate and defeat any objections that come up.

Often, I will attend an appointment, and the homeowner over anticipates an event and how that event will affect them. As you review the full scope of the market data with the seller, you will be able to help them better understand how the information will impact them. If you can do this before they attach themselves to the meaning of the local news, you will cut them off from making inaccurate assessments.

I sell real estate in Northern Virginia, which is a subsection of the Washington DC metro area. There are more than 6.25 million people (34) in this area.

In 2014, one of the area's largest employers, ExxonMobil, moved its headquarters and its 2,100 jobs from Fairfax County, VA to Houston, TX. (35) I recall the pessimism of the sellers that I met with at this time and counseled them to understand that 2,100 families are a tiny section of millions of people.

There was zero impact on the real estate market as a result of ExxonMobil's move. When the oil and gas company vacated the Northern Virginia region in 2014, the prices increased locally by 1.26% (36) (which is a small loss when you consider inflation measured by the Consumer Price Index for 2014 was 1.6%.) (37)

This past year, Amazon announced it was opening its second headquarters in our area. It will be a good thing for the market, yet it seems the sellers have over-calculated the impact this will have.

Each month since Amazon's announcement the area's inventory consistently has been down twenty-five percent to sixty percent, year over year. The days on the market have dropped to half, and prices have increased by 17.7% in many areas as of a year ago. (38)

Amazon claims they will implement a slow growth plan through the years, and they will hire residents as much as possible.

Those sellers who are sitting on the sidelines might consider the opportunity presented to them and understand that the 24,000 jobs Amazon will bring will be in increments of 2,000 per year over 12 years. (38)

The knowledge that I share with you about ExxonMobil and Amazon is the type of information that you would need to know when you advise your seller. A part of your job would be to help your sellers (and prospective sellers) to interpret how this type of information impacts them.

- **Review the tax record to get into what's called a 'Yes-set.'**

In the Yes-set Close, you will ask a series of questions that will solicit a, 'Yes,' and then you should dive deep to guide them in the direction that you intend.

You say,

> "I see that you own the home with your spouse, Julie. Is that correct?"

Seller assumes,

> "Yes."

You ask,

> "And you bought in June 2016?"

Seller,

> "Yes."

You,

> "And I see that you bought for $567,000, is that right?"

REAL ESTATE EVOLUTION

Seller says,

"Yes."

- **Review the CMA**

Use your tablet or computer to show the other homes that are on the market. You must show these homes on a computer that allows you to view each home. Slowly slide through photographs of the comparable properties.

As you are sitting in the dining room or at the kitchen table, it will be easy for you to compare their kitchen with that of the homes you are using for comparison.

When you land on a photo of the neighbor's superior kitchen, pause on the picture to allow the contrast to sink into the seller. It becomes challenging for them not to acknowledge the truth.

This approach will eliminate the seller's natural response that their home is better than the neighbor's.

Ask,

"Have you been inside any of these homes?"

(This will remove the chance that they have been in the other homes and know more about them than you without you knowing that they know more.)

"So, Mr. Seller, how do you think your kitchen compares to this one?"

The seller will view a photograph of the other property you are displaying. They will see their living room, bedrooms, baths, and other areas as compared to others on the market and those that recently sold. If the carpet is worn, they will see it.

If it is possible, show them a photo of a comparable property that the home seller staged and one that is not.

If this scenario is not feasible, wait until after you complete the CMA review and then show them before and after photos of a non-comparable home that you sold for another seller that you staged.

The homeowner will understand how staging will drive an emotional appeal. They will be able to see other appropriately staged homes and better understand how the emotional appeal of a staged home will help.

>Ask,

>"Which of these houses attracts you more?"

The seller likely will choose the staged property.

>"And what about that one is more appealing?"

I typically will not dive deep about staging at this point. You already got the seller to confirm that staging works, and you can come back to this part of the conversation later.

Show them where other homes show better than theirs. Say,

>"Don't overlook these areas of your home when preparing to sell it on the market. It just might make all the difference in your sale.
>
>"When selling your home, there are specific attractive points that buyers seek. There are also factors that buyers will take little interest in or, worse, that will drive them away.
>
>"Mainly, there are two areas of the home that buyers will be most interested in, and the first is the kitchen.
>
>"Buyers will expect you to have an updated kitchen, with granite countertops, stainless steel, and a modern look."

Some sellers will want to offer an allowance for the buyer to improve items such as carpeting, etc. Before you propose that they make any improvements, proactively advise them,

>"We want to appeal to the feelings of the buyer because logic makes you think, and emotion makes you act. We want a buyer to take action when they come into this house."

When you make suggestions for improvements, consider which will give the most significant return. You should share tips that will get more than a dollar-for-dollar return. Typically, this includes paint, carpeting, light landscaping, clean up, and cleaning.

If the home has equity, you probably can find a contractor who will take payment for any improvements when the property sells; this will be an added value. If you have money in the bank, you could loan them money to be paid back with interest.

When you're advising the client, you will encourage them to declutter and consider that "Less is More" when presenting their home for sale.

- **Agree on a price**

They must select the price so that if it is wrong, they will not be able to turn that onto you.

If you have done your job correctly to this point, they will select a reasonable price. If, in the rare situation, they choose an amount that does not make sense, ask them a series of questions to guide them.

> "If you were a buyer, which of these homes would you select?"

"What would cause you to select that home?"

The answer will either be price, location, or amenities.

> "So, based on that reasoning, where should we price your home so that it will sell?"

- **Close**

There are a few ways that you can close at this point.

- **Use the hard close.**

The **Hard Close** is a direct way to gain commitment. When you have rapport with the seller, and you feel that they are ready to move forward, say,

> "Do you feel comfortable and confident that I can help you?"

Seller says,

"Yes."

You,

"The next step is to just OK the paperwork, and we can get started."

- **Use the assumptive close.**

When you follow the processes step by step, this is a natural closing to an agreement. Assuming the close is my favorite way to get the sellers to sign the listing.

Say to the seller,

"We agree that we should list it at $599,000. Is that correct?"

Seller replies,

"Yes."

Close,

"Tell me about the personal property that will convey. How many ceiling fans do you have?"

At this point in the sales process, you merely start filling out the listing paperwork.

When you take the listing, tell the seller to keep their insurance current and utilities on. I learned this the hard way when I listed a home for sale.

Shortly after the seller hired me, he abandoned the house without telling me and turned off the utilities.

I soon visited the property and found spores of blackish mold infesting each surface, from top to bottom. Since the electricity was turned off, the sump pump was not operating, and that period had excess rain, which caused significant moisture, resulting in the mold.

The mistake significantly diminished the value of the property.

- **Overcome any objections.**

As you become a better salesperson, objections will become fewer. When you are proactive in the process, difficulties will be fewer. The process is designed to understand the priorities of your seller deeply and to address any future opposition proactively.

Even when you implement everything correctly, there may be times when an objection occurs.

If you did not uncover and overcome all the seller's objections, you probably would have the challenge of getting hired. If the seller seems confused throughout the process, you should review your presentation skills.

A simple and direct question that you could ask to uncover an objection is,

> "What would stop you from moving forward?"

When you do receive an objection, you always should repeat the opposition, affirm what is being said to you, isolate the complaint, and then handle the doubt.

Here is an example of how the objection-handling strategy works.
The seller shares their concern with the agent.
The agent repeats the objection.
Then the agent affirms,

> "That is a great question, and I understand why you would ask that."

The agent isolates the objection,

> "Is there anything else other than that objection that would stop you from moving forward with me today?"

You want to understand that there is no other concern that the seller may have before you handle the objection so that another complaint does not sideswipe you after you deal with the first objection.

Then you handle the concern.

A seller may have a few common objections.

Common Seller Objection 1 -- "We have to think about it."

This objection is most often a smokescreen for a more profound concern. Your job is to dig deeper.

> **Option 1 to Handle the Objection** -- "We have to think about it."

Agent says,

> "I understand you have to think about it. That is smart to be certain that you are making the right decision. Other than thinking about it, is there anything else that would stop you from moving forward today?"

Seller,

> "No, nothing else."

Agent says,

> "Great. So, out of curiosity, exactly what is it that you will think about?"

Then you can handle their real objection.

> **Option 2 to Handle the Objection** -- "We have to think about it."

Agent says,

> "Tell me more about that."

Then you handle the genuine concern following the pattern of repeat, affirm, isolate, handle the objection.

Common Seller Objection 2 -- "We have other agents to interview."

Agent,

> "I can appreciate that. I understand that you have other appointments scheduled. Is there any other reason besides the appointments that you have scheduled that would stop you from moving forward with me today?"

Seller,

> "No."

Agent,

> "At this point in my conversation with a seller, they say they are comfortable and confident to move forward with me, yet there are other appointments scheduled. They feel obligated to the other agents. Is that the case now?"

Seller,

> "I do feel that I should keep those appointments."

Agent,

> "I respect that. Let's do this. I wouldn't mind making it easy for you.
>
> "Let's agree to work together now. I will call the other agent and let them know that you hired me and that we will share the commission with them when they bring us a buyer. That way, we do not waste any time finding you a buyer because the buyer for this property might be looking tomorrow, and we want to get you on the market as soon as possible."

Common Seller Objection 3 -- "The other agent says that they can get more money."

Agent,

> "I can appreciate that, and I understand that you want to get the most money for your sale.
>
> "Besides the price, is there anything else that would stop you from hiring me today?"

Seller,

> "Well, we want the highest price."

Agent,

> "What you should understand is that most agents will take a listing just so they can use your property as bait to attract buyers.
>
> "Yes, you want an agent who will tell you the truth, and I am telling you the truth.
>
> "What the market indicates is that other properties such as yours are selling for $450,000 to $465,000.
>
> "If you list above market expectations, then you will sit on the market until the agent who promised you a higher price gets you to drop the price.
>
> "This strategy will hurt you because when your listing lingers on the market, a buyer will be more aggressive, which ultimately will net you LESS money.
>
> "Let's do this. Let's pay attention to what the market is telling us and list it with me today at a price that will cause it to sell at the highest dollar that the market will bring."

Common Seller Objection 4 -- "Will you list it for less of a commission?"

The other agent says that they will list it for less of a commission.

Option 1 to Handle the Objection -- "Will you list it for less of a commission?"

If you have a rapport with the seller and feel confident, they understand the value that you will bring to them, say,

"No."

Pause and then take back control by asking a question and then close them.

Option 2 to Handle the Objection -- "Will you list it for less of a commission?"

Agent,

"Ouch! I understand that you want to net the most money. Is there anything other than the commission that would cause you not to HIRE ME today?"

Seller,

"No, just the commission."

Agent,

"Well, I say, 'Ouch!' because if an agent will not protect their compensation, how do you think that they will represent your interests in a negotiation?

"Let's do this, let's agree to work together now, and I promise that I will put my experience in consultation to your benefit to get you the most money for the sale of your property."

Common Seller Objection 5 -- "I have a friend/ aunt/ uncle/ neighbor/ golf partner who is an agent."

Agent,

> "I understand that you have loyalty to another. Is there anything besides your concern for your friend that would stop you from hiring me?"

Seller,

> "Well, I do not want to hurt my friend."

Agent,

> "Are you willing to risk your friendship?"

Seller,

> "No, of course not."

Agent,

> "Well, you owe me nothing, and you owe your friend nothing except friendship, but you do owe yourself the best.
>
> "After all, if your friend is not successful, how will that impact your relationship?"

- **After you get hired, send a handwritten thank you card.**

Step 6: Connect the Buyer with the Seller

Way to go, you got hired! You are on your way to **C.P.I.!**[*]
   Now it's time to exceed your clients' expectations, provide them value, and earn referrals. It is time to advocate for your clients.
   Each year Amazon founder and CEO Jeff Bezos hosts an event called MARS, which is an acronym for Machine learning, Automation, Robotics, and Space. Bezos invites leaders in these areas together to share thoughts. (39)
   On June 6, 2019, at the MARS Conference in Las Vegas, Bezos declared, "If you want to be an entrepreneur, the most important thing is to be customer-obsessed."
   Bezos continued, "Don't satisfy your customers, figure out to how to absolutely delight them. That is the number one thing. Whoever your customers are." (40)

---

[*] C.P.I. = Consistent, Predictable Income

Your efforts should be to exceed your clients' expectations. To be successful in real estate sales, you must have this mindset.

Bezos also shared at the MARS event that a business owner or salesperson should be a missionary, not a mercenary.

He said that entrepreneurs who champion their clients' interests "always end up making more money... ...they always win." (40)

If the strategy of obsessing over your clients works for Jeff Bezos, you might consider doing the same. As you continue reading, think about how you can over-deliver the steps.

Be a Fiduciary

In your real estate licensing class, you learned that a client is someone who hires you, and a customer has not hired you. You owe a duty to both, but your responsibility to a client is greater.

You can recall those duties required to serve a client when you remember the acronym, **OLD CAR**.

When the buyer or seller hires you and becomes a client, your obligation to them includes:

Obedience

You will follow your client's instructions and do all the legal activities that they ask of you regarding helping them to buy, sell, or invest in a property.

Loyalty

You will place the client's interests in front of all others, including your own. If you or a close relative has any interest in a transaction that you represent, you must make sure that all parties understand your relationship with the property.

Disclosures

The agent is responsible for advising about the appropriate disclosures. These will differ from state to state, and your broker can advise on the documents that will be necessary.

When in doubt, you should disclose.

REAL ESTATE EVOLUTION

I once met a seller who was getting his home ready for sale. At our first meeting, I noticed a severe crack on the exterior foundation wall in front of the house. I told the seller that he should repair the damage.

After the seller made the improvements, I returned to the home and noticed a trio of freshly planted purplish Azaleas in front of the wall with the crack.

I thought to myself, "That is not what I meant!"

I explained to the seller, "Those are pretty bushes. Now, let's remove them or disclose."

We had to make sure that any buyer would know about the flaw in the wall.

You should disclose latent defects and material facts.

A latent defect is a flaw that is not easily seen, such as seasonal flooding or a carpet that covers a foundation crack.

A material fact is something that a buyer would want to know and if they knew it, might change their mind about buying the home.

You also must disclose any affiliated business arrangements or joint ventures that you or your brokerage have with a mortgage financing or title company.

Confidentiality

You never will share anything that you learn about your client without their permission, particularly knowledge that could hurt your client during a negotiation. Anything that you learn about their financial situation, personal matters, or motivation to buy or sell should not be shared.

Accounting

You will need to care for any money entrusted to you that is related to the transaction. For example, if you must hold money in escrow (a third-party account), the agent has an obligation not to mix personal funds with their private or business capital.

When you place money in escrow, you can release it in one of three ways:
1. When the principals finish the transaction or exit the contract as previously agreed when they do not meet a contingency.
2. Each party agrees to release the funds.
3. A court tells all parties to disperse the money.

Reasonable Care and Due Diligence

It would be best if you have a high degree of knowledge about real estate and understand the factors that drive the market.

Current interest rates, financing options, supply and demand, economic issues, government policies, social factors, local infrastructure, and the impact of the media on the real estate market are all some topics that you should know.

When you are not a qualified expert, you should share with your client that you are not the resource for their needs.

For example, if a buyer asks you if a home has mold, you should refer them to a qualified mold inspector. If a seller asks for financial advice, you should connect them with a CPA or financial advisor.

For things that fall outside of your expertise, you should be the source of the resource.

Care Owed to Client and Customer

You must act in good faith and be fair and honest with both the client and the customer.

Buyers - Write an Offer that Gets Accepted

As you work with the buyer, remember that the buyer is less interested in you and most interested in the homes for sale. As you work together and provide excellent value, a relationship naturally will occur.

Prepare for home showings.

You have now fully consulted your buyers, and they hired you. It is time to show homes and then write an offer that gets accepted.

Be prepared for your appointment no later than one hour ahead of any showing. To get ready to show homes, you should complete these tasks:

- Identify all the homes that you will show.

- Obtain showing instructions for each property.

REAL ESTATE EVOLUTION

- Review the local market data for the areas where you will be showing a property.

- Speak with each listing agent of the homes that you will show to gather information.

- Identify the short sale and REO properties and do an extra assessment of these properties that includes reviewing the listing agent's record of success with these types of listings.

- Put together a showing packet for each person who will be viewing the properties. The showing packet should include a printed copy of the client view of each MLS listing, a clipboard and a pen for each client and a **1 to 5 Home Tour** printout for each home that you will show. (See Bonus Resources).

- Use a showing packet when you show homes.

Show the homes.

Each time that you show a home for sale to a buyer, you should strive to write a contract that gets accepted.

When you arrive at a home, knock on the door, and announce yourself.

Trust me, even when you have scheduled the showing, you will be grateful if you follow this advice. I have a few stories of homeowners surprised during a showing that the censors would not allow me to share with you in this section.

When you enter the property, get in front of your buyers, and turn on every light in the house. Go to the kitchen and allow the buyers to view the home.

Listen to 'buying signals' from the buyers as they view the home.

Signs that indicate that the buyers might be interested include them mentally beginning to place the furniture in various places. Financial questions such as, "How much do the utilities cost?" also are useful clues.

When the buyers spend a lot of time in a home and look at every nook and cranny, it could mean they are interested.

When you hear some of these signals, ask if the house feels like home.

If they say, "Yes!", you are ready to get the paperwork together.

If the buyers view the home in silence and ask no questions, this is not a good sign. When this occurs, suggest moving onto the next one.

These are the steps to follow to write the offer that will get accepted.

Many years ago, a buyer's agent that worked with the **Greetings Virginia Sales Network** was working with a husband and wife to buy a home.

The agent found the dream home for her clients and she was preparing to write an offer. The house was on the market for more than nine months. The average time on the market in our area at the time was about 30 days.

The husband and wife who were buying the home debated for a day on what offer they would make.

The next day, all parties on our end were in alignment, and our agent put together an offer. Meanwhile, another buyer saw the same home and wrote a proposal that the sellers accepted.

Our buyers weren't just disappointed – they were pissed off.

They assigned blame squarely on us and could not believe that a home that was on the market for more than three quarters a year would go under contract with another buyer.

"How could that be?" they asked.

And frankly, we had no right answer for them.

No matter how long that the property has been on the market, be sure to communicate,

> "There may be another buyer writing an offer on this property. I have had clients write an offer on a property that was on the market for many months. They were disappointed that another buyer got the home.
>
> "I suggest that you write the highest and best offer the first time. No matter what the situation is with the home, we may only have one shot."

When your buyer selects a home that they are ready to make an offer on, you should call the listing agent immediately so that another buyer does not write an offer without yours having the chance to compete.

REAL ESTATE EVOLUTION

Say to the listing agent,

> "Mr./Mrs. Listing Agent, I wanted you to know that I will be presenting an offer today from a serious well-qualified buyer. If you receive another offer, please let me know and ask your sellers to wait to receive our offer before proceeding with another."

If the offer that you will be presenting will be a lowball offer, then state,

> "Mr./ Mrs. Listing Agent, I will be presenting an offer on your listing later today. It's not quite what your sellers are seeking. Yet, lets you and I figure out a way to make this work."

This approach will encourage a counteroffer instead of a rejection from the sellers.

As you prepare your offer, you should make sure that you do your due diligence on the home as well as the listing agent. Your intention should be to identify any potential challenges that could occur so you can avoid them and to write an offer that gets accepted.

Before you write the offer, verify the value, and have a current and updated CMA. Review the comparable homes for sale and that have sold recently and seek to understand the market statistics.

You already should have discussed this information with your buyer during the consultation phase of the **80/20 Buyer Consultation**. Now you should remind the buyers of the data.

If the market is suggesting that homes that sell, sell for 99.7% of the original list price, you should remind the buyers of that fact.

If you neglected to consult the buyers earlier in the process, it would be challenging for you to do so now. Because it will appear that you do not have their best interests at heart and that you only intend to do another deal.

- How many transactions has the listing agent completed during the past six months?
- Have you or a colleague worked with them before?
- Will you be working with the agent or her assistant?

You will want to know the scenario of who you will be working with so that you may prepare your client's expectations for the next thirty days.

Call the listing agent and ask,

> "Do you have other offers?"

If yes, ask all the details of the other offer conversationally,

> "What are the terms of the other offer?"
>
> "Can you tell me about the contingencies?"
>
> "What type of financing does your current buyer have?"
>
> "How much earnest money deposit did they offer?"
>
> "What amount of down payment did they provide?"
>
> "What is their offer price?"
>
> "What is their closing date?"

The listing agent's job is not to answer your questions (unless directed to do so by their seller). Your job is to find out as much information as possible so you may best represent your buyer's interests.

If there are no other offers, ask the listing agent,

> "Please ask the seller to wait until we present our offer for them to make a decision, and if you receive any other offer, could you let me know while I am getting the paperwork together for my clients?"

Ask the listing agent what else that he or she can share about the property and the sellers.

Ask a question, and then, **KEEP YOUR MOUTH SHUT!** You will be amazed at what a listing agent will divulge.

"Why is the seller selling?"

"Where is the seller moving?"

"What closing date will best meet the seller's needs?"

"What is important to the sellers?"

Prepare the offer

As with all suggestions in this book, follow your Broker's guidance if it differs from these recommendations.

When you prepare the offer, it is essential to do so in the most professional manner possible so that it will be easy for the listing agent and seller to understand.

Your job is to write an offer that gets accepted. Following a few proven strategies will improve your buyer's position.

Fill in EVERY blank on the offer.

ALWAYS have one other agent review the offer before submitting it.

Get pre-approval (not a pre-qualification) letter from your preferred lender.

A pre-approval is when your client completes the application process, and your lender has reviewed the documents. From this, the lender will be able to state the specific mortgage approved for versus a pre-approval, which does not include a credit check or thorough analysis of your client's ability to buy a home.

Submit an offer that will get accepted.

Use the following checklist to submit your client's offer:

- Use an offer cover page and share how they may contact you. Highlight the details of the offer and point out the best points. For example, if your client is using a conventional loan, say so.

- Share a copy of the earnest money deposit check.

- Include the pre-approval letter from your lender of choice.

Provide a copy of proof of funds for the down payment.
- Complete the purchase offer and always have one other agent review it before submitting it. Fill in every blank.

- Ask your client to write a compelling letter to the sellers.

When preparing an offer, coach your client that one of three things will happen when you present the proposal to the seller:

Say to the buyer,

> "Mr. Buyer, I have submitted our offer to the sellers, and I will keep you updated throughout the process.
>
> "The sellers now can reply in one of three ways.
>
> 1. "The sellers will accept the offer.
> 2. "The sellers will counter the offer.
> 3. "The sellers will reject their offer."

And then you physically cross your fingers and deliver my favorite script that I learned from my wife, Traci,

> "Let's keep our fingers crossed."

Present the offer.

Ask the listing agent to please confirm receipt and ask when he or she will be presenting the offer to the seller.

If the buyer is experiencing stress, it would be entirely typical. Update the buyer about when the listing agent will present the offer and keep them informed throughout the negotiation. When you communicate excessively with them, it will help alleviate their anxiety.

I often have seen agents misunderstand their role in the transaction and become overzealous in a negotiation. Your job is to facilitate an accepted offer and get to a successful closing.

When things go wrong, it is common to lay blame on another party in the transaction. **You NEVER should engage in conflict with the listing agent, lender, title company, or any other party to the transaction.** These people are working toward the same outcome.

Ask your lender to call the listing agent and share the financial health of your clients. When he or she makes this phone call, the listing agent will better understand that your buyers are well qualified and will more likely push your offer to the sellers.

Sellers – Get the Listing Ready for the Market

For a seller, a comprehensive marketing campaign is essential to getting the most for the sale of a home. Promotional costs such as photos, brochures, advertisements, MLS insertion fees, printing, direct mail, directional signs, personal Internet websites, and virtual tours all are offered by the top agents.

Administrative staff will help you greatly to get your listing to market and to sell it for the highest profit for the sellers.

I suggest that you review the section in this book, **Step 9: Build, Support, and Guide Your Team** to understand how to get support for behind the scenes responsibilities.

I highly suggest that you consider hiring a Virtual Assistant to help you. If cash flow is a challenge to hiring, then give thought to partnering with another agent or two and sharing a VA.

Some of the tasks that will need done to sell your listing are:

- Look up the tax and other property information.
- Research the area.
- Order the signs.
- Take photos of the property and the neighborhood.
- Enter into the MLS.
- Coordinate a time and date with the seller to post the listing live.
- Place signage and the lockbox.
- Announce locally.
- Announce to the list of people that you market to.
- Activate the marketing plan.
- Email the top agents in your marketplace.
- Post on Facebook.
- Schedule the broker's open house.
- Schedule an open house.
- Monitor social media activity.

Sellers – Officially on the Market

You may have heard the general truth that many agents will take a listing, put up a sign, and place the property into the Multiple Listing Service. Those agents then wait, hope, and pray they find a buyer.

I believe this strategy represents negligence. A proven plan will best serve you and your sellers.

Selling a home can be a very emotional experience. A seller often is scared about their upcoming move. They are probably anxious about the process.

Your job is to make sure the seller knows the plan and strategy, and that you follow through upfront and proactively.

Reassure the sellers by letting them know,

> "We will create a 'Buyer Frenzy' for your house. That is quite simply the only way to create a situation where you have an abundance of offers to ensure that you get TOP DOLLAR for your home.
>
> "We will position your property in the best possible way, providing lots of visibility with qualified buying prospects. We will create scarcity and urgency on the part of the buyers so they will feel compelled to submit highly qualified offers with as few contingencies as possible."

While the house is on the market, you should advise your seller to do the following:

> "When agents use the lockbox for entry to the home, they will coordinate directly through our showing service.
>
> "When you let an agent into your home, please call our Seller Hotline at 703-555-1212 with the agent name, company, phone number, and email address so we may obtain feedback from them.
>
> "If you have any questions or comments about what is going on, please feel free to give me a call. Open communication is the best way to solve any problems that may arise.

REAL ESTATE EVOLUTION

"Your needs will be taken care of BEFORE the selling process, DURING the selling process, and AFTER the selling process – in other words, ALL THE TIME."

No matter how skilled you are in pricing a home, there will be times when the market disagrees with you. When you touch base with the seller at least six times per week, it will be hard for them to blame you when the house does not sell and it will be more comfortable for you to convince them to adjust the price when needed.

Let the seller know what to expect for a showing. Tell them,

"When a buyer schedules a viewing, these are the best steps:

1. Approve the showing.

The buyer will always be accompanied with a real estate agent.

2. Ten minutes before the buyers are scheduled to arrive, turn on all the lights and exit the property.
3. You can go to the local coffee shop or take a walk while the buyer is viewing the home. The maximum time that an agent will be at your property is one hour.
4. Then you can come back home, turn off the lights, and relax until your next showing.

A few times, a buyer will show up unannounced. If this happens, let them see the house only if it works for you. If it is not convenient, ask them to schedule the showing properly.

Sometimes agents are running late or don't let us know if there's a cancellation. It can be inconvenient, but the benefits to you will outweigh the negatives.

As you market the home for sale and solicit offers, you should over-communicate with the sellers. At a minimum, each week, you should call them twice, email them twice, and text them twice about the actions you are taking. Excessively communicating will help in all aspects of the sale.

Consistently let your sellers know about your marketing efforts, feedback from those who show the house and attend an open house, data about new homes on the market, and properties that go under contract.

Set an auto-search on your MLS to email you when new homes in the community come to the market or go under contract. You should be the first voice that the seller hears when there is activity in the neighborhood.

On the 14th of each month, share the market statistics from the previous month's information, and help the seller to interpret what the data means to them.

If you have an assistant, he or she should set you up for most of the information that you will communicate. If you do not have an assistant, you will have to do the work. You should do so in the afternoon so you can block your time for lead generation in the morning.

Each morning between 9:00 a.m. and noon, Monday to Friday, call all agents who have shown the listing, get specific feedback, and update the seller.

Sunday - Host an open house.

Monday – In the morning, send a text to your clients saying you will solicit feedback from the agents who showed the house over the weekend, and you will share what you learn with them later in the day.

In the afternoon, share a comprehensive update about the comments received from any agent who showed the property.

Also, share the feedback from the open house. How many people attended the event?

What did they like, and what did they not like about the property?

Tuesday – Host a broker's open house. Map out any open houses that you are planning to host during the upcoming weekend. If you plan to do more than one, ask another agent from your brokerage to help.

Share what you learn from the broker's open house with the seller.

Wednesday – Share about your recent marketing efforts.

Let them know about any social media platforms, such as Facebook, Pinterest, Google+, Craigslist, and other places where you have posted the listing.

Update them if you have planned for an open house.

Thursday – Share market statistics from your MLS, such as absorption rates in the area.

Friday –. Update the seller on emails that you sent to agents.

If you mailed any postcards promoting their listing, let the sellers know.

Saturday - Spend the day with your family, friends, or take a rest day.

Sellers – Accepting Offers

When an offer is received, you should summarize it with the seller so they can make a smart decision. Explain the pros and cons of each offer to the seller.

You will want the seller to consider the terms of the proposal, the ability for the buyer to execute, the closing date, contingencies, and the price. You should explain the differences between financing options and alternatives.

Behind the Scenes – Receiving and Evaluating Offers

1. Follow up with the lender to verify the status of the mortgage pre-approval process.
2. Create a point-by-point comparison of multiple offers and make recommendations.
3. Help the seller to develop a counteroffer when appropriate.
4. Discuss with the submitting agent.
5. Review the contingencies with the seller.

Step 7: Clear the Path for Closing

You or your assistant should follow up with all parties associated with the sale throughout the process. Continue to update your client consistently.

You will want to touch base regularly with the lender, buyer's agent, title company, any inspectors, appraisers, and more.

You should coordinate all items to help you make a smooth transition. Share resources to change utilities, post office address, get new insurance, arrange the movers, and provide any other support needed.

Over-communicate with the agent who represents the other party in the transaction. Creating an excellent relationship with him or her will help the sale close more smoothly and set you up for cooperative deals in the future.

REAL ESTATE EVOLUTION

Buyers

You will want to be sure that the buyer understands all the details about their mortgage.

Be sure that they know where to go.

There will be a lot of moving parts that occur at the end of a transaction. Buyers often are anxious; the last thing you want to do is have the buyers stress about where the closing will take place.
    Make sure that a few days before the closing you confirm the time and location and that your buyer understands the details.

Let them know to bring their identification.

Tell the buyers to bring their driver's license or other government ID. The settlement company will need to make copies of these for the lender and other parties to verify that the buyer is who they say they are. Make sure that the identifications are valid and not expired.

The buyer should bring certified funds.

Before I was a real estate agent, I bought my first home. On the day of the closing, I showed up with my checkbook, ready to write a big check for my down payment.
    I learned a lesson that I share with all my buyers today.
    The title company seldom will accept a check for a significant amount. Prepare your buyers to bring the exact amount in a certified or cashier's check to the closing to cover the down payment and other closing costs.

Help the buyers get insurance.

Connect the buyers with a property and casualty insurance agent to get the adequate protection needed. If the buyer is getting a mortgage, the lender will require proper insurance.

Prepare the buyer for the closing.

Tell them that they will be signing many documents at the closing. The buyers will have to sign the property transfer paperwork and an abundant amount of loan paperwork.

Review the closing disclosures.

Three days before closing, you should review the closing disclosure (CD) with the buyer. The CD will explain the final terms, fees, and costs of the loan that the buyer will get, and this will be shared directly with the buyer and seller.

Sellers

When the property goes under contract, you will want to share planned updates from the parties about the status. Place all contingencies and inspection dates into a calendar so you can keep track to be sure that you remove those contingencies on time. Let the seller know when you complete those tasks.

If there is a condominium or homeowner's association, be sure that you get the disclosures from the association to the buyers as soon as possible. Double-check to make sure that there is not more than one association.

The seller's closing is typically quicker than the buyers. They have fewer documents to sign.
The same as the buyers, the sellers should bring proper identification, and you should be sure that they know where to go for the closing.
The sellers should contact their utility and insurance companies and arrange to cancel the policies. I typically recommend that they arrange to cancel the plans the day after closing.
They should bring any keys, garage door openers, etc.
If the sellers have any warranty manuals or handbooks for any appliances, they should leave them on the countertop in the kitchen.
Advise the sellers to clean the home before they leave. The sellers should 'broom clean' the house, and it will be good karma for them if they take a step further with the cleaning.

Step 8: Have Others Sing Your Praises

Get Referrals

When I teach, I often ask the classroom, "When should you ask for a referral?"

More times than not, the consensus that I hear is, "All of the time!"

While I appreciate the assertiveness of this thought, I suggest a more strategic approach.

I recommend that you ask for a referral any time that your client thanks you for doing something right.

The natural inclination for us is too often reply to a 'Thank you' with a 'No problem.' Instead, respond to gratitude with,

> "You are welcome. And by the way, who do you know that is in the market to buy a home, sell a home, or invest in real estate that also would like this high level of service?"

As your business matures, it should be your intention to get more and more business from referrals; this will allow you to have more excellent stability.

Get Reviews

Recently I traveled to San Diego, CA, for a business conference, and I wanted to grab a bite to eat. As I was not familiar with my immediate surroundings, I visited Yelp! on my phone and took a suggestion for a local restaurant.

When a home buyer or seller does not have a relationship with an agent, they will start in the same place as I did when I was hungry. They will look online.

Where will a buyer first look for a home? Zillow.

Whether you use Zillow or not, you should have a strategy to solicit positive reviews on your profile.

When a consumer looks you up, they understand that you are a qualified resource through the reviews that they see. They're going to trust Zillow more because that's just the way the consumer thinks.

In this day and age, 100% of prospective clients will look you up online. You should get positive reviews on portals such as:

- Zillow
- Facebook
- LinkedIn
- Soundcloud
- Google

When asking for a review, here is a script that you can teach your clients to use:

> "I had a 'problem' or 'goal.' I found **YOU** or **YOUR COMPANY**, and they helped me solve the problem or achieve the goal by... If you have a 'problem' or a 'goal,' you should call **YOU** with **YOUR COMPANY** today."

After you close the sale, **send a handwritten thank you card.**
Film a testimonial video from each client on or before each closing.

Step 9: Build, Support, and Guide Your Team

Should I Build a Team?

Even if you're a solo agent and you don't want to build a team, you should seek to surround yourself with great people. Because if you are successful at getting business, there will come a day when you either get help, ride the roller coaster of sales/no sales or hire out of desperation.

Selling real estate without help can be dangerous.

You can get distracted from serving your clients and not be available to support them in the manner that they deserve. It is unlikely that you simultaneously will be skilled at selling and paying attention to details.
  When you are overworked, you can make mistakes.

Missing the support that you need can cause you to work endless hours.

There is an easier way.

You don't have to build a big business yet. I suggest that you hire help as soon as you can, even if it's a Virtual Assistant.

I would recommend hiring at least two assistants. Why do I say two instead of one?

1. They can specialize.
2. You can get better leverage.
3. You want to hire two because if you lose one assistant, the other can-do double duty for a short period and you don't go back to doing those administrative tasks yourself.

You could choose to have one of those assistants manage your client care as well as your contracts to close and the other to manage your marketing. It would help if you cross-trained both in the administrative and marketing roles, which will make your business more secure.

I suggest that you continue reading this section of the book because you will find shortcuts to hiring and leading. You will understand that when you follow a plan, the process of getting help can create predictable results.

Understand Purposeful Leadership

To be purposeful means that you have an intention and a resolve to achieve a goal. These people are determined, enthusiastic, and enterprising; they have a plan. They are aware of their own strengths, as well as their team's, and they understand how the people they guide impact each other.

> Purposeful Leadership = Intentional Awareness.

When you have a purpose, you will create a more predictable outcome.

Choose to be intentional, and you will have more control over your result.

There are many forms of leadership. Morals and intentions have no bearing on the ability to lead.

I polled a few of my friends and asked who they thought were the worst leaders of all time.

The response included people such as Branch Davidian cult leader **David Koresh**; the Supreme Leader of North Korea, **Kim Jong Un**; and former Enron CEO **Jeffrey Skilling**.

And how could we exclude the man who intended to create a new "master race" by eliminating Jews and others through torture and extermination, **Adolph Hitler**, from the list of the worst?

OK, maybe I am getting carried away with my examples of horrible leaders. Indeed, there are no leaders in the real estate business that compare to those described above.

The point that I intend to make is that a **leader is simply someone who another follows**. It does not matter if they are an excellent or miserable leader.

As you understand that a leader is someone that another follows, you will realize that you should vet those who you follow and seek to be the best for others to support you.

Great leaders run into the storm because they know that they will be in the wind for a shorter time. They are optimistic and know that at the end of the day, they can carry the day. **They are authentic and keep it real. They have great relationships.**

If you are not sure if you are a leader, look over your shoulder.

Is there anyone there?

If someone is there, would they follow you into a storm?

Many people in leadership positions never deeply study how to inspire others. A leader's job is to teach others to think so that they may get what they want.

When you study **Purposeful Leadership**, you maintain awareness about the choices that you make. **A purposeful leader shares instruction and direction**; they help others understand how to think so that another may get what they want when they want it.

Build a Foundation

You can Google, "How to build a team in real estate?" and come up with all the brokerages' versions of how to build a team.

You seldom will find a quick and secure structure to do so.

The following Evolved Sections, "Build Your Team" and "Lead Your Team" discuss actionable real-life steps that you can take.

I will not dive deep into the **Organizational Model** of your business. The *Millionaire Real Estate Agent* by Gary Keller, Jay Papasan, and Dave Jenks is the best resource available to describe the models of success for real estate sales. In that book, they outline the **Organizational Model** of a team that you should emulate.

To be successful in your leadership, you can follow purposeful steps. These steps are:

- Gain clarity about your values
- Set the vision
- Understand the culture
- Define the people
- Create the mission
- Find and hire the right people

Gain Clarity About Your Values

As you develop and understand what is meaningful to you, you will gain clarity. The better that you define what is important to you, the less hard your decisions will be.

For example, I have a **Moral Compass** that guides me to make conclusions and act based on what is best for most rather than what is best for one. I can make simple choices when threatened by a squeaky wheel of someone who I lead.

As I maintain my guideposts, it enables me effortlessly to understand the best options when otherwise I would have dwelled on a decision.

When you gain clarity on your values, you will be able to communicate them effectively, seek people who share those values and surround yourself with them.
Ask yourself:

- "What are my core values?"
- "What matters most to me?"

- "How do I spend my time?"
- "What is essential to my clients?"
- "What is necessary for those I lead?"
- "Who surrounds me?"
- "Are the people I am around holding me back or pushing me forward?"
- "What are my goals?"

Every company has politics. Often alliances are formed. Manipulation is used to achieve an individual's objective, such as a raise, promotion, or to enhance their power or control. There is regularly a formal or informal hierarchy of influence present.

As a leader, you should understand the natural tendencies of multiple people to feed into these politics. When you do, you can address and label them.

I have found that it is useful to define politics, so we are more likely able to allow the dynamics to be helpful. The politics of the **Greetings Virginia Sales Network** are the politics of performance.

To lead, you should be the kind of person other people want to be around. Your mission should be to help other people to get what they want, and as a result, you will get what you want.

As a leader, some of your most important questions to ask of yourself will be:

1. How do I think?
2. Who will I know?
3. What words will I choose?
4. Will I have the discipline to follow a schedule?

When I started in real estate sales, I asked myself,

"How can I get more business?"

I now realize that business is abundant. I can post a few Facebook advertisements, knock on some doors, visit some FSBOs, and I will get hired. I just need to make a few more phone calls to find that business. I understand that strategy and mindset will determine success.

Then I asked,

"How can I get people to work with me?"

I had success and struggles with hiring people, and I realized that the right people should push you through a ceiling instead of you having to pull them.

I learned that I want to hire people that say,

> "I want Dan's job. And I will do whatever it takes to push him up so that I may earn it."

Next, I wondered,

> "How can I duplicate my gifts for others? Who do I need to be in business with to mutually succeed?"

I understood that the journey to success would be through others and by devoting my time and energy to their growth.

I learned to set a vision, provide the tools for others, agree on expectations, clear the path of obstacles for those I lead, and then get out of the way. I learned to lead, train, and provide them value and accountability.

My coaches challenged me to get clear on my vision. They said to make it bigger. They suggested that I build my 20-year plan.

They challenged me to ask better questions:

> "How do I create a business that will transform people's lives so that it will leave a lasting impact on their legacy?"

I realized that the company with the most leaders wins. So, I asked,

- "What am I doing to foster an environment that attracts elite leaders?"

- "Who can partner with me?"

- "Who can I build this for?"

- "How will I find people like that?"

- "How can I serve others?"

- "Who already attracts that level of talent?"

- "Who do I need to be to lead four leaders that earn $1 million a year who lead others so that all achieve their highest destiny?"

- "How will the money that I earn allow me to help others and have a better life?"

I identified a half dozen of these leaders and vowed to copy them.

Set the Vision

Effective leaders set and communicate their vision often and then recruit a team to that vision.

To attract the very best people, you must a grand idea and be able to share your vision and aspirations passionately so others can see the opportunity that you offer.

Consider making your vision so big that when another person becomes a partner with your organization, they will be provided with a vehicle to allow them to achieve every aspiration of their dreams.

When you create a vision aligned with your passion that is big enough to change lives with endless opportunities, then you will attract the best talent. You will notice top performance from those people.

Communicate your vision often. Jack Welch was the chairman and CEO of General Electric between 1981 and 2001 (41) and known as one of the best business leaders of modern times.

About vision he said,

> "Good business leaders create a vision, articulate the vision, passionately own the vision, and relentlessly drive it to completion.
>
> "Above all else, though, good leaders are open. They go up, down, and around their organization to reach people. They don't stick to the established channels. They're informal. They're straight with people. They make a religion out of

being accessible. They never get bored telling their story." (42)

During Welch's time with GE, the company's value rose by more than 4,000 percent. (43)

Understand Culture

In a team, culture is everything.
When I hear people speak about it, I often observe that they perceive it as a positive attribute.

Culture is neutral. It is neither positive nor negative; it is merely the way that you treat another.

As a leader, you will have the most significant impact on the way that your team treats each other. You define your culture.

> **Culture is the way that we treat each other.**

Today I focus much attention on my ability to lead so that I may lead others to achieve their deepest desires.

I recently asked the Facebook Mastermind Group https://www.facebook.com/groups/RockSolidagents/.

> "What is the one characteristic that you believe every leader should possess?"

Here are some answers I received from a few agents who participate with the group:

- At the risk of stating the apparent, leadership
- Integrity
- Passion!
- Honesty
- Caring
- Empathy
- Confidence

An array of people from different perspectives described the above characteristics to me. **It is essential as a leader to understand multiple points of view.**

Define the People

Establish each member's role that will achieve the vision and hold the team accountable to the actions and results that will drive that vision. **When issues arise that threaten the vision, respond quickly.**

Seek people who want to do good and make an impact in an environment that supports the mission. People who desire to learn and grow and to work with other talented people are ideal for driving your vision.

The right people serving in the right roles will contribute to the success of each other so that they may achieve their destined greatness.

Create the Mission

A mission is the goal of your company. It is a map of how you intend to achieve your vision. After you define your vision, ask, "How will I get there?" and then ask, "Who will help to get us there?"

It would help if you gained clarity to understand their personal goals and then make it your mission to help those you serve to achieve those goals as they help you achieve yours.

Find and Hire the Right Talent

Your key to success is to get into a relationship with the right people.

The gap between where you are and where you want to be is in the 'Who.' When you resolve to make your life about the 'Who' rather than the 'What,' your life becomes unlimited.

A great reference that explores the hiring process in greater detail than I outline below is *Who: The A Method for Hiring,* by Geoff Smart and Randy Street. I recommend that you read it.

How do you hire people who will be the right people and own the outcome?

You do so through following a process that most likely will predict success in a hire. When you follow a hiring system, you will be more purposeful in developing your new relationships. **Even above-average leaders can't get above-average results from marginal people.**

You should seek to be in business with highly skilled people. **A talented person is motivated to do the job that they are best matched to do.**

If you desire to be the best, you should model the elite. Surround yourself with champions.

Meet one successful agent each week. At the very least, you may learn from them. They might be a future partner or refer an agent or staff to you.

I regularly host a Facebook Live interview with a top performer in real estate sales, marketing, hiring, leadership, or entrepreneurship each week. The dialogues have been intense.

When I started these conversations, I intended to add value to the agent marketplace. As I developed my ability, I changed my perspective. Today, I focus the interviews on what I want to learn rather than what I think that others want to know. I make videos available to others to watch.

If you want to eavesdrop on the conversation, visit our agent coaching website www.GetRockSolidCoaching.com.

The past interviews with people such as Wendy Papasan, Jennifer Young, Haro Setian, Aaron Kaufman, Grant Wise, Lars Hedenborg, and other geniuses of the industry are archived there. All are offered to you to view for free.

The interview that I did with Adam Hergenrother changed my life, and you should watch it.

It takes others (and the right others) to achieve ultimate success. The wrong others can hurt you exponentially in ways that you cannot easily control.

I have internally debated which example I should include in this book relating to the top nightmare hire I have made.

Was it the drunk agent who swayed side to side in the middle of the business day after showing a client of mine homes for sale?

Perhaps it was the disheveled agent who resembled Kramer from *Seinfeld* who I caught in the office at 10 p.m. in his underwear?

Was it the CFO who embezzled tens of thousands of dollars from my company?

Yes, these all happened. Those are just the top three that come to mind; I could go on.

Now to think back about those events, I would like to say that they were amusing to recall. I would say that they were funny if I was not so irresponsible regarding my business and family when I brought those people into my life. I don't know how I missed the signs.

Build Your Team

Assess. Gain Clarity. Move Forward.

If you're interested in living the most beautiful life possible and being a part of something larger than yourself so you'll always have opportunities ahead of you, then you could choose to build or join a team. When you consider joining a team, you should critically review how they will help you.

If you want to start a team, you should understand the financial risk, time that you will invest, and other challenges that you likely will experience. Seek to evaluate your current needs in real estate sales. Have clarity on where you are and where you want to go and then take substantial action.

ALWAYS Look for Talented People

To grow, you will want to attract high ability people. Ultimately, another person will ask,

> "What value do you provide?"

They will want proof of concept. Your agents care more about how you will help them than how you will change their business and how it is different from any other brokerage or broker as a person or as an office.

People will join you when they feel good about you.

You will need to have a big plan and be able to paint the picture of the future to others.

You already should have established a value of employing successful assistants and mastered a lead generation system before you hire an agent.

Attract the Right People to You

I often mastermind with other business owners to learn how we may help each other. I can tell what phase their organization is in when I ask, "What is your greatest challenge?"

I only hear three answers, which reflect their company's maturity.

1. "I do not have enough business."
2. "I do not have the right people/employees/team members."
3. "I do not retain the people I hire."

As a salesperson, the foundation of success is to find buyers and sellers to work with you.

For the past decade, I have had a quote posted on the office corkboard that reminds me,

> "I am not in the real estate sales business. I am in the lead generation business, specializing in real estate sales."

I do not know who to attribute the quotation to. It was one of the first things that I learned as a new real estate agent.

At the introduction of this book, I mentioned,

"In real estate school, they seldom (unless you were a student of mine) tell you that after you graduate, you will be starting a lead generation business specializing in real estate sales."

Throughout this book, I speak about how generating leads is the foundation of your sales business, and it is. As you grow, your highest focus will build on top of lead generation. At a point, you will shift your attention to find the right people and then develop them into the very best leaders while you are a conduit for them to achieve their aspirations.

If you desire to build a significant (or moderate) real estate sales business, you will have to devote a substantial amount of time to recruiting and selecting talented people and then train, lead, inspire, and hold them accountable for their success.

You should seek knowledge to develop yourself. Because, without it, you will struggle. If you are not growing, you will not attract flourishing people to you. Look for people with unlimited beliefs.

You might make mistakes along the way, and when you do, you can learn.

When you follow a proven method and model, you more likely will be able to hire effectively. When hiring, it's not just about matching the right skills; it's about finding the right people to fit your culture that will achieve a set of goals.

Many agents spend their careers working in the industry and find it impossible to take time off. Often, this causes them either to have limited success or work eighteen hours a day.

> Limited beliefs =
> Limited results.

Life is not about working 120-plus hours a week in real estate.

Time will be a limiting factor since hours are not a scalable resource. At some point in your sales career, you will hit a ceiling of achievement.

When you run into this ceiling, you will have three choices.

1. Continue to bounce up and down as you bop your head on the limit set by the cap and quit in frustration.
2. Accept that achievement as your best.
3. Hire people and use systems to help you grow.

Of those choices, which would be easiest for you?
If you decide that you do want a bigger life and want to obtain more sales or more choice of how you spend your time (or both), then you will have to focus on leading other people to achieve their goals.

To best lead, you need the right people to lead.

You should be in the business of searching for talented people each day. When you find the right people for the right roles, your life will change, and so will the lives of those who you lead.

You should agree on expectations with the team member who you contribute to and then hold each other accountable to that agreement.

When growing a team, there likely will be challenges, because it involves people. When you build a real estate sales business, you must maintain your sales while adding the right talent and systems to continue reaching your goals.

> *Years go by fast. So, I choose not to spend them acting small.*
>
> *I understand that to impact people's lives in a massive way and for me to live the most meaningful life possible that I will have to succeed through others.*
>
> *Moving forward, when I do an activity in my business, I will always first ask,* **"How else or who else can get this done?"** *(notes from my journal).*
>
> - Dan Rochon

Top real estate salespeople start their business by seeking business **(Lead Generation)** and then move to hiring **(Organization Building)**. When they lead their team **(Leadership)**, they realize the highest achievement.

Being a salesperson and being a leader takes different skills. If you are a qualified salesperson, you might not have a natural gift to hire. The essential skills that allow you to find clients often conflict with the competencies that you will need to build a team.

The qualities of relating to people, making quick decisions, and influencing others will serve you well in your success generating leads. These same characteristics often will conflict with the skills that you need to hire the right people.

You do not want to "win" a bad hire. If the candidate is interviewing with your competitor, you will have to keep your competitive spirit at bay and **stay curious.**

As a new agent, I thought that my only job was to find listings. I did not emphasize hiring the right people; I believed that if I did the heavy lifting to find ready, willing and able buyers and motivated sellers, that almost any agent who joined my team then could serve them well. I was wrong.

Today, **I understand that it is as important to have the right people in place as it is to have great clients.** Having the wrong person in place can at best be an opportunity cost and, at worst, will devastate your business and reputation.

I spend fifty percent of my lead generation time looking for sellers and fifty percent searching for talented people in the real estate sales business that I may help. If you spent twenty-five hours a week recruiting and selecting the best talent, how would that change your life?

I have found that **it is easier to find the right person than to make a good person.** The foundation to be a great leader starts with the relationships that you choose to develop.

I once heard a recollection of a conversation between Gary Keller and a group of his top agents that went something like this:

> **Gary Keller**, "Do you have enough leads to reach your goal?"
>
> **Agent**, "No."
>
> **GK**, "OK, great, then that is your ONE Thing, go get enough leads."
>
> **Agent**, "OK, Gary, I got enough leads."
>
> **GK**, "Great! Do you have enough people to work on them?"
> **Agent**, "No."
>
> **GK**, "Well, that's your problem. Fix that. That's your ONE Thing."
>
> **Agent**, "OK, Gary, I now have the people."
>
> **GK**, "Great, are you hitting your numbers?"
>
> **Agent**, "No."
>
> **GK**, "Then you have the wrong people. Fix that. That's your ONE Thing."

Agent, "Geez!"

I liken elite real estate sales teams to those top teams in the military. I do not intend to take away from the honor of veterans and those serving with the previous statement. I share this comparison to convey that if you want to lead a Special Operations Forces team, you will need a selection process that will graduate the best in the world.

I once heard real estate agent icon Ben Kinney say,

"If you want to lead a Navy SEAL, you have to have a navy."

I understand Ben's comment to mean there are very few people who will qualify for the elite forces.

If you want to lead those top people, you will have to weed through many, many people who will not be eligible. You will need to be in a relationship with many individuals who could be a candidate to work with you.

Only about six percent of all SEAL applicants meet the requirements to start training, and then only one out of four who go through the training graduate. That means that for every sixty-five men who apply, there is only one graduate. (44) (45)

Does your hiring process weed out sixty-four of sixty-five?

Do you want to be the best in our industry?

Build a Bench

You are at the mercy of your first hires if you do not have talented people who could replace them if they quit or you dehired them.

Build a bench of talent. As an NFL football fan, I notice that all teams lose players during the season. Those teams that thrive have a deep bench. Those teams that have injuries with nobody to step up the struggle (i.e., my beloved Washington Redskins).

To fully protect your business, you should have a pool of talent and a bench. Every NFL general manager has a depth of players on their roster. **Your backup quarterback should be talented enough to be a starter on another team because he might end up as your starter.**

Professional football teams have at least two to three players in each role that can come into the game at any time. If the top player breaks a leg, the second-stringer comes in, and they hire another player to fill in for the next game.

The GMs of football teams maintain a practice squad of players who do not play in games but practice with the team. If the unit needs a qualified player quickly, these players are considered "Plan C." The teams are ready if any player, or even a couple of players, at the same position go down.

Scouts and personnel directors continuously keep tabs on talented players to be ready to pick up the right person when the need arises, and the situation presents itself. The teams always are preparing for changes. They invariably have a contingency plan.

There are many lessons to learn from professional football teams.

Are you ready to lose a key player in your organization? If not, what will you do about it?

If you have a bench, your business will have more safety and predictability. You will be a much better leader when you have choices.

How do you Hire the Right Person?

Check with your brokerage to see if they have classes to teach you the hiring process and guide you through training your people, leading them, and motivating them. If they do not have a course of study to support you, ask if they will offer one and, if not, seek another brokerage if you want to learn the skills to build a business.

Keller Williams Realty offers a hiring and training curriculum that includes a class called **Career Visioning.** When you take this class, you will learn how to hire the right people.

A follow-up class called **30-60-90** is designed to teach you to get your people into productive activity immediately by focusing on guiding them through the essential activities of their job during their first ninety days.

Success through Others is the last class of the series. It teaches you how to lead your organization, so its members achieve their goals and vision, which then allows the team to succeed.

Know the Traits of Success

All candidates should go through the following process.

At the end of each step defined below, ask yourself,

1. Will this person likely succeed in the role?
2. Will they likely consistently achieve the set goals?

If no, STOP the interview.

If yes, go to the next step.

If, at any time, at the end of any step, do not proceed without an affirmative answer. There are no "yellow lights" at the end of each level. If it is not a bright, "green light," then it is a "red light," and you should leave the interview gracefully.

My MAPS coach, Tara Smith, taught me that about hiring. **"If it is not a 'Hell yes!' it is a no."** You can apply that philosophy to many areas of life.

If at any time during the interview process, you have doubts about your candidate, stop the interview and exit it with class.

End the conversation in a manner that you honor the person you are interviewing and leave them empowered. Tell them that it is your responsibility to match the right role to the right person and that you would be doing them a disservice to place them into the position that you are hiring.

If you have another role that might fit the candidate, transition the conversation to that opportunity. If you have no role that suits them, do your best to help them find another opportunity with another company.

Identify what Level of Talent you Seek

Talent can be defined as:

> **Potential Talent** has not done anything in this industry yet. They have the right behavior for the role. They will be your riskiest hire and most affordable. Use caution when you consider someone at this level. Yet, do not overlook them, because they could be the future leaders.

> **Emerging Talent** has succeeded in other similar or smaller-scale roles. They have a record of success in other areas. These people will be more affordable than a Proven Talent and more likely to succeed than a Potential Talent.

REAL ESTATE EVOLUTION

Proven Talent has established themselves in the role for which you are hiring. The return should almost be immediate. You will incur less risk, but they will be more expensive.

The Steps to Follow to Hire Talented People

Step 1: Identify a record of success in the role that you are hiring.

Success leaves clues, and so does failure. When you are hiring, you first should look for a record of success. If you're looking for a buyer's agent, they should have a track record of success in self-generated sales.

Focus on past patterns since they most likely will predict the future. When you seek the right fit, the first step is to review their record of success.

Review their work history.

- What have they done in the past?
- Where have they succeeded?
- Where have they failed?

If they have not been in the workforce for a while, you could look for clues in other areas. For example, if they have been a stay at home mom or dad, see what social activities they have embraced.

Have they volunteered with their kid's school or led the Boy Scouts or Girl Scouts?

Did they serve on the PTA?

Were they in a leadership position?

Ask yourself,

1. Will this person likely succeed in the role?
2. Will they likely consistently achieve the set goals?

If no, STOP the interview.

If yes, go to the next step.

Step 2: Do an Initial Interview

Have a deliberate conversation with the candidate. Pay attention to their behavior, thinking, and, most importantly, if they are a potential fit for your culture.

Ask open-ended questions to learn more about them. Make the conversation casual.

Seek to understand if this person has the potential to succeed with you and your team. You can have this first conversation on the phone or face-to-face.

The initial interview identifies the following

- What is their work history?
- What educational background do they have?
- What professional roles have they worked?
- What do they like to do when not working?
- What are their interests?
- What are their goals?

It is important to ask open-ended questions so they can display examples of their past actions, since these will be the most telling.

Calculate if the candidate has the following behavioral qualities:

- **Competitive** – Do they strive to win?

    Ask questions such as,

    - Did you play sports in high school?
        - If yes, "Tell me about when you won? What about when you lost?"
    - Tell me about a time that you were in a contest.

- **Learning-based** – Is learning a foundation of their DNA?

    Ask questions such as,
    - What seminars have you attended recently?
    - Do you like to read?

- If yes, "What is your favorite book?" (You are looking for answers such as, *Think and Grow Rich, Rich Dad/ Poor Dad, The Millionaire Real Estate Agent,* not books such as *50 Shades of Grey.*)
  - What podcasts do you enjoy?

- **Assertive** -- Will they take charge?

  Inquire,
  - Has there been a time when you gave a presentation to a large group?
  - Can you share a time that you made a mistake? What did you do about it? (You are seeking whether they took personal responsibility).
  - Has there been a time when a friend, relative, or colleague disappointed you? What did you do? (You are looking to see if they appropriately addressed their concern with another.)

- **Relationship-based** -- Do they enjoy spending time with others? Does spending time with people take or provide energy to them?

  Ask,
  - "What do you do when you are not working?"
  - "Who do you spend your time with on the weekend?"
  - "How do people give you energy?"

- **Team players** – Will they drive your business forward in partnership with others?
  Ask the candidate the following questions,
  - "Have you played sports in the past?"
    - If yes, "What type of sports?" (You are seeking team sports such as football or field hockey as opposed to individual sports such as tennis.)
  - "What does it mean to be a team player?"

- **Self-starter** – Do they exhibit critical thinking skills and the ability to solve problems? Will they take responsibility for their actions? Will they take the initiative?

    Ask them,

    - "Has there been a time that you needed help in the workplace?" (You intend to understand how they handled the problem.)
    - "Tell me about a time when you acted without permission."

Ask yourself,

1. Will this person likely succeed in this role?
2. Will they likely consistently achieve the set goals?

    If no, STOP the interview.

    If yes, go to the next step.

Step 3 (a): Administer a behavioral assessment

In the 1920s, Dr. William Marston at Harvard University developed the DISC assessment, which is the foundation of behavioral evaluations today. Dr. Marston also invented the lie detector test and was the comic book writer who created Wonder Woman. (46) (You now are prepared to win your next Trivial Pursuit bout).

There are MANY instances where people's behaviors do not align with the role they serve. These people can often achieve success through perseverance, or an overwhelming reason to succeed.

If you want to build a predictable business, you more likely will have success when you hire people with the right behavioral match.

While behavior is not black and white, in general, great salespeople tend to be high "D's" and "I's" and, occasionally, high "ISC's" and administrative/operations people will be high "S's" or "C's."

REAL ESTATE EVOLUTION

Dr. Marston identified traits as:

- (D) Dominant
- (I) Influence
- (S) Steadiness or Safety
- (C) Conscientiousness or Correct

I describe these behaviors to you below.

(D) Dominant

A person with a **Dominance (D)** behavior wants to accomplish results. He or she is confident and focuses on the bottom line.

They are often very blunt and direct in their communication style. Dominate people tend to be fast-paced and have a high level of confidence. These people will be the drivers of a business and often are in a position of authority.

High D's often see the big picture and face challenges comfortably. They quickly take charge of a situation and are comfortable taking risks.

They have a challenge with being patient and paying attention to details. They fear that someone will take advantage of them.

High D personalities often wear black or dark, solid color clothes and drive a white or black car. If you call their phone and receive a voice message, it will directly state something such as,

"Leave a message."

(I) Influence

Someone with an **Influence (I)** style aims to shape his or her environment by influencing or persuading others. This person values openness, friendship, and building relationships.

High I's are enthusiastic and optimistic.

High I's want to be the center of attention, and they do not like it when others ignore them. They tend to be very excited and love to collaborate.

They love fun and energetic environments. Group settings where many people surround them are ideal for a **High I** personality.

Sometimes they do not speak directly and will need help with the details. They fear rejection.

Many times, **High I's** will wear flashy clothes and jewelry and drive fancy cars. If you visit their home or office, you will see many photos of THEM! Sometimes when you get their voice message, there will be a lot of noise going on in their environment.

These are the **people who EVERYONE knows** were at the party.

(S) Steadiness or Safety

A person with a **Steadiness (S)** style wants to work with others within existing circumstances to carry out tasks. He or she values cooperation, sincerity, and dependability.

High S's can be humble and often are accommodating. They tend to seek safety and be slow to change. They do not like to confront others and will avoid conflict at all costs. Stability is a high value to a **High S**.

High S's will remain loyal, and you can depend on them.

High S's will have many photos of their family and friends in their home and office. Sometimes when you call them, the message that is on their phone has their entire family as a part of it.

(C) Conscientiousness or Correct

Quality and accuracy are most important to **High C**. **High C's** value details and are very analytical. A **High C** personality values expertise, competency, and objective reasoning. They want to be precise and correct. The procedure is essential to them.

High C's are afraid of criticism and unnecessary change. You can motivate a **High C** by logic – think, "Mr. Spock" from Star Trek. They are not very social and are happy to work alone.

High C's will leave a voice message such as,

> "Hi, this is Daniel Francis Rochon.
>
> "Please leave me a detailed message and tell me your phone number with your area code, and the exact time and date of your call.
>
> "Repeat your number to me twice and spell your full name – even if you think that I know you."

REAL ESTATE EVOLUTION

There are many assessments online that you could use, including:

- www.tonyrobbins.com/disc/
- www.michaelabelson.com/take-assessment/
- www.wizehire.com offers a behavioral matching system in conjunction with an online recruiting platform.

If you are a Keller Williams agent, you likely have access to the **Keller Personality Assessment (KPA)**. Your Team Leader can let you know if you have access and if there is a cost.

- The **KPA** is a more comprehensive assessment that has modeled the most successful characteristics of people in specific real estate roles. It compares the candidate's traits to a job.

The **KPA** will review:

- Behavior
- Logical thinking
- Critical thinking
- Cognitive thinking

Step 3 (b): Review the behavioral assessment with the candidate.

You will sit down with the applicant and review the assessment.
Be clear that this is NOT A TEST. It is an assessment of someone's behavior, and there is not a Pass/Fail result. Make sure you communicate with the candidate that their results were perfect (as we are all ideal creatures, in some manner).

It is vital to sit with the applicant and review the results with him or her. It is incredibly disrespectful to administer a personality assessment and then not discuss it with the person, since this risks them thinking they have a flawed personality.

You should thoroughly read the report and prepare for the meeting.

Meet at your office and be sure that you will be in a space with zero distractions. If the meeting takes place in a conference room with a glass wall, have them sit with their back to the wall to avoid distractions. Leave your phone outside.

Review the results with your candidate and ask them to help you understand if it is accurate. Ask specific questions about what you are discovering such as,

- Tell me about a time in your life that you displayed that characteristic.

It is imperative to ask follow-up questions. Because the assessment might not tell the entire story. Ask them,

- How do you feel about the results? Are they accurate?
- What is accurate?
- What is not accurate?

Seek examples of when they used the behaviors in the workplace and other areas of their life.

Ask yourself,

1. Will this person likely succeed in the role?
2. Will they likely consistently achieve the set goals?

If no, STOP the interview.

If yes, go to the next step.

Step 4: Conduct a Full Interview

In-person interviews are vital so that you can see the body language of the other person. If it is not possible to get together in person, then you should do a video conference interview.

You may find excellent interview questions on sites such as www.Monster.com or other hiring portals.

Some questions that you could ask include,

1. Tell me about you.
2. What are your strengths?
3. What are your weaknesses?
4. What did you learn from your life journey?
5. What makes you the right candidate for this role?

6. Where will you succeed?
7. Where have you succeeded in the past?
8. Where will you struggle?
9. Where have you failed in the past? What did you learn?
10. What are you most proud of that you have accomplished in your career?
11. What do you take pride in that you have personally accomplished?
12. Who do you admire? Why?
13. When I speak with your last three bosses (refer to them by name), what will they tell me about you?
14. What is one thing about you that only your mother knows?
15. When you thrive, what is your preferred environment? What setting do you not enjoy?
16. What is a specific example of when you got into a conflict?
    a. What was the situation?
    b. What did you do?
    c. What did you learn?
17. What advice would you give the ten years younger version of yourself?
18. What do you know about my company? How will you contribute?
19. What would cause me to want to hire you?
20. What would cause me not to want to hire you?
21. What would make this relationship a success?

Dig deep in the full interview.

Your job is not to treat the discussion like a beauty contest, where the prettiest girl wins. It should be treated in a manner that you are identifying if the candidate likely will succeed in the role you are hiring for and fit your culture.

Ask follow-up questions and make statements such as:

- Tell me more about that.
- What does that mean to you?
- When was a specific time that you experienced that?

Ask yourself,

1. Will this person likely succeed in this role?
2. Will they likely consistently achieve the set goals?

If no, STOP the interview.

If yes, go to the next step.

Step 5: Check References

The essential step that you do not want to skip is to ask other people about the candidate. Be sure that you get the applicant's permission to do this.

Do not ask questions about anything that is a protected class, such as age, race, etc. Keep the inquiries related to their ability to succeed in the role that you offer.

Ask the reference,

1. How do you know the candidate?
2. Briefly describe the position and then ask, "Will this person likely succeed in the role?"
3. What are the candidate's strengths and weaknesses?
4. If I was working to develop the candidate, what advice can you give me to best lead them?
5. How did the candidate get along with their co-workers and supervisors?
6. If you had the opportunity, would you work with or hire this person again?
7. Will they likely consistently achieve the set goals?
8. Is the candidate reliable and dependable? If yes, how would you describe how they display those traits?
9. Who else should I speak to about the candidate who can provide different insights?
10. What else do I need to know about the job candidate that I didn't already ask?

When you have the conversation with the reference, listen for "Red Flags." Listen to what the person is saying to you and be aware of what is unsaid. Notice if there are long pauses in the referrer's responses that might be telling. Thank the person. Offer to help them in the future if the need arises.

No applicant will provide you references that will say something wrong about them. When you review recommendations, go three-deep. In other words, ask the first reference, "Who else should I speak with who may give me perspective about the candidate?" Then ask the second person who the first reference refers to you to introduce you to a third.

When you get to the third level that is where you want to pay attention.

Ask yourself,

1. Will this person likely succeed in the role?
2. Will they likely consistently achieve the set goals?

If no, STOP the interview.
If yes, go to the next step.

Step 6: Team Interview

In a casual setting, you want to have the candidate meet other people who they might be working with and other people you know that have successfully hired before. This can best be done off-site in a coffee shop or for lunch, and you should not attend this meeting.

Share any concerns with the group before they meet. Prep them that, while this will be an informal dialogue, they should pay attention to determine if this person is a good fit. Have them focus on whether the person's motivation, team fit, and work pace will match yours, as well as anything else that is important to your culture.

You should not attend the group interview. While you maintain the final veto or approval right in the hiring process, you would be foolish not to listen to the feedback given to you from your colleagues who engage in the group conversation.

Ask those from the group after the interview:

1. What do we know about this person?
2. What do we not know?
3. Would you stake your job on the success or failure of this candidate in this role?

Ask yourself,

1. Will this person likely succeed in the role?
2. Will they likely consistently achieve the set goals?

If no, STOP the interview.

If yes, go to the next step.

Step 7: Set the expectations and hire.

Share with the new hire what you want them to do. Explain what defines success in the role that they are taking and agree on those metrics.
When a person who works for you understands the definition of success, it allows you to be a better leader. If you meet weekly with the person and review their status of success, then they either will perform and thrive or self-select out.

Go Virtual

Where can I Find a Virtual Assistant?

As a business owner, your business only can grow at the pace that you increase sales while maintaining a profit.

For more than ten years, I've worked with multiple Virtual Assistants (VA's) with my real estate sales company, **The Greetings Virginia Sales Network**. Expanding talent selection across the globe has helped our business to increase revenue, manage expenses, and to thrive.

I have hired virtual help that was based in the United States, as well as across the world. Currently, we employ five full-time people and have a cadre of part-time resources. Almost all our virtual team members head their households. The average time that our Virtual Assistants work with our team is more than three years.

It is vital that when you interview a candidate who lives in another country that you test their English, vibe, and design skills. They should have a computer with enough processing power, a smartphone with a headset, and the ability to make calls via Google Voice and reliable high-speed Internet.

The most significant qualifier for an employment match is a culture fit; a culture fit means that the behavior and beliefs of those you employ match your and your company's values.

Virtual team members are vital in helping us to generate opportunities, convert leads, expand our services, and provide value to our clients.

Our VAs performs clerical tasks to support our agents and clients. These duties include compiling reports for market data reports; writing advertisements, brochures, and fliers; designing websites; helping with SEO; posting property listings in the MLS; placing classified ads for our listings; managing our social media content; answering our phones; and more.

Connect with your VA via email, chat, text, phone, and video. The more methods you use to communicate, the better. It would help if you were approachable and committed to their learning process as well as embracing them as a close member of your team. They have families, lives, and ambitions.

Please make sure you appreciate and recognize them as valuable people.

If you need some help with the sourcing and management of your virtual staff, you can use a resource such as:

- www.MyOutDesk.com.

You can hire your virtual staff directly at:

- www.vivahr.com
- www.virtualstaff.ph
- www.manila.craigslist.org.

To find people who will be able to do short-term task-oriented projects, you also may use a company such as:

- www.UpWork.com

The Greetings Virginia Virtual Team

I describe below the team that currently works with me. I hope that you take the pieces that I explain here that best would support you and duplicate them in your business

The Full-Time Virtual Team

Our full-time Virtual Assistants are genuine members of the team. We speak face-to-face via Google Hangouts several times each day and are as close as can be. My commitment to them and their success is equal to my dedication to our local team members. Our full-time VAs are full team members of our business and operate in that capacity.

Director of Operations

Juleene Dela Cruz is the Director of Operations of **Greetings Virginia Sales Network**. She is responsible for keeping the business profitable and exceeding internal and external client expectations.

She lives in San Mateo, Rizal, Philippines.

Juleene and her husband, Sev, recently had a daughter, Sabrina, who we call, 'Baby Boss.' They also have an older daughter, Leigh.

Working from home allows Juleene to care for her new child while she stays employed full-time.

Juleene has worked in various places across the world. She worked in Kuwait as a training manager for a restaurant company for five years. After that, she decided to go home to The Philippines so she could be with her eldest daughter and started her career in Business Process Outsourcing as a Customer Service Representative for Telecommunications in the US. She grew in this company, and she got promoted as a Quality Analyst, then Team Lead, Revenue Manager and, finally, as an Operations Manager.

Having a teachable heart is one of the traits that a leader should have. When we have an open heart to learn, we can receive wisdom from God and others. And this is one of Juleene's core values. Juleene says about herself, "No matter how great you are, if you're not open for feedback, then you will not grow."

Keen attention to detail is important to Juleene, and she accomplishes tasks wholly and accurately. She is results-oriented, a self-starter with the ability to work independently, with general direction. She can identify issues, obtain relevant information, and relate and compare data. She is a continuous seeker of knowledge, and she is wired to improve systems and efficiency.

As the operations leader of the sales team, she implements systems that are not redundant, which allows for high productivity. She understands that client care is the front-facing representative of our business and understands that many clients are very detail-oriented. Juleene understands the value of communication for the good of the company.

Juleene's most recent efforts have been to get us up and running with a new system called KW Command.

KW Command is an Artificial Intelligence-enabled CRM provided by Keller Williams Realty. It allows us to track goals and organize the activity of our business.

With KW Command, we manage our online lead generation activity, maintain contacts, support our listing consultations, manage our documents, and manage our offers and communications, and more, in a simplistic manner.

Before KW Command, we used an array of Google Drive documents and spreadsheets as well as multiple other systems.

Director of Hiring

A key component to the success of the **Greetings Virginia Sales Network** is our continuous pursuit to develop a relationship with talented people who serve in the right roles.

A year ago, I was having dinner in San Diego with the CEO/Owner of Vyral Marketing, Frank Klesitz. Frank and I masterminded about business, and he suggested that I hire someone to take charge of recruiting and selecting staff.

I implemented Frank's suggestion, and I met and hired **John Karlou Villamil**. John oversees hiring, training, consulting, and holding accountable all staff members.

John lives with his partner, Maria Margaux, in the southern the Philippines Islands city, in Dumaguete City, on Negros Island. He is the eldest son and has a younger sister, Jessa, who lives in Australia.

John grew up in The Philippines in a family of engineers in a small house located in a massive field. His early childhood was simple. They had a farm with a couple of livestock and horses.

When John turned nine years old, his mom left him and his sister with their dad. His father was a civil engineer and always was working and not physically present. It was rough for John growing up with a father who he got to see once a month, and without a mother.

However, John did not let his childhood negatively affect him. He used that life experience to fuel him for success and making a name for himself. John's experience helped him develop the resilience that serves him today. His determination has allowed him to be a vital leader in our organization that is helping us to make a name for ourselves collectively.

John delegates appropriately and manages all the hiring systems. He oversees our company's training calendar, coordinates the team training while communicating to all team members, and ensures 100% participation.

John's most common and most necessary work activities are:

- Hiring and Recruitment
- Quality Analyst
- System development, implementation, and management
- Information management
- Checking in with team members to check for happiness

John manages details well and often takes care of problems before they occur. He plans activities and follows through. He knows how to get the job done and stay on track.

He is task-focused to complete his work, because he most likely is working on projects while handling requests for support and assistance from other teammates.

Many real estate agents who want to gain certainty and predictability in their sales business contact us regularly to apply to work together. To manage the interview process, we host a weekly Exploratory Call that John leads.

If you would like to attend a call, email, info@GreetingsVirginia.com with the subject line, 'Exploratory Call,' and John or another member of our team will coordinate.

Marketing Team

Our marketing team supports our real estate sales team to have a prominent online presence and helps with online activities.

They focus on graphic design, spreading our material across social media, managing website content, managing websites, and helping all our marketing to create an omnipresence on the Internet.

They contribute to developing relationships with top people in the marketplace and help to promote them consistently.

Our marketing team oversees the graphics and design in our marketing and promotion and represents our team image in a manner that makes us look good — they assist in organizing campaigns and developing marketing strategies.

The team's priority is promoting our listings in a way that allows for high visibility to the general public who might be in the market to buy a home and communicating those efforts to our listing clients twice per week. They implement marketing programs such as our listing promotions, direct mailings, social media campaigns, client seminars, online webinars, and publicity events.

The team members in our marketing department are savvy in social media, skilled with branding and marketing, and can recognize leads. They are responsible for systematically building raving fans. They lead our promotional activities selected to support the brand and marketing strategy; this includes the creation, design, and distribution of print materials such as brochures, and ads.

Marketing activities include planning, developing, and executing our marketing programs, such as direct mailings, social media campaigns, client seminars, online webinars, and publicity events. The marketing team is responsible for maintaining our online exposure and telling our story.

Other tasks and activities that the virtual marketing team performs include:

Graphics, video and web design, and graphic designing for the following:

- All websites including:
  www.GreetingsVirginia.com and
  www.GetRockSolidCoaching.com
- Open Houses
- Listings
- Closed Sales
- 'Coming Soon' Properties
- Real Estate Classes
- Agent's Marketing
- Special Initiatives
- Online Interviews
- Hiring and Recruitment Ads

- Events to be posted onto www.GetRockSolidTraining.com and www.GVAppreciatesYou.com
- Postcards and Newsletters to be mailed systematically to our sphere of influence and local neighbors on the 15th day of each month.
- Company Banners and Logos
- Real Estate Memes and Quotes

They also complete the video editing for the following:

- Vlogs (Four Q and A videos each month)
- Local business owner Facebook Live interview (Weekly)
- An influencer in the real estate agent community interview (Weekly)
- Online Interviews
- Property Walk-in Videos
- Agent's Marketing
- Company Advertising Videos

Inside Sales Agents

The main job of our ISA team is to set appointments for us.

They seek to pair buyers with sellers in a proactive way and provide consistent follow-up with leads. They call expired listings, FSBOs, and our Internet leads. Members of the ISA team love learning what a buyer or seller desires about their real estate needs and goals.

There are different ways our ISAs help other people, and they always start by listening and understanding what others need. The simple philosophy that the ISAs have is to make you feel good by hearing what another says. When they help another, they understand that they also help themselves. So, they put themselves into a prospect's shoes and think of possible solutions that will resolve their problems or help them to achieve their goals.

Our Part-Time Virtual Staff and Project-Based Contractors

We also employ part-time resources who either work on specific projects or a case-by-case basis. We also have relationships with a cadre of virtual vendors who help on project-based activities, such as website design/SEO, online research, database entry, travel research, email management, scheduling, meeting preparation, social media reports, and more.

We work with people across the world and locally to have a high-functioning support staff to help our agents achieve their success. Our team allows our agents to focus on the top activities that will drive results, which are:

1. Lead generation
2. Lead conversion
3. Going on appointments
4. Negotiating
5. Scripts and roleplay

More importantly, our agents can have a better choice of how they spend their time. Most of our agents have families, and as a result of the support that our Virtual Team provides, they can have more time with their families.

We also use the services of vendors who offer specialized care. Some of those companies include:

Streamlined Business Services

This is a bookkeeping company based in Phoenix, AZ. They have worked successfully with clients in a practical aspect for quite a while. Streamlined provides us with financial reporting that allows us to be more profitable and act as a liaison with our CPA.

The reports that they provide to me include:

- Profit & Loss Reporting
- Budget vs. Actual
- Lead Source Tracking
- Percentage of Income/Expense Reporting
- Account Reconciliations
- Accounts Payable & Receivable

LRB Business Center

This company is based in Alexandria, VA, and provides us with receptionist services. They answer our phones during office hours, screens the calls, and then transfer them to the appropriate person, which allows us to offer a professional image to clients, agents, and prospective clients who call our office.

Acknowledge Your People

You must appreciate your people's efforts. When you acknowledge them, you will increase their allegiance and production. If any issues arise, you should be approachable, and you want them to call you. You also should meet one-on-one each week to hold them accountable for the goals and to coach and mentor as necessary. Inspect what you expect from your team members. Hold accountability conversations with them every week. Hold high standards and protect your culture.

Our team does **daily video chats each morning** to help each other. At **seventy-thirty a.m.**, a team member shares an inspirational video from Dianna Kokoszka, Darren Hardy, John Maxwell, or me.

At eight fifty-five, our team discusses the video and share our thoughts and what we learned from watching the video. At nine-oh-five a.m., we review the previous day's activity, and from nine-fifteen a.m. to nine-thirty a.m., we practice scripts. Often, the local team meets **before the eight fifty-five a.m.** start of our meeting to get extra script practice together.

Each Thursday **from eight fifty-five a.m. to twelve p.m.**, we host a team wide training that local and virtual staff attend.

People who work virtually will not have a chance to get to know you outside of the work environment. It will be vital that you take extra effort to understand who they are and let them know who you are. Take the time to lead them the same as you would your local teammates.

It would be best if you relied on video chat as often as possible, because you want to be sure you answer any questions in real-time.

When you can see the other person via video, you can observe their physiology, including their body movements, tone, verbal pauses, tempo, and different postures that will allow you to pick up on cues of understanding or confusion.

Rely on email or text chats for quick communications.

REAL ESTATE EVOLUTION

The last thing I suggest to you is to be sure to say thank you often. Your team members must understand that you appreciate them for the time that they spend helping.

Lead Your Team

In real estate sales, you most often will show the way for your clients. There will be times that you will lead the cooperating agent on the other side of the transaction. Sometimes you will persuade the lender, home inspector, appraiser, or other people who are a part of the sale. If you have a team, you will lead them.

Everybody leads another in some manner. At times, you might direct your spouse, and in other instances, he or she will guide you. You might lead a child or a friend.

The nature of influence allows for a ripple effect. You can impact people who you never have met through the way you lead those who are close to you.

To build a great business, you should focus on growing your people, and then they will create a great company.

The team should believe that what they do is important and has meaning. People need to have clarity about what they are supposed to do and need to be able to depend on each other. They should feel safe to express their concerns and thoughts.

Have the right people in the right roles performing at the right level. The people you lead have more impact on your outcome than you.

As a leader, **your job is not to meet people in the middle. It is to meet people where they are and then help bring them to where they want to go.** Come from the position of providing value to people so they can receive the most out of life.

> I do it >> We do it >> They do it = Exponential.

When problems arise, offer a solution by pointing to the way to fix the problem. **When stressful situations occur, be sensitive, and be present**. Provide praise in public and critical recommendations in private. Remember that the intention is to help. **Give care, then candor.**

At the beginning of your sales career, the only resource that you have is yourself. Then you hire one or two people, and you do the business together. When you develop your ability to lead others so they may get what they want, then they will lead your business, and you will grow exponentially.

About Working Together

> *"Two are better than one because they have a good return for their work: If one falls, his friend can help him up. But pity the man who falls and has no one to help him up! Also, if two lie down together, they will keep warm. But how can one keep warm alone? Though one may be overpowered, two can defend themselves. A cord of three strands is not quickly broken." -Ecclesiastes 4:9-1*

Being a part of a group does not make you a team. When you form a group, the result is often a setback. When that group becomes a team, the propulsion can be exponential.
Your success is mutual with those you lead. The team should be engineered to succeed at an optimal level, with each member entirely taking on their duties you are responsible for understanding that your actions impact others.

This practice applies to your extended team, including lenders, title companies, home inspectors, etc. Together you will achieve more. Insist that your organization use your preferred vendors when they can. Because when they do so, team members can be confident they are working with an individual committed to the same outcome.

Tips and Tricks

Throughout the years, I have learned more lessons than I ever could have believed. I have experienced 'messy' in the past as well as success.

Some of the most valuable lessons I have learned while building a team are:

1. Set expectations for your relationships. A complaint reflects an unfulfilled expectation.

2. Stand for the greatness of those you serve. Lead to people's strengths, not their weaknesses. Know their strengths and hire for your fault. Help others to identify their power.

3. Listen. As a leader, **LISTEN to another person's perspective**. Learn from criticism. When someone disagrees with you, listen twice as hard. Always ask, "What can I do differently?"

Always strive to hear. Consider all opinions and then select an option of direction based on what is best for the whole group or team. Examine what will allow us to reach our goal more quickly.

4. Respond instead of reacting. When a problem arises, think about the best solutions before you act.

A well thought out response will allow for greater success than a quick reaction. Real estate business leader Mo Anderson conveys, "A leader always responds appropriately."

5. Every problem has a solution. Face challenges head-on.

6. Move obstacles out of the way. Move the constraints.

7. As a leader, do not interrupt a team member when they speak. You best can demonstrate that you are listening by being quiet and then restating what someone says after they say it. Always be sure that all speak before a meeting concludes.

How do you remove the restrictions?

Where are your bottlenecks?

8. Teams succeed when everyone feels they can speak up and have a voice.

9. Create opportunities for others.

10. Understand that your job is to lead so that others can think and act in the manner that they desire to reach their goals.

11. Attract people who believe in themselves and act. I noticed that those who thrive possess competitiveness, like to learn, are assertive, relate to others, are team players, and are self-starters.

12. Be 100% accountable and authentic to your responsibility for the results. Measure on results, not effort. Strive to obtain incremental gains.

13. As a 'Rainmaker,' your job is to find listings, find talented people who have unlimited thinking, and then train, lead, and develop them.

14. As a leader, when there is failure, look in the mirror. When there is a success, search through a window.

15. You never get paid to be right. You get paid to persuade.

Holding on to being right will create a barrier and keep you from listening.

This does not mean you must negate the conviction of your beliefs, just that when you are more committed to achieving the outcome than being right, you will get a better understanding of another and be more likely to collaborate.

What I have learned that poisons a team:

1. Gossip.

2. Incompetence.

3. Lack of unity.

4. Personal ambitions that outweigh those of the team.

5. Missing cohesion.

Retain Talented People

Top people are attracted to a high value. People are only loyal to the extent that they get what they want.

If your benefit to another is supplying leads through Boomtown or Zillow, then your value is weak. Your agents easily can copy this, and you are at the mercy of the lead owners.

When your database is producing your business, it provides insulation and helps with retention. Another cannot easily duplicate the opportunity of your sphere of influence.

Most people can stick with you when things go well.

What do they do when there are struggles?

How do you create an inner circle that will create an elite outcome, no matter how hard?

People will leave you for one of these reasons:

1. They do not receive the benefit/money.
2. They do not align with the culture.

Competing at the highest level is not about winning. It is about preparation, courage, understanding, and nurturing your people with heart. As a result, you will win together.

Strive to see the best in people. Choose to do your best. Choose to be calm and peaceful.

Speak greatness into others. The most successful people do not rely on their own willpower to determine their success.

Leadership vs. Management

Management is the method of overseeing or regulating people. Leadership is different because it refers to your mastery to train, inspire, and motivate others toward a common goal.

If you seek to understand, and if you are a leader or a manager, ask yourself, "**How many people come to me for advice?**"

A leader will have many people seeking guidance, and often, these people will be outside of those who report directly to you. You should model the behavior that you expect others that you lead. A leader's actions are always under a microscope.

When I was a young man, I was the Food and Beverage Director of a small luxury hotel and marina on Chesapeake Bay.

I led three restaurants as well as food service to the hotel and marina. I was new to management. (And I intentionally refer to the experience as 'management' as I had not yet understood the difference between management and leadership).

One of my first leadership lessons was that even a casual comment by me would blow out of proportion my intention. I quickly learned to be very careful with my words, as I did not always recognize the impact of my statements.

I once casually commented that we should upgrade our table linens. I was thinking out loud, and the next week, the manger that I was speaking with had replaced all the laundries. That was not my intention.

You do not have the liberty to slack.

I recently attended a development course offered to its agents by my company. Forty-eight people participated in the seven-week program. The instructor divided us into groups of seven.

I was volunteered to lead our small group, which included leading my broker.

The broker was distracted by some illnesses and events from home, and she missed two classes. I reached out to support her, and she told me that she was going to quit the course.

I encouraged her to continue and was unsuccessful. I asked her boss, the CEO of the 200-plus person brokerage, for help. Then I received education on leadership.

The CEO spoke with the broker and shared with her that she had free choice. The CEO asked questions designed for the broker to reflect on the impact of her decisions. As the broker realized that agents looked up to her, she recognized that her actions impacted others more than herself.

The CEO did not tell her that she had to continue. Instead, the CEO led and encouraged. I believe the broker understood that even though she was uncomfortable in the setting, her actions as a leader would leave an emotional wake for others.

The following week, the broker was at the class, and she stayed until graduation.

You should lead people and manage systems.

REAL ESTATE EVOLUTION

Standards and Accountability

If you are running a sales team and you intend to win, you should keep score. If you do not know your performance, you never intentionally will improve.

First, define your standards. A standard is the absolute bottom performance marker that you will accept for a team member to be on your team. If you allow anything below your 'standard' to occur, then you have created a new standard, because you are accepting less.

After you define your standards, you will meet one-on-one with your team members to understand their goals. If you have high-performing people on your team, they probably will have personal goals that exceed the standards set.

As you agree on what the floor of production will be for your organization, and you understand everyone's intentions, inquire about what is important to them about achieving their goals.

Why do they want to achieve those goals, and what will they do with the money that they earn?

For administrative staff, it should be clear to them how to earn more money and opportunity.

All the people you lead will have to earn their opportunities. Your job is to stay committed to helping them to achieve their intended destination.

I am writing this section in October. At the beginning of the month, my team and I agreed that we would take fifteen listings this month, and when we do, I will take them skiing. To qualify for the trip, each person who will attend the prize event will have to take at least one listing.

As we approach the last week of the month, a team member has not yet taken his listing. As a result, it is an all hands-on deck approach to help him get his listing so he and his family can join us.

Our inside sales agents are calling every FSBO, expired listing, absentee owner, and any other person they can come up with to solicit an appointment. Our other agents are volunteering to help him convert those appointments. We all are committed to helping him succeed.

After you understand what is essential to those you lead, you should set weekly accountability meetings with them. These meetings should be no more than thirty minutes. During the time that you meet, you will want to focus on the highest-level activities they could do to create the outcome they desire.

When you meet in this manner, it will be a leadership opportunity for you to help each person hit his/her goals. You will find that you will enhance your relationship, and they will work hard to achieve their intentions.

If a person is not consistently meeting their goals, it will set up the conversation for a very natural transition for them to move away from the role. When this occurs, see if you can find another position on the team for them that they may be better suited for, and if none exists, you will have to part ways.

About Training/ Coaching

The best leaders look at their roles as if they are a coach. They lead through asking great questions. Some questions to ask include:

> "Are we winning?"
> "What do you think we should do in this situation?"
> "How can we achieve our goals?"
> "What is getting in the way?"
> "How can we move this out of the way?"
> "How may I help you?"
> "What do you need from me for you to succeed?"

Plan your questions before you meet. When you have the weekly conversation, know what your goal is, and keep focused on one question before you move to the next. Dive deep into the conversation to learn what the real opportunity is. Say,

> "Tell me more about that."
> "And what is important to you about that?"

Ask, 'How,' 'What,' and 'When' questions. Do not ask, 'Why' questions (unless you are inquiring about why they want to achieve a goal). 'Why' questions mostly will solicit a defense rather than a solution from the person you lead.

Read the examples below and choose which question is most empowering,

REAL ESTATE EVOLUTION

Example A:

> "Hey Bob, I noticed that you haven't hit your goal of taking one listing this week. What can you do so that you reach your goal?"

Example B:

> "Hey Bob, I noticed that you haven't hit your goal of getting hired by a seller this week. Why haven't you taken a listing yet?"

I know that as you read the examples above, you do not hear my voice inflections in my head as to how I am asking those questions. I intended that you heard **Example B** as accusatory. If not, reread the two examples and listen to recognize that **Example A** is more empowering than **Example B**.

Start the weekly meeting where you review the prior week's goals and the progress toward them the person you lead has made. You could ask

> "Last week, you said that you would have two first time appointments, and you had one. What can we do together so that this week, you get three appointments to make up for only getting one the prior week?"

Sometimes, if you get an adverse reaction to your leadership, it is probably because the other person is not connecting the dots of how the actions, they take will allow them to achieve their, 'Why.' Your job is to help them reconcile this.

> "Bob, you told me that you want to take your wife on that great vacation in three months. You said that you want to sell one home in addition to the number you normally sell to help you pay for this. How can I help you achieve that extra sale so you can take your vacation?"

This approach will allow the other person to understand how the actions that they take will create the outcome they want.

After you set goals, understand what drives your people, and host weekly meetings, your job is to remove any obstacles to their success.

It should be your priority that those on your team are as successful as they can be. You should strive to provide those you lead with the necessary education, training, development, staff, systems, structure, and support. You might not be in the position to fully support another with those resources, yet you should intend to move toward sharing as much as possible.

People can achieve more than they believe, and when they are led to think and act so they can reach what is essential to them, they often will be grateful to you.

As people strive for higher goals, they typically will maintain a higher level of achievement. Once something is stretched, it does not go back.

To teach another person, you first should show them how to do it, then have the other person show you and, finally, do it in a live-fire with your support.

Role Model = You demonstrate to another how to do it = Awareness.

Role Play = They practice with another = Confidence.

Real Play = They do it with your guidance = Courageous.

> *You can't put motivation in anyone. It must come from within. You can teach the skills, and you can reinforce, but you can't make someone want to do something."*
>
> -Jean Burgdoff, co-founder of Burgdorff Realtors in Murray Hill, NJ, with 30 offices and $2 billion in sales, as well as the owner of the #1 ERA franchise in the world.

I choose to let others know what conversations I will engage in and which I will not have. I love the day to day conversation with my teammates, and I enjoy the professional relationships that the team develops.

I view each member of the team as an extended family that I should guide to achieve their highest destiny.

Most days, I have every moment of my time scheduled. I am intentional in my communication -- I get to the point as soon as possible. That works for some but may not work for all.

REAL ESTATE EVOLUTION

I intend to be the most productive and useful. **My most pressing concern is in who others become and in them to be the most refined version of themselves as possible.**

In my sales network, I am available to discuss with our teammates:

- Acknowledgment of Team Member individual success
- Training
- Development
- Coaching
- Goal setting
- Prospecting
- Prospect conversion
- Writing offers that get accepted
- Negotiating
- Having fun and ideas to promote the enjoyment
- Opportunities for improvement in systems or structures
- Proactively avoiding obstacles in a transaction*
- Overcoming obstacles as they occur in a sale**

*The better a team member succeeds with this task, the less this conversation ** will be required.*

About the operations of our business, **I never will discuss**:

- Gossip
- Rumors
- Other team members with team members in anything less than a positive manner. (Unless if involves an action that is illegal, unethical, immoral, or harms others or the company; these situations ALWAYS should be brought to leadership's attention ASAP.)
- Lead distribution
- Anything that takes away from the fun, positive, productive environment

I ask team members that if you ever have a business concern that needs a conversation with a member of leadership, please present it to them with at least two possible solutions. **Matters presented without at least two possible solutions will not be considered.**

If they ever have a business concern that needs to be addressed, first, share it with the appropriate person who can make a difference.

Feedback Loop

I think it's crucial to have a feedback loop, where you're always thinking about what you've done and how you could be doing it better. You also should have systematic feedback to help your people.

We embrace **End of Day Reports** from our inside sales agents and staff. These reports allow us to understand where they perform well and where opportunities for improvement exist.

Once each week, our Director of Hiring touches base with each team member to solicit their feedback. He asks,

- What is the most valuable thing you receive from the team?
- How could the team increase its value to you?
- How could you increase your value to the team?

Step 10: Choose Profit

You have achieved a **C.P.I.**,* now what?

Real estate agents tend to fall into one of two categories. They are either an entrepreneur or a salesperson. Often, in neither case are they a good manager. For many agents, having the skill to build or sell is a hindrance to achieving a profit.

A lot of the agents that you look up to are selling a ton of homes. Podcasts feature them, and people are listening. But many times, these agents are not making money. Selling a bunch of houses for the sake of feeding an ego is a bad idea.

Seldom do we hear about profit goals instead of sales goals. It seems that most focus on the transaction or volume goals.

Many will boast about the sales that they have. Few people talk about the profit they have earned. Your family does not care that you sold $20 million in volume when you lose or take-home little money.

---

*C.P.I. = Consistent, Predictable Income

Some Rainmakers have fallen in love with the idea of having a vast team. When you build an organization, you must pay attention to the expenses. To survive, you must be profitable.

When you started your sales career, how much time and effort did you invest in mastering the sales game? Did you devote the same time to becoming an outstanding businessperson?

Often, agents do not focus nearly as much time on being astute in business as they do on sales. In addition to achieving mastery in sales, you could be a student of business.

A foundation of being good in business is to make money. Many salespeople and business owners are living paycheck to paycheck to survive. I have been there! When you cannot pay your bills, then something is radically flawed with your business.

As a group, real estate agents are making less money than we were five years ago. As a result, we must make more sales to achieve the same income.

The challenge is that while our income has gone down, our expenses have not.

Since we have less revenue, it becomes harder to make a profit, but there is a simple formula that you could follow. Take the following few steps and you will be set to succeed:

1. If you do not have a bookkeeper, hire one today. (Ask a few top producers in your office who they use. If you get stuck and cannot find one that is affordable and will help, email me at info@GreetingsVirginia.com with the subject line, 'Bookkeeper Recommendation,' and I will help you.)

2. If you do not have a business account separate from your personal account, set one up today. Call the new account, **BUSINESS ACCOUNT**.

3. After you have your bookkeeper and business account up and running, set up a second and third business account.

    a. Call these new accounts, **PROFIT**, and **TAXES**.

4. When you get a commission check, deposit three percent to five percent of it into the **PROFIT** bank account and another twenty percent to thirty-three percent into a separate **TAX** bank account.

REAL ESTATE EVOLUTION

If you are a solo agent, deposit thirty-three percent to the **TAX** account.

If you run a team, start to save thirty-three percent and then scale it back each quarter to as low as twenty percent, as your taxes require. As a team owner, you will have expenses that will allow you to save proportionately less of the gross income.

The team owner will need less as a percentage of the gross income in reserves for taxes because she will have other expenses and will pay the government from the net income, not the total.

5. Pay your estimated taxes each quarter from your **TAX** account.

6. Pay yourself a regular salary from your **BUSINESS ACCOUNT** to your personal account. **Do not change the amount that you pay yourself unless you have earned a raise** and can feel confident that you can sustain paying yourself more money.

7. Celebrate at the beginning of each quarter of the year by distributing your profits and treating yourself and your family.

8. In your original **BUSINESS ACCOUNT**, save three months of your business expenses.

    a. After you have three months of reserves saved in your **BUSINESS ACCOUNT**, increase the percentage that you allocate to profit.

Follow the above system and make this a habit. You will have a healthier financial outcome.

Dan Rochon

Next Step: The Evolution

The Speed of Change

The evolution of real estate sales is happening so rapidly that it has evolved more quickly than I could finish authoring this book. Though I placed this section near the end of the book, it was one of the first that I wrote.

When I originally wrote this section, I shared a concern that many of my real estate agent friends expressed in an online debate about the disrupters. There was great rumbling in the agent community that our industry was being upended and burned to the ground.

Disruption is happening to us, yet the real estate sales business is not being burned down.

We should be aware of the threats to our survival, and to survive, **we will have to evolve -- FAST!**

Earlier this year, I had lunch with a very successful RE/MAX agent whom I respect very much. At our lunch, he made sure I knew that RE/MAX recently announced an exclusive partnership with Redfin across the US and Canada.

RE/MAX partnered with Redfin on March 18, 2019. Two months later, RE/MAX ended the exclusive partnership with Redfin. (47)

When I started authoring this book, discount broker **Purple Bricks** was entering the US market in New York, Orlando, Phoenix, and various areas of California. The fear expressed in the agent community was that **companies such as Purple Bricks were going to put us out of business.**

I originally included my thoughts about the impact that the outsiders might have on our industry. As I began to edit this book, **Purple Bricks had announced they would leave the US and Australian markets** and I had to rewrite this section.

During the foray into the US and Australian real estate markets, Purple Bricks lost at least $25 million in six months. (48) (49)

The stranger, Purple Bricks, was here and gone in a flash.

I guess that they decided it is a good idea for a business to make a profit. And having a website such as this following website:

www.PurpleBricksSucks.com

Having named your company probably after that website probably did not help.

Does a publicly-traded company need to earn a profit?

A publicly-traded company can lose money for a long time if it has raised enough money to spend, but it cannot lose money forever.

In 2018, Redfin lost $42 million. (50)

In May 2019, Redfin CEO Glenn Kelman said, "There's a feeling now among Wall Street investors, and perhaps the general public, that everything's up for grabs, that real estate's really going to change, and when you have twenty percent of the U.S. economy at stake, you're going to see companies take larger losses and bigger risks to try to win the prize." (51)

In the first three months of 2019, Zillow has lost $67.5 million. They lost $750,000 every day for ninety days! I had to check my math three times to be sure that I included enough zeros. (52)

Other public real estate brokerages that I am choosing not to name are in the same boat as Redfin and Zillow about loss. If you work for a publicly-traded real estate sales company, you might check to see what their last twelve months' profit or loss has been.

Certainly, the real estate sales companies that continue to lose money hope to be the next Amazon or Microsoft or Google.

Granted, Microsoft and Amazon are the two US companies that rolled the Yahtzee of a market valuation north of $1 trillion. (53) But, Amazon lost money for years in pursuit of market domination.

And what are the odds of success of market domination?

REAL ESTATE EVOLUTION

In the early 2000s, thousands of technology companies lost money while chasing the dreams of becoming the multi-(tr)billionaire company.

According to Webmergers, Inc, by the end of the dot-com burst of the early 2000s, nearly 5,000 tech companies that were chasing market share instead of profit went bankrupt or out of business.

Is it possible for a publicly traded real estate sales company to tumble?

The highest stock price of Realogy -- which owns Better Homes and Gardens Real Estate, Century 21, Coldwell Banker, ERA, and Sotheby's International Realty -- was $53.53 per share on May 17, 2013. As I write this today, on September 10, 2019, it is $5.97. (54)

But what if a company like Realogy got into a relationship with a mammoth such as Amazon?

In July of 2019, Amazon partnered with Realogy. Non-Realogy agents predicted gloom and doom again.

On July 22, 2019, the day before the announcement, Realogy's stock price was $5.18 per share. On September 11, 2019, the stock rose to the $5.97 that I already mentioned.

I guess we will have to wait and see how the Amazon/Realogy marriage proceeds.

Will the companies losing money going to keep pace with the rate of evolution in the marketplace?

Will, the speed of change, beat their growth?

If a privately-owned company or another publicly owned company disrupts the industry in a significant way, would investors still invest money in those other companies? And if investors stopped investing in companies that lose money, what happens to those companies?

The Evolution Explained

When I started selling real estate in 2007, the consumer relied heavily on the agent to guide them.

Today, our world is an advanced digital one. Homebuyers can view photos of a property, experience virtual tours of homes, and obtain neighborhood data online. A buyer quickly can narrow their search based on location, price, and type of home. Houses for sale may be viewed online before a potential buyer considers contacting an agent.

Technology has allowed buyers and sellers to perceive that they can transact real estate with little guidance. What the consumer often overlooks is the experience that they lack in marketing, local market conditions and trends, negotiating, and more.

Uber killed the taxi. Technology has changed, and the pace of its growth increases. In 1965, the co-founder of Intel, Gordon Moore, created Moore's Law (55), which states that every two years, the capacity of transistors on a microchip will double. This prediction proved correct from about 1975 to around 2012, when the growth of the transistors slowed, because nothing can rise forever. (56)

As a young boy, I spent hours with my friends playing the Atari table tennis game of Pong. Just a couple of kids, a television, a console, two dials, one knob, and one button were all that we needed, for hours of entertainment of bouncing a square ball with a rectangle paddle across a screen.

Today, a significant increase in technology since Pong allows me to work with amazing people from several countries and time zones. On a five and a half-inch screen displayed on a contraption that fits in my back pocket, we interact face to face in real-time each day.

In his 1999 book **The Age of Spiritual Machines**, Ray Kurzweil, futurist, inventor and Google's Director of Engineering suggests that when technology reaches its limitations, new technology will replace it, allowing for an exponential evolution. He believes that by around the year 2045, we will experience "technological singularity." (57)

Singularity, as described by Kurzweil, is collective machine intelligence that will combine all human knowledge with machine intelligence to be more potent than all humans. (58)

The concept that Kurzweil described received much criticism in 1999; in 2019, his suggestions seem more viable, since we already have combined all human knowledge available since history has been documented and can access it just by stating, "OK, Google..." The rate of technology growth continues to rise.

> "Technology goes beyond mere tool making; it is a process of creating ever more powerful technology using the tools from the previous round of innovation." (71) –Ray Kurzweil

Today, aggregators have entered the marketplace, and they might be the most significant disruption to the real estate sales industry. An aggregator is a website that collects data from multiple sources and displays those results in one portal to allow the consumer to hire based on the price.

Buyers will be significantly swayed

REAL ESTATE EVOLUTION

by paying lower rates. Airlines, car rental companies, hotels, and cruise lines most often have their websites where you can book travel and accommodations.

Consumers can search for multiple sites by visiting one website. with such as Expedia, which will then search for the best price offered on individual websites. On the face of it, this seems like a good plan, but there often are unintended and unexpected consequences.

Companies such as HomeLight, and others aggregate real estate agent's services. Consumers visit those sites and agents bid for their real estate business. When buyers and sellers decide based on price alone, with no regard to the services offered, convenience, or experience that a real estate agent provides, they can end up paying a much higher ultimate price for the cheapest agent.

My wife Traci and I often take spontaneous trips. We enjoy staying at the beach during the offseason because it is quiet, has no crowds, and when we visit, we get to act like locals.

A few years ago, on a day early in December, Traci booked a spur of the moment weekend getaway to Ocean City, MD. Like many travelers, she wanted the best deal and booked the journey on an online travel aggregator website.

Late on a Friday night after a long day in the office, we left our home in Virginia to visit our beach destination. We drove past dying cornfield after cornfield of the flat Eastern Shore of Maryland and finally arrived at our hotel by the ocean.

I was exhausted after a long day of helping clients, followed by a tedious drive across a distance, and I was looking forward to some rest.

When we arrived at our destination, there was very little activity in the area; the streetlights flickered, and an officer on watch sat in a lone police car parked in the lot. It reminded me of a setup for a Stephen King novel.

We wearily approached the hotel's reception area, and nobody welcomed us. Traci and I lingered for a bit, and there was not a person to check us in. Discouraged and exhausted, we gave up on the option to stay at the booked hotel and ventured off to find a new spot to sleep.

We checked into another hotel and enjoyed the rest of the weekend, marveling in the restaurants and entertainment at night and sipping coffee in peacefulness each morning.

When we returned home, we called the first hotel, explained our experience, and asked for our money back. The lady I spoke with was empathetic, yet unable to help, since we had arranged for the hotel on the travel website.

It took us almost four months to obtain our deposit. The experience was frustrating and time-consuming. Call after call after call to the representatives of the online portal born little results. Only my persistence allowed for an eventual refund.

When I think of online real estate aggregators, I remember our beach hotel experience.

The most significant difference is that our experience at the beach could have resulted in the loss of one or two hundred dollars, while a buyer or seller having a comparable experience risk much more. When a home buyer or home seller chooses an agent on price alone, they will get the cheapest agent, which might cost much more in the long run.

Years ago, when real estate agents wanted to view homes for sale for their clients, they had to come to the office to see a library of bound MLS books. The books only were updated every couple of weeks.

The brokers owned the data, the search, and the transaction. Many homes sold before agents from their companies could view them.

In 1975, the first computerized MLS began (59), and by the 1990s, the online MLS had replaced the physical books that previously were used by agents. During this time, the real estate community collectively owned the data, search, and transaction.

In 2004 we saw the launch of Redfin and Zillow (60) and a few years later, they owned the search, while agents controlled the inventory and transaction data.

We must face the reality of how our society is changing and understand how that impacts the real estate sales industry.

Three significant revolutions have affected our world in the past. These shifts altered the way we communicated, traveled, worked, and generally transformed our lives. We now are entering the fourth era of significant change.

Once upon a time, the world primarily was centralized around farming. In about the mid-1700s, the steam engine allowed the factory to take precedence in society. Mechanical machines, production processes, and machine tools allowed people to be more

REAL ESTATE EVOLUTION

productive. As a result of the transition that became known as the **First Industrial Revolution**, the population rapidly grew.

In the late 1800s mass production began as a result of the discovery and use of electricity and the assembly line. The railroads expanded, and Alexander Graham Bell obtained the first patent for the telephone. Many other inventions followed, such as the airplane, the refrigerator, and the car, which allowed us to enjoy a more comfortable life and do more. Communication and travel expanded in mass during this time. (61)

This period became known as the **Second Industrial Revolution**. (62) (61)

Technology impacted us during the **Third Industrial Revolution**, which started in the 1950s. Today, in my daughter's second-grade classroom, she studies reading, writing, and math on an iPad and learns about 3D printing and coding and uses robots. (61)

Genetic sequencing has been developed, and we widely use Artificial Intelligence. Inventors have developed computers, semiconductors, and digital technologies.

Gordon Moore taught us that technology would grow rapidly until it no longer can evolve. Ray Kurzweil explained that when technology no longer can improve, new technology will replace it.

New technologies are emerging today to replace those technologies that have reached their limits. In his book, *The Fourth Industrial Revolution*, the founder of the World Economic Forum, Klaus Schwab, suggests that we have entered a **Fourth Industrial Revolution**.

When you drive your car, you can avoid every pothole on the road and avoid traffic when you use your Waze app. Waze shares real-time information about traffic conditions, police speed traps, and vehicles stopped on the shoulder by combining data from more than 50 million people.

Amazon Prime can predict your next purchase by mining, analyzing, and interpreting data. They almost know that you need a pair of shoes before you realize that the midsole has lost its cushion.

Technologies are becoming intertwined. Big Data, robotics, Artificial Intelligence, and self-driving cars are a reality.

At the 2018 Inman Connect in San Francisco, CA, Brad Inman had a conversation onstage with Gary Keller. (63)

Some consider that Keller was combative in the interview; I perceive that he was agitated because he has certainty of our future and was ineffective in persuading Inman to acknowledge our reality.

During the Inman talk, Keller claims that Big Data powered by AI will be our future,

"The challenge is that the people who are in the digital space wake up every morning, and they say, 'What's the least I have to do physically to kick your physical butt?'"

Gary continued, "This is the battle. The battle is over Big Data powered by Artificial Intelligence."

Gary Keller continued the dialogue with Brad Inman,

> "You're going to be one of two people. You're either going to be an agent who is enabled by tech, or you're to be the agent that is enabling the tech."

A fiduciary acts on behalf of another and places their interests in front of all others, including their own. Moving forward, either you, the agent, will be the fiduciary, or the technology will be the fiduciary.

Keller expanded the conversation to discuss when our world started with the use of physical components of computers,

"Hardware was invented. At some point, you had software to run the hardware."

He continued, "One of the most interesting decisions in the world is that IBM, who created the hardware, decided not to own the software, and they gave one of the greatest deals of all time to Bill Gates and Paul Allen to own the software.

"Then, suddenly, at some point, you're using your hardware, your phone, and you're using the software, and you get this offer to buy a data plan because you were out of space.

"Someone came up with the idea of 'how about if,' and they called it 'the cloud.' How about if we just string computers together, and we put all your data there so you can access it from any technology hardware that you want to use, right?

"Well, here's the interesting thing about that. That's a commodity. For about $1,000 or less, I can buy a piece of hardware. I can buy a piece of software, and I can buy a data service, and I'm in business, right?"

Gary Keller expanded to share about how Big Data and Artificial Intelligence will change our world,

REAL ESTATE EVOLUTION

"Data [will be] powered by Artificial Intelligence.

"And, by the way, it doesn't matter what industry you're in. It doesn't matter if you're in real estate. This applies to all industries. The medical profession, the legal profession, the architecture profession, any profession you want to name at this moment."

> "Dude, that's a problem" -GK.

In summary, Keller said,

"You have two worlds that we live in. The first one is the physical world, and the second one is the digital world. What happens is [that] everybody who's physically based, all their businesses, they [will] wake up.

"The fatal question they [will] say is, 'What's the least I have to do in the digital world to protect what I currently have physically?'"

Gary Keller continued in the talk with Brad Inman,

"Technology, and only that technology, and putting technology that works in their hands, is the only thing that we're focused on" about his relationship with his agents.

Keller claimed, "You have the ability to build a platform that talks to each other, where everything is integrated. I mean, when Berkshire Hathaway calls us up and wants to rent our cloud service, dude, that's a problem.

"Well, the truth of the matter is, is that the entire real estate experience is gonna come online."

Keller is correct to explain that technology has rewritten the rules. The money and resources needed for an average brokerage to compete are well beyond their supply.

As a real estate agent, you will be best served to align with a company that is keeping pace with the changes, and you should place a high emphasis on communicating systematically with your sphere of influence in a manner that you contribute value to them.

The social media conversation between agents at different brokerages online is often a debate over the pros and cons of Profit Share vs. Revenue Share, Zillow vs. Redfin, 'My Daddy can beat up your Daddy,' etc.

I believe that those agents are missing the point.

The war that we are fighting for is for the eyeballs of the consumers. It is for the adoption of a platform.

Companies such as Amazon, Facebook, Uber, and Airbnb have challenged the status quo of business. These companies act as a platform to connect the user with the provider. The ecosystem flourishes when it is intertwined. The traditional model quickly is becoming invalid.

When a company can completely intertwine the real estate experience with the user so that the consumer would be able to use it as a one-stop-shop, that company will triumph over other real estate sales companies.

Currently, Zillow and Redfin are in the front, with most consumer mindshare.

Keller Williams is pushing its tech platform by combining Big Data and Artificial Intelligence to integrate all. KW plans to pass the current leaders and obtain full integration with its agents, brokerages, affiliated companies and consumers first.

The company that develops and obtains the adoption of a platform by consumers first will win. It is tough to get into the platform game after the consumer already has adopted a platform.

Does it matter which company is first?

It seems Bill Gates thinks so.

On November 6, 2019, at the New York Times DealBook Conference Andrew Ross Sorkin of the New York Times and CNBC interviewed Gates.

During this conversation, Gates said about the lost opportunity for Microsoft in the smartphone marketplace, "We were so close, I was just too distracted, and I screwed that up... We were just three months too late with the release that Motorola would have used on the phone. So, it's a winner-takes-all game, that's for sure, but now nobody here has even heard of Windows Mobile ...so instead of using Android today, you would be using Windows Mobile."

Three months! That is the time that Gates said his company was too late to launch into the smartphone race. Gates believes that if his

> "A **platform** is a **business** model that creates value by facilitating exchanges between two or more interdependent groups, usually consumers and producers. In order to make these exchanges happen, **platforms** harness and create large, scalable networks of users and resources that can be accessed on demand." (65)

company acted three months earlier, Microsoft would have made the mobile device that you currently use.

What do the trends of technology, Big Data and Artificial Intelligence mean to you the real estate agent?

It means that moving forward, you will drastically have to adapt the way you do business. The consumer will dictate who will be on the top at the end. The end-user will dictate which real estate companies survive, based on the digital experience that sticks best with user.

The real estate company that is first to develop a platform that successfully integrates the agents, brokerage, consumers, and other real estate related services will win.

I suggest you understand who you are in business with matters.

Complete your research.

Ask your broker,

- "How they will compete?"

- Do they own their own technology?

- How will they integrate it onto a platform?

Do they understand what a platform company is, and can they explain it to you?

Commoditization

Our industry has become commoditized, meaning that in the absence of value, the consumer will make a buying decision based on rates charged.

There have always been discounted brokers. Today they are more prevalent, and they have been able to gain attention by using the Internet.

When the consumer does not discern between expertise and discount, compensation will be pushed downward for real estate agents. The consumer will tend to hire the cheapest.

To prevent this, you must be able to communicate with your people in a systematic manner. You also must serve your clients at the highest level and effectively communicate with prospective clients about how you best can help them.

If you do not protect your database by providing them high value and contributing to them, you risk the possibility of becoming a simple commodity.

What can you Control?

In our industry, there are many things we have no control over. We can fear change, or we can realize what we have power over.

When it rains, you have no control over the storm. You only have power over your actions; you can bring an umbrella.

Today, your experience as a real estate agent is more important than ever before. The downside is that experience is gained only through repeating tasks, which often takes time.

The real estate sales business has evolved and continues to change. We do not know how technology will commingle nor how this will impact our future. To best prepare, bring your umbrella -- focus on what you can control.

Here are a few things that you can control:

- **Your database is your business**

When you provide value and contribution to your people in a systematic manner and add to your database regularly by lead generating as your priority, you will protect your business.

- **Your adoption of technology**

We must be tech-savvy. Companies who have a good handle on technology will be our ultimate competition. If you affiliate with a tech-driven real estate sales company, you will be ahead of the game.

Technology makes it easy to get visibility, but the challenge in a real estate transaction is that you must pay attention. In an attention-deficit world, the difference between a stress-free and a stressful transaction (if it closes at all) is the willingness and competence of you as a real estate agent to anticipate and proactively solve problems (before those challenges become "hair-pulling-out" nightmares).

In today's world, you need to embrace the use of technology. Technology should enhance consumer experience -- not replace the agent. You should remain the fiduciary of your client's experience, while technology plays a functionary role. Placing the client's interests first is different than the world where tech replaces the agent with software and systems that claim to act in the consumer's best interest, while the agent plays a functionary role.

- **Your mindset, skill, and motivation**

I firmly believe that the key to success in business (and life) rests within having a growth mindset, strong motivation, and talent. For many people, this means taking the time to develop.

You can improve your mindset by developing personally.

Your thoughts, beliefs, attitudes, experiences will define your existence. When you focus on the activity described at the beginning of this book in **Step 1: Flourish**, you will be able to guide your mindset toward good health.

You can enhance your skills through learning and practice. You might have a lower ability in an area. Yet, if your motivation is high and you have a mindset full of energy, you can choose to work hard to compensate for any skill deficiency.

To best identify your motivation, ask yourself, 'Why am I doing what I am doing?' When you can answer that in a meaningful manner, you will be able to succeed in almost any situation.

Some people take pride in that they sell real estate to make a lot of money. While having money or power, in of itself, is not a bad thing, it will restrict massively you if it is your predominant motivation.

When things get tough, and they probably will, the money will not continue to push you. Instead, I have noticed that those who are driven by a profound, purposeful reason achieve greater results.

Conclusion

During my career, I have had fun. I have experienced success and setbacks, discovered, planned, retook action and, sometimes, I hit the mark. **I have evolved and I continue to do so.**

To the best of my ability, I shared with you a few of the most important lessons that I learned along the way. I also suggested specific tactics for you to better succeed in real estate sales. As I summarize, there are a few things that I believe have affected me the most that I would like to highlight.

- Understand your priorities.
- Choose to live your life with meaning.
- Develop, learn, and grow.
- Understand your worth.
- Be committed to an outcome – not attached.
- The people you surround yourself with have an exponential impact on who you are.
- Pay attention to the right people.
- Supplement your weaknesses.
- Understand that gratitude and negativity cannot co-exist.
- Focus on one priority at a time.
- Embrace your passion.

REAL ESTATE EVOLUTION

Understand your priorities.

On a personal note, my sobriety has been the most significant thing that has impacted my life. My priorities are Sobriety, God, Health and Fitness, Family, Business.

I believe that without sobriety, I never adequately could have focused on my other priorities.

I sincerely hope that God understands that I placed sobriety in front of Him in the pecking order. Heck, it is not like I have anything important depending on my risk in our relationship – only eternal peace in the afterlife -- did I mention that I am a risk-taker?

Choose to live your life with meaning.

I long ago shed the destructive behavior that ruled my youth. I am still sober, and my life has meaning. Each day, I wake up and consider, 'How I may do better today?'

Develop, learn, and grow.

My devotion to personal development and growth has kept my life fun.

To say that I have evolved over the past years of real estate sales and leadership would be an understatement. Today, I strive to let go of being right and listen to others as I place my trust in the outcome. I have learned to pull, instead of push, to influence.

Through my real estate sales journey, I have learned much. I am grateful that I have evolved. I have developed personally and professionally. There are a lot of areas of this business that I have immense knowledge. There is still much for me to learn and much for me to give.

Understand your worth.

I understand that I am worthy of achieving my goals.

Be committed to an outcome – not attached.

As I reflect on the perceived successes and failures of my career, I realize that it would have been impossible for me to have invested more time, energy, and resources into the tasks that I have embraced. I have struggled at times, and when I did, I never gave up – until I did.

The people you surround yourself with have an exponential impact on who you are.

I have learned to be careful about the relationships that I keep. I understand the value of partnering with the right people.

I have been in relations with good people in which we were not the right for each other. Many setbacks that I experienced have been as a result of my being in the wrong relationship.

Pay attention to the right people.

I quickly fall in love with someone who I lead. I have struggled to get out of a relationship with someone who I care about when they are not performing. I understand the importance of staying in contact with the right people and not the wrong people.

Supplement your weaknesses.

As I understand my weaknesses, I have supplemented it with other people's strengths. I have hired a Hiring Director/Success Coordinator named John Karlou Villamil. His full-time job is to seek talented people who want to make a larger impact in the world while they realize their dreams.

John helps me to take a stand for the greatness of those we partner with so that they thrive. He also recognizes that if we allow a nonperforming person to partner with us, it deteriorates the organization and is a disservice to the person. I appreciate how John supports me and the team so we can rely on each other.

Understand that gratitude and negativity cannot co-exist.

When I made mistakes in my business, and I felt my head dragged through the gravel as I banged it over and over, I sought appreciation. At worst, I would get a bloody nose. At best, I could appreciate the fact that if I were to learn from the mistake, I never would have to experience the challenge again.

REAL ESTATE EVOLUTION

Focus on one priority at a time.

I have learned the critical lesson to focus on one priority at a time — my mind races with the velocity of light speed, and often, I am challenged to implement one ambition at a time. I know that it is a better strategy to focus on only one major initiative at a time.

A few years ago, my friend Abraham Walker and I had the privilege to sit with Gary Keller and Jay Papasan in Gary's private office as they wrote the ***Millionaire Real Estate Agent 2*** book.

To say that Gary Keller created a bunker to allow him to focus on his highest-level priorities would be an understatement.

When we arrived at Gary's office in the basement of Keller Williams Realty International's headquarters in Austin, TX, I noticed on the left side of the massive entryway door to Keller's office what appeared to be a retina scanner security system. There was a buzzer that we pressed, and GK's chief protector inquired through the intercom about our credentials and verified that we had a valid appointment to enter.

As we passed through the first guard post, an assistant who acted as the next bulwark against distractions met us and then confirmed our identities again.

When we entered Gary's office, a flat-screen projector sat on top of the eight-seater table to the left, where Gary and Jay sat. To the right was a display of about twenty guitars from Gary's collection. Behind the guitars sat Gary's desk, and behind the workspace was a bookshelf that spanned from the floor to the 14-foot ceiling. Housed on the bookshelf was a collection of books that looked to be costly collector's items.

Gary glanced at us as we entered and motioned to the leather couch that I believe was the same that he and Joe Williams bought when they opened the company. He said, "Sit down." We sat. Gary went back to work with Jay.

For the next hour and a half, we observed Gary and Jay as they wrote and debated concepts. From time to time, he would ask for feedback, but it was clear that he was hyper-focused.

As we sat, I noticed on the dark deep wood easel was a note, "Until my ONE Thing is done, everything else is a distraction." I thought that this level of focus was a myth. Gary focused on the task at hand intently.

It amazed me that the owner of the largest privately-owned real estate sales company in the history of the world would be able to focus on one activity at a time without distraction. That day, I learned an essential lesson about focus.

As they finished their task, Gary turned his beast of a chair toward us and asked, "What did you think that the founder of the largest real estate company is doing now? Playing golf?"

Gary was doing his ONE Thing.

Gary and Jay have not yet published their book. I suspect that GK looked at the landscape of the business environment, and consciously decided that building a technology company that happened to sell real estate was a higher priority than finishing the book.

I would predict that Keller will get back to authoring the book with Papasan after his company's platform is more developed.

Embrace your passion.

Choose to embrace your passion for the choices that you make of how you spend your life. I encourage you to ask,

"What should I be doing today so that, ten to twenty years from now, I still could be living my passion?"

I do not know the future. Yet, I do know that, to the best of my ability, I will create a meaningful one. I will wake up tomorrow morning, and I will ask again, "How may I do better today?" I encourage you to do the same.

To your success!

The Real Estate Agent's Hack

I am glad that you read my book. Thanks for taking the time to develop yourself and to learn.

I shared a LOT of information with you and I know that it can seem overwhelming. Do you want help implementing these steps to gain more certainty and predictability in your sales business?

Do you still get a bit nauseous when you think about riding the real estate roller coaster?

Very often, when I teach, real estate agents ask me to coach them. For years, I have resisted this call to action. I have chosen to spend my time and energy otherwise.

Well, guess what? I STILL am resistant to coaching one-on-one!

Why do I resist?

Because for now, I still spend my time in the trenches of real estate sales, where I help our clients to solve their problems or achieve their goals, and I support the agents on my team to accomplish every aspiration of their dreams.

I still wanted to deliver massive value to the agent community. So, I masterminded with some of the best agents in the world, and asked them, 'How I can do both?' I learned that I could help agents across the globe with the help of other high achieving, successful people. Together, we offer **Rock Solid Real Estate Coaching**.

I have asked ten of the best real estate agents and coaches in the country to partner with me to help real estate agents like you.

We host ten training classes each week covering the topics that will help you.

1. Flourish
2. Look for Leads
3. Focus on Conversion
4. Nail Your Presentation
5. Get Hired
6. Connect the Buyer with the Seller
7. Clear the Path for Closing
8. Have Others Sing Your Praises
9. Build, Support, and Guide Your Team
10. Choose Profit

By now, you should see a clear pathway of how to succeed in real estate sales. But, if you want to fully maximize your ability to earn predictable income, month after month, we have something more for you.

Imagine the thrill of seeing commission check after commission check.

Rock Solid is a paid service, and the price is affordable. If at any time you cancel your coaching, we will refund you your last thirty days payment.

Visit www.GetRockSolidCoaching.com, to learn more. While you are at the site, view some interviews from the top agents in the world at the 'Superstar Interviews' section. We offer tons of free content on the site.

Enjoy it and use it as a tool to learn.

For Agents in Virginia, and the Mid-Atlantic Region

Dear Real Estate Agent,

If you're a **solo agent and you have sold at least six homes**, would you be interested in **tripling your business in the next twelve months?**

Would you **like to sell more homes; earn a more consistent income; have certainty in your business?**

Would you like to **be more productive**, **spend more time with your interests**, and **work less**?

If you answered yes to the questions above, read on.

You can **decide today** that you will be a success. It is possible to choose to be the best father or mother possible. You could want to be the best brother, sister, uncle, nephew, aunt, or niece; be the best version of yourself that you could be. **Be the best real estate agent**.

Decide to give the best service to your people, to your clients, to those who work for you. Decide that you want to be a millionaire. And then do the work.

> Success is tough.
>
> Being broke is tough.
>
> Which toughness will you choose?

It's a known fact that eighty-seven percent **of all real estate agents** fail within their first five years in the business, either because they run out of money, get too distracted, or **don't have the guidance or mentorship they need to succeed**.

Right now, **you may not have a system or culture in place that allows you to live as the best version of yourself or the direction to attract more business**. There are a million and one things to do when it comes to real estate sales, and sometimes everything outside our job description can get in the way of creating results and a predictable income stream.

I started the **Greetings Virginia Sales Network,** affiliated with KW Realty, because I noticed that **many real estate agents experience the pain of uncertainty in their business**.

Many don't have the clarity to solve this problem because they're busy paying their bills and trying to do everything themselves. If this problem goes unsolved, they have no choice but to go back to a nine-to-five job in another industry.

Here's where I can help you. I've been in real estate sales for twelve years and have helped more than 250 agents get their license. I'm an associate broker in Virginia and Maryland. I have spent my entire career helping agents to be successful because that's my highest focus, and I can help you be successful too.

Do you want to close three transactions every month naturally?

We have a position open on our team for an agent who wants to win, and we'd like you to **apply to join us**. Email info@GreetingsVirginia.com with the subject line, 'Exploratory Call.' **This invitation is extended to agents that want to achieve NOT to people that boast idle words and we are selective.**

My priority in the relationship with those I work with is to empower them. I have complete faith in agents we hire because we are discerning in who we take on.

My job is to provide you with the opportunity for you to succeed massively. If we were to work together, your job would be to take advantage of the chance and to contribute at the highest level.

We're different than other brokerages and sales teams in that we already have the systems, processes, and leads in place for you to succeed. **Our inside sales agent team will develop seventy-five percent of your business for you**.

We also have an extensive media presence, including radio advertisements on top radio stations and a comprehensive CRM that we use to make sure our agents always have business and effectively can communicate with clients.

Our administrative department focuses their time on writing offers for you to negotiate, overseeing contracts to close, marketing, and all administrative tasks.

We use proven and repeatable systems based on evidence – not emotion. We have developed these systems as a result of years of experience and studying successful models. Our agents use these systems with all prospects and clients.

When you join our team, you'll enjoy the benefits of:

- Constant, continuous, high-quality leads
- Full administrative support by our coordinators of chaos
- Consistent training
- A team-oriented and learning-based environment
- A career track to earn a six-figure income
- A fun, enjoyable place to work
- An environment that embraces lead generation and accountability for you to lead generate each day
- Access to MOJO triple line auto-dialer
- Listing administration
- Use of the support of our runner to deliver Pre-Listing packages, hang your signs, hang lockboxes, and visit your listings
- Use of a proven system of doing business predictably to allow for you to sell more homes and to net more money
- A fully staffed call center for leveraged lead generation and follow-up
- Listing administration
- Paid Facebook advertising to generate a massive amount of leads
- Access to the highly customized Command CRM that includes Action Plans, Templates, and more
- Tools to allow for systematic tracking of client opportunities
- Effective and engaging lead generation campaigns
- National agent referrals
- Support to help you track your goals and the progress made toward reaching them
- Ability to add, touch, and manage your contacts from your tablet or phone

- Hyperlocal data to show clients unique insights about the specific home and their market
- Signs, riders, directional signs
- Opportunity to work with both buyers as well as sellers
- Daily support around scripts and role play
- High leverage
- Database management
- Transaction management
- Social media support
- Weekly one on one coaching
- Lockboxes
- Marketing management
- Reduced stress
- Certainty
- More time back
- Reputation and strength of a successful team
- Branded apps
- Team 800 number
- IT support
- Web management
- Fliers
- Printing/paper/toner
- Mailings
- Four client appreciation events each year
- Care for business while you take a vacation
- Access to and use of Team Showing Agents, who give you more time to:
    - Lead generate
    - Convert those leads
    - Go on appointments
    - Negotiate
- Scripts/ roleplay
- Local, regional, national training
- Unlimited income potential, with the ability to leverage your business within our business
- Presentation materials
- Video marketing
- Leadership
- Vendor relationship

- An environment committed that you grow personally and professionally
- A true TEAM. NOT a collection of individuals who DO NOT help each other
- Future opportunity to become a leader within the organization, a coach, an owner/ investor in Keller Williams brokerages, an investor in other businesses, an investor in property ownership, and more
- No administration or marketing expense
- Reduced/ little risk
- More

For Team-Showing Agents

- Part-time opportunities
- Allow for a Lead Agent to take leadership of the transaction

With weekly coaching, listing and marketing assistance, customer care assistance, office space, an extensive CRM, branded apps, a checklist, scripts, leadership presentation materials, and a supportive culture, **you'll never again fall through the cracks**. The goal is to allow you to focus on activities that allow you to help people and to produce dollars.

You may well notice how wonderful it feels when you have the support that you need – when you do not have to worry about,

"How will I pay my bills?"

Your other options are to try achieving success on your own or joining another team that may or may not have the tenure, maturity, or systematic approach that's produced a decade of success for us.

This approach allowed an agent on our team who joined us to work only part-time while being the manager of a major retail shopping center and still close twenty-one transactions in a single year.

Last year, an agent who previously had worked for a competing real estate brokerage sold nineteen homes with us during her first six months. Before joining us, she sold zero homes.

If you have not increased your take home pay in the past twelve months by at least $100,000, or if you are not earning at least $250,000 each year, then we should talk!

You will have **ZERO marketing costs, ZERO money that you pay for our staff or supplies.** Ask yourself,

> How will I spend my time when I have the support for success?
>
> Who can I be when I have an organization that has my back?
>
> Who do I need to be to reach my goals?

After you join our team, you'll follow our 100-day orientation process that's developed specifically for you and your success. You'll read "***The Millionaire Real Estate Agent***" and "***The One Thing***" by Gary Keller and learn our buyer process from A to Z.

If you're interested in living the most fabulous life possible for yourself and being a part of something larger than yourself so you'll always have opportunities ahead of you, don't hesitate to apply.

Here are a couple of FAQs we typically get from agents wanting to join our team:

What other opportunities are there outside of just being an agent?

You'll have leadership and expansion opportunities within the **Greetings Virginia Sales Network** system. You will have Team leadership opportunities to lead the Sales department or Lead Generation department or become a Regional Director. When appropriate, you could have the chance to partner in investment, business ownership, and real estate ownership ventures.

What's an average day look like?

We start each day with a power-up meeting via video conference, which lasts from 8:55 a.m. to 9:30 a.m. on Mondays through Fridays. Every weekday from 9:30 a.m. to noon we generate leads. From noon to six p.m. we service our clients, do more lead generation, and pursue educational opportunities.

REAL ESTATE EVOLUTION

It doesn't cost a penny to apply, and we're offering more than just money in return. We're here to help you fulfill your potential, reach all your goals, and be the best person you can be.

Who are we?

The mission of the **Greetings Virginia Sales Network** is to have a profitable and fun business that serves us with grace and ease, so that you have a life of abundance, freedom, choice, and can realize full self-expression.

Where will we go?

We will exceed expectations be the real estate sales team of choice for home buyers and home sellers of Virginia.
    We will be omnipresent about real estate sales in Virginia.
    We will open doorways for our clients and those on our team.

How will we get there?

We will generate a massive amount of leads, convert those leads, close at a high level, and have the very best people in the business in our business.

What is the Greetings Virginia Play?

Our agents play the following play each workday and each week:

- Attend one face-to-face appointment each workday.
- Attend one networking event each week.
- Attend two first-time appointments each week.
- Generate leads for three hours each day.

What is the Greetings Virginia Marketing Plan?

Our organization has a very systematic way to stay in touch with our past clients, friends, and sphere of influence. Here is the **GV Marketing Plan**:

- The Team builds the database by adding 50 people each day.
- We email four educational videos each month to our people.

- Our inside sales agents call all the people who watch the videos.
- We host four client appreciation events annually.
- We teach at least twice per month (Quantum Leap for Kids, Licensing Class, VHDA Class).
- We mail postcards to our closely known people each month.
- Our inside sales agents call our entire database each quarter.
- We service all the leads that come into our company.

What do we value?

We value God, family, and business.

What do we believe?

We believe that each transaction should be a win-win, and we value each client with the highest level of care. Through people, lead generation, and systems, we achieve our success. We do the right thing every time and serve others.

What is our perspective?

We are an organization that fosters an environment of open communication and feedback. We work from goals, action plans, standards, and accountability to the team.

I am sure that you are just like me and that you seek the very best fit for who you are to decide who you should be in a relationship.

Agents who partner with us are provided with a vehicle to allow them to achieve every aspiration of their dreams.

As real estate agents, we are professionals. Our clients are our priority.

Together, we can achieve more. We can alter destinies and our legacy; we will impact the world in a significant way. My dream is more worthy than any of my other gifts.

Won't you join me?

Schedule a 15-minute Exploratory Call to see if this might be the right fit for you and if you might be the right agent for us.

REAL ESTATE EVOLUTION

If you would like to **schedule a 15-minute Exploratory Call**, do so. You may contact me at info@GreetingsVirginia.com with the subject line, 'Exploratory Call'.

Mastermind Together on Social Media

Are you looking for training that teaches you precisely what you need to do to sell more homes? Are you frustrated with your real estate sales career?

I invite you to join the **Rock Solid Real Estate Agent Mastermind Group** on **Facebook** and subscribe to our YouTube channel. This group is open to high-minded real estate agents across the United States and Canada.

You may find us at www.facebook.com/groups/RockSolidagents/.

In this Group, agents discuss:

- Real estate agent success stories
- Question and answer videos
- Highlights of our team training
- Our favorite technology tips
- Interview videos and podcasts with the very best Icon Industry icons
- Lead Generation
- Lead Conversion
- Presentation
- Buyer and Seller Onboarding
- Transaction Management
- Referrals/Reviews/Past Clients
- Team Building/Hiring
- Personal Development
- Interview videos and podcasts with the top agents

REAL ESTATE EVOLUTION

Network with other agents and learn specific strategies and actions that they employ that allow them to sell more homes in less time.

Q&A videos answering the FAQs.

Replays of the training and meetings we hold are shared so you can attend 24/7.

Invites to special events with guest speakers (exclusive discount codes often are provided to **Rock Solid Real Estate Agent Mastermind Group** members).

Copies of operations manuals, checklists, and more are shared.

Market updates that we publish that you can copy and paste to use in your marketing.

This group is specifically for real estate agents who want to grow, learn, and want to dominate their market with a local brand and expert presence.

If you want to improve yourself, make more money, and you feel you can do more and need the tools, this is for you. This group is not for part-time agents who are happy with their income.

So, if you're interested in knowing what we're up to here, and you'd like to stay current on the latest strategies to:

- Generate qualified seller leads
- Attract buyers who want to buy
- Convert more leads to appointments
- Win more listing presentations at full commission
- Systematize your administrative processes
- Earn more referrals and reviews for repeat business

I invite you to subscribe.

Most importantly, everything posted in this group is designed to start a conversation. If you have any questions about selling real estate, you can email me at Info@GreetingsVirginia.com with the subject line, 'Question for Dan.'

First, I'll answer your question in the group, and if I think it would be of benefit to more people, I'll explain it in a video.

Fully 100% of the advice given is educational. I'd like you to get to know what we're up to here so we can grow the size of the real estate pie. And, of course, the group is open to all agents across the country.

If you want to view the interviews from Icon agents who sell thousands of homes each year and learn how they do it, **SUBSCRIBE** to our **Rock Solid Real Estate Coaching YouTube channel**.

You may find us at:

www.youtube.com/RockSolidRealEstateCoaching

Like' the videos that give you value and feel free to comment. I look forward to staying in touch. Let's raise the standard and training of all real estate agents.

Bonus Resources

When you visit www.GetRockSolidCoaching.com, you can access and download copies of the forms and letters that my team and I use that you can customize with your logo.

People often ask me, "Dan, aren't you worried that you're going to help the competition?"

First off, I don't see agents as competition. I see other real estate agents as partners to help my clients sell their houses for the TOP DOLLAR.

And secondly, success is all about the execution. You are either the type of person that will act or not. If you act, you will do so with or without my support, so I mind as well be a friend and help you.

Please rip off and duplicate the resources that I share.

If you want to reciprocate, consider my team and me as your resource for your real estate sales referrals in Virginia, Washington DC, and Maryland.

You may introduce a buyer, seller, or investor to me by emailing me at Dan@GreetingsVirginia.com. I promise that I will take great care of your referrals, treat them like gold, update you throughout the process, and, most importantly, make you look good.

At www.GetRockSolidCoaching.com/free-resources, you will receive free access to the following resources, and more:

Bonus Resource - 1 to 5 Home Tour

Bonus Resource - The GV Promise

Bonus Resource - Questions to Ask the Lender

Bonus Resource - Follow up with the Lender During the Transaction

Bonus Resource - Letter to Share Prior to Closing

Bonus Resource - Pre-Listing Email 1

Bonus Resource - Pre-Listing Email 2

Bonus Resource - Pre-Listing Email 3

Bonus Resource - Shock and Awe – Pre-Listing Plan

Bonus Resource - The Pre-Listing Plan Cover Page

Bonus Resource - The Table of Contents - Pre-Listing Plan

Bonus Resource - Pre-Listing Cover Letter

Bonus Resource - Pre-Listing Long Form Letter

Bibliography

1. Tony Robbins Quotes. *www.brainyquote.com*. [Online] [Cited: October 20, 2019.] https://www.brainyquote.com/quotes/tony_robbins_132532.

2. About Dr. Robert Cialdini. *https://www.influenceatwork.com/*. [Online] [Cited: December 23, 2019.] https://www.influenceatwork.com/.

3. **Kruse, Kevin.** The 80/20 Rule And How It Can Change Your Life. *https://www.forbes.com*. [Online] March 7, 2016. [Cited: October 10, 2019.] https://www.forbes.com/sites/kevinkruse/2016/03/07/80-20-rule/#33df54bd3814.

4. **Robert B. Dilts, John Grinder, Richard Bandler, Judith DeLozier.** *Neuro-Linguistic Programming, Volume I: The Study of the Structure of Subjective Experience.* s.l. : Meta Publications, 1980. 9780916990077.

5. **Tripp, James.** NLP and the 3 Principles - A Perspective. *www.jamestripp.co.uk*. [Online] December 3, 2015. [Cited: March 8, 2019.] https://www.jamestripp.co.uk/blog/blog/nlp-and-the-3-principles-james-tripp-interview.

6. **Chiarella, Tom.** Just Throw the Damn Ball, Tom Brady. *www.esquire.com*. [Online] August 6, 2008. [Cited: March 10, 2019.] https://www.esquire.com/sports/a4883/tom-brady-0908/.

7. **Philip, Christopher.** Non Verbal Body Language Dictionary ::M::. *www.bodylanguageproject.com*. [Online] March 10, 2010. [Cited: October 20, 2019.] http://www.bodylanguageproject.com/dictionary/bodylanguage-dictionary-m-microculture-mirroring-the-mirror-neuron-military-man.

8. **Roche, Steve.** Deletions, distortions and generalisations. *www.alchemyassistant.com.* [Online] [Cited: March 13, 2019.] https://www.alchemyassistant.com/topics/VKSWRiWxcLWMhBrf.html.

9. Physiology. *www.britannica.com.* [Online] Encyclopædia Britannica, Inc. [Cited: October 20, 2019.] https://www.britannica.com/science/information-theory/Physiology.

10. Military Quotes John Hackett – Charles Horner. *www.military-quotes.com.* [Online] [Cited: October 20, 2019.] http://www.military-quotes.com/database/h.htm.

11. **Trump, Donald J.** @realDonaldTrump. *www.Twitter.com.* [Online] August 8, 2016. [Cited: February 22, 2020.] https://twitter.com/realdonaldtrump/status/762781826549030912.

12. **Smith, Chris.** Ben Kinney Shares His Secret Sauce: The Business Model Of The Future Is Already Here. [Online] December 9, 2011. [Cited: February 17, 2019.] https://www.inman.com/next/ben-kinney-shares-his-secret-sauce-the-business-model-of-the-future-is-already-here/.

13. John Wooden. *www.sports-reference.com.* [Online] , November 17, 2019. https://www.sports-reference.com/cbb/coaches/john-wooden-1.html.

14. **Fishbein, Mike.** John Wooden: Success Is Becoming the Best That You Are Capable of Being. *www.entrepreneurs.maqtoob.com.* [Online] September 29, 2017. [Cited: November 17, 2019.] https://entrepreneurs.maqtoob.com/john-wooden-4d68c1a42348.

15. **Phatak, Omkar.** *www.bodytomy.com.* [Online] December 21, 2017. [Cited: October 21, 2019.] https://bodytomy.com/reticular-activating-system.

16. **Editors, Biography.com.** Andre Agassi - Biography. *www.biography.com.* [Online] October 8, 2019. [Cited: October 22, 2019.] https://www.biography.com/athlete/andre-agassi.

17. **Schawbel, Dan.** Jocko Willink: The Relationship Between Discipline And Freedom. *www.forbes.com.* [Online] October 17, 2017. [Cited: March 5, 2019.] https://www.forbes.com/sites/danschawbel/2017/10/17/jocko-willink-the-relationship-between-discipline-and-freedom/#3bedadc46df8.

18. Alaska Salmon Viewing Spot. *www.alaska.org*. [Online] [Cited: June 5, 2019.] https://www.alaska.org/things-to-do/salmon-viewing.

19. **McNicholas, Kym.** Warren Buffett's former pilot launches Visionary Airlines in Silicon Valley. *www.pando.com*. [Online] June 14, 2013. [Cited: August 24, 2019.] https://pando.com/2013/06/14/warren-buffetts-former-pilot-launches-visionary-airlines-in-silicon-valley/.

20. **Szramiak, John.** This story about Warren Buffett and his long-time pilot is an important lesson about what separates extraordinarily successful people from everyone else. *www.businessinsider.com*. [Online] December 4, 2017. [Cited: August 24, 2019.] https://www.businessinsider.com/warren-buffetts-not-to-do-list-2016-10.

21. Steve Jobs: Get Rid Of The Crappy Stuff. *www.Forbes.com*. [Online] May 16, 2011. [Cited: August 24, 2019.] https://www.forbes.com/sites/carminegallo/2011/05/16/steve-jobs-get-rid-of-the-crappy-stuff/#633979267145.

22. **Mann, Sonya.** Tony Robbins Says Success Is Only 20 Percent Skill--and the Rest Is All in Your Head. *www.inc.com*. [Online] September 28, 2017. [Cited: July 19, 2019.] https://www.inc.com/sonya-mann/tony-robbins-says-entrepreneurship-is-not-for-everyone.html.

23. **Eveleth, Rose.** There are 37.2 Trillion Cells in Your Body. *https://www.smithsonianmag.com*. [Online] October 24, 2013. [Cited: July 25, 2019.] https://www.smithsonianmag.com/smart-news/there-are-372-trillion-cells-in-your-body-4941473/.

24. **Ferriss, Tim.** https://fhww.files.wordpress.com/2018/09/72-paul-levesque-tfs.pdf. [Online] [Cited: July 19, 2019.]

25. **Mayweather, Floyd.** Floyd Mayweather vs Juan Manuel Marquez ?? September 19, 2009 MGM Grand, Las Vegas, Nevada, USA. *www.youtube.com*. [Online] December 17, 2017. [Cited: June 17, 2019.] https://www.youtube.com/watch?v=QPKH9hgMawo.

26. **National Association of REALTORS .** *Real Estate in a Digital Age, 2019.* 2019.

27. **FTI Consulting.** *The Allstate/National Journal Heartland Monitor Poll.* s.l. : Atlantic Media, 2015.

28. Oreo's Super Bowl Tweet: 'You Can Still Dunk In The Dark'. *www.huffpost.com/.* [Online] February 4, 2013. [Cited: September 27, 2019.] https://www.huffpost.com/entry/oreos-super-bowl-tweet-dunk-dark_n_2615333.

29. **Watercutter, Angela.** How Oreo Won the Marketing Super Bowl With a Timely Blackout Ad on Twitter. *www.wired.com.* [Online] February 4, 2013. [Cited: September 27, 2019.] https://www.wired.com/2013/02/oreo-twitter-super-bowl/ .

30. **Calfas, Jennifer.** Here's How Much It Costs to Buy a Commercial During Super Bowl 2019. *www.money.com.* [Online] February 3, 2019. [Cited: September 27, 2019.] http://money.com/money/5633822/super-bowl-2019-commercial-ad-costs/.

31. **Attom Staff.** Digital Conversion Rates in Real Estate: What's Considered "Good"? *www.attomdata.com.* [Online] April 25, 2018. [Cited: July 5, 2019.] https://www.attomdata.com/news/company-news/digital-conversion-rates-in-real-estate-whats-considered-good/.

32. Prospecting Conversion Rates for Real Estate Agents. *www.therealestatetrainer.com.* [Online] March 8, 2015. [Cited: July 5, 2019.] https://therealestatetrainer.com/2015/03/08/prospecting-conversion-rates-for-real-estate-agents/.

33. Home Buying and Real Estate Professionals. *www.nar.realtor.* [Online] [Cited: December 21, 2019.] https://www.nar.realtor/research-and-statistics/research-reports/highlights-from-the-profile-of-home-buyers-and-sellers.

34. Washington-Arlington-Alexandria, DC-VA-MD-WV Metro Area. *https://censusreporter.org.* [Online] [Cited: October 9, 2019.] https://censusreporter.org/profiles/31000us47900-washington-arlington-alexandria-dc-va-md-wv-metro-area/.

35. **Heath, Abha Bhattarai and Thomas.** Exxon Mobil moving Fairfax operations to Houston in 2014, taking 2,100 jobs. *https://www.washingtonpost.com.* [Online] June 6, 2012. [Cited: October 9,

2019.] https://www.washingtonpost.com/business/capitalbusiness/exxon-moving-fairfax-operations-to-houston-in-2014/2012/06/06/gJQA7o00IV_story.html.

36. Market Stats by Showing Time. *http://www.getsmartcharts.com.* [Online] [Cited: October 9, 2019.]

37. Consumer Price Index, 1913-. *https://www.minneapolisfed.org.* [Online] [Cited: October 9, 2019.] https://www.minneapolisfed.org/community/financial-and-economic-education/cpi-calculator-information/consumer-price-index-and-inflation-rates-1913.

38. **Levy, Nat.** With Amazon's HQ2 on the way, a housing boom begins in Northern Virginia, echoing Seattle. *https://www.geekwire.com/.* [Online] 24 May, 2019. [Cited: October 9, 2019.] https://www.geekwire.com/2019/amazons-hq2-way-housing-boom-begins-northern-virginia-echoing-seattle/.

39. https://marsconference.com/. *https://marsconference.com/.* [Online] [Cited: October 13, 2019.] https://marsconference.com/.

40. **Datoo, Siraj.** Tips on How to Succeed in Business From Jeff Bezos. *https://www.bloomberg.com.* [Online] June 7, 2019. [Cited: October 13, 2019.] https://www.bloomberg.com/news/articles/2019-06-07/amazon-ceo-jeff-bezos-gives-tips-for-success.

41. **Kagan, Julia.** Jack Welch. *www.investopedia.com.* [Online] June 25, 2019. [Cited: October 25, 2019.] https://www.investopedia.com/terms/j/jack-welch.asp.

42. **Charan, Noel Tichy and Ram.** Speed, Simplicity, Self-Confidence: An Interview with Jack Welch . *https://hbr.org.* [Online] September - October 1989. [Cited: August 2, 2019.] https://hbr.org/1989/09/speed-simplicity-self-confidence-an-interview-with-jack-welch.

43. GE: The Importance Of Timing. *www.seekingalpha.com.* [Online] [Cited: October 25, 2019.] https://seekingalpha.com/article/4082100-ge-importance-timing.

44. **Tahmincioglu, Eve.** Want to be a Navy Seal? Tough is just a start. *www.nbcnews.com*. [Online] May 2011, 5. [Cited: August 7, 2019.] http://www.nbcnews.com/id/42884153/ns/business-careers/t/want-be-seal-tough-just-start#.XbLhauhKhPY.

45. Navy SEAL Requirements. *www.military.com*. [Online] [Cited: August 7, 2019.] https://www.military.com/special-operations/requirements-for-navy-seals.html.

46. William Moulton Marston's Legacy. *www.discprofile.com*. [Online] [Cited: September 8, 2019.] https://www.discprofile.com/what-is-disc/william-marston/.

47. Exclusive Redfin and RE/MAX Partnership Ends. *www.investors.redfin.com*. [Online] 13 May, 2019. [Cited: 18 October, 2019.] http://investors.redfin.com/news-releases/news-release-details/exclusive-redfin-and-remax-partnership-ends.

48. **Lane, Ben.** Flat-fee real estate agency Purplebricks shuttering U.S. business. *www.housingwire.com*. [Online] July 9, 2019. [Cited: October 18, 2019.] https://www.housingwire.com/articles/49508-flat-fee-real-estate-agency-purplebricks-shuttering-us-business/.

49. **Schlesinger, Larry.** Purplebricks to quit Australia. *www.afr.com*. [Online] May 7, 2019. [Cited: October 19, 2019.] https://www.afr.com/property/residential/purplebricks-to-quit-australia-20190507-p51kzo.

50. **Levy, Nat.** Redfin posts $487M in revenue in 2018 as losses balloon to $42M for the year. *www.geekwire.com*. [Online] February 14, 2019. [Cited: October 18, 2019.] https://www.geekwire.com/2019/redfin-posts-487m-revenue-2018-losses-balloon-42m-year/.

51. **LEVY, NAT.** A new era for home-buying: How Zillow, Redfin and their rivals plan to revolutionize real estate, again. *www.geekwire.com*. [Online] May 25, 2019. [Cited: October 25, 2019.] https://www.geekwire.com/2019/new-era-home-buying-zillow-redfin-rivals-plan-revolutionize-real-estate/.

52. **levy, Nat.** Zillow 2.0 era begins: Real estate giant posts $454M in revenue in first quarter since major business shift. *www.geekwire.com*. [Online] 9 May, 2019. [Cited: October 18, 2019.] https://www.geekwire.com/2019/zillow-2-0-

era-begins-real-estate-giant-posts-454m-revenue-first-quarter-since-major-business-shift/.

53. **Monica, Paul R. La.** The stock market now has two $1 trillion companies: Amazon and Microsoft. *www.cnn.com.* [Online] July 11, 2019. [Cited: November 29, 2019.] https://www.cnn.com/2019/07/11/investing/amazon-microsoft-trillion-dollar-market-value/index.html.

54. *Market Summary > Realogy Holdings Corp.*

55. Moore's Law Explained . *www.OnDigitalMarketing.com.* . [Online] [Cited: October 25, 2019.] https://ondigitalmarketing.com/learn/odm/foundations/moores-law-technology-growth-rate/.

56. **Akers, L.D.** MICROPROCESSOR TECHNOLOGY AND SINGLE. *www.digitalcommons.usu.edu.* [Online] [Cited: April 23, 2019.] http://digitalcommons.usu.edu/cgi/viewcontent.cgi?article=2493&context=smallsat.

57. **Reedy, Christianna.** Kurzweil Claims That the Singularity Will Happen by 2045. *www.futurism.com.* [Online] October 5, 2017. [Cited: April 24, 2019.] https://futurism.com/kurzweil-claims-that-the-singularity-will-happen-by-2045.

58. RAY KURZWEIL. *www.singularityhub.com.* [Online] [Cited: April 23, 2019.] https://singularityhub.com/ray-kurzweil/.

59. **Yale, Aly J.** Is The MLS Dead? The Threat Of Tech And New Homebuying Habits. *www.forbes.co.* [Online] June 18, 2018. [Cited: August 12, 2019.] https://www.forbes.com/sites/alyyale/2018/06/18/is-the-mls-dead-the-threat-of-tech-new-homebuying-habits/#4a95b1245851.

60. **Abrosimova, Kate.** What Technology Stack do Zillow, Redfin and Realtor.com Use for Property Listings? *www.medium.com.* [Online] August 5, 2015. [Cited: 12 2019, August.] https://medium.com/yalantis-mobile/what-technology-stack-do-zillow-redfin-and-realtor-com-use-for-property-listings-b6b1ba695618.

61. Meet the Three Industrial Revolutions. *www.trailhead.salesforce.com.* [Online] [Cited: October 26, 2019.]

https://trailhead.salesforce.com/en/content/learn/modules/learn-about-the-fourth-industrial-revolution/meet-the-three-industrial-revolutions.

62. Section V: Europe from 1815 to 1914: The Nineteenth .... [Online] [Cited: October 25, 2019.] https://www.cram.com/flashcards/section-v-europe-from-1815-to-1914-the-nineteenth-century-488625.

63. Gary Keller at Inman Connect 2018. *www.youtube.com*. [Online] July 19, 2018. [Cited: October 26, 2019.] https://www.youtube.com/watch?v=IoHwEgo7CUg.

64. www.the1thing.com/. *www.the1thing.com/*. [Online] [Cited: August 24, 2019.]

65. **Moazed, Alex.** Platform Business Model – Definition | What is it? | Explanation. *www.applicoinc.com*. [Online] May 1, 2016. [Cited: September 11, 2019.] https://www.applicoinc.com/blog/what-is-a-platform-business-model/.

66. Two Capitalists Worry About Capitalism's Future. *www.maddyinstitute.com*. [Online] April 25, 2019. [Cited: October 22, 2019.] https://www.maddyinstitute.com/april-25-2019/.

67. **Smith, Connor.** Hedge Fund Billionaire Ray Dalio Says Capitalism 'Must Evolve or Die'. *www.barrons.com*. [Online] April 5, 2019. [Cited: October 22, 2019.] https://www.barrons.com/articles/billionaire-ray-dalio-income-inequality-education-u-s-at-risk-51554468777.

68. **Robertson, Reece.** Think Big, Go Small: How to Get the Most Out of Your Work and Life. *www.medium.com*. [Online] May 5, 2019. [Cited: 17 2019, June.] https://medium.com/swlh/think-big-go-small-how-to-get-the-most-out-of-your-work-and-life-fdade374a10b.

69. Where Is Idaho Falls, ID? *www.worldatlas.com*. [Online] [Cited: October 25, 2019.] https://www.worldatlas.com/na/us/id/where-is-idaho-falls.html.

70. **Hicks, Mike.** About Me. *www.zillow.com*. [Online] [Cited: October 25, 2019.] https://www.zillow.com/profile/mikehicks/.

71. **Dorrier, Alison E. Berman and Jason.** Technology Feels Like It's Accelerating — Because It Actually Is. *www.singularityhub.com*. [Online] March 22, 2016. [Cited: April 23, 2019.]

https://singularityhub.com/2016/03/22/technology-feels-like-its-accelerating-because-it-actually-is/.

72. 87% Of All Agents Fail In Real Estate! *www.tomferry.com.* [Online] [Cited: March 3, 2019.] https://www.tomferry.com/blog/87-of-all-agents-fail-in-real-estate/.

73. Quick Real Estate Statistics. *www.nar.realtor.* [Online] May 11, 2018. [Cited: March 3, 2019.] https://www.nar.realtor/research-and-statistics/quick-real-estate-statistics.

74. Yogi Berra Quotes. *www.brainyquote.com.* [Online] [Cited: March 4, 2019.] https://www.brainyquote.com/quotes/yogi_berra_391900.

75. John Wooden. *www.sports-reference.com.* [Online] [Cited: November 17, 2019.] https://www.sports-reference.com/cbb/coaches/john-wooden-1.html.

76. **Fishbein, Mike.** John Wooden: Success Is Becoming the Best That You Are Capable of Being. *www.entrepreneurs.maqtoob.com.* [Online] September 29, 2017. [Cited: November 17, 2019.] https://entrepreneurs.maqtoob.com/john-wooden-4d68c1a42348.

About the Author

Dan Rochon is a Certified Practitioner in the Art and Science of Humanistic Neuro-Linguistic Psychology and Neuro-Linguistic Programming from the Washington DC Hypnosis Center.

Dan's purpose in life is to help people achieve their greatness and to open doorways for their success through his teaching, coaching, and mentorship. He leads the **Greetings Virginia Sales Network** for our agents and Staff to exceed our client's expectations.

As a real estate sales agent, Dan and his team are consistently top producers in their marketplace and provide solutions for their clients. Through their investment company, Dan and Traci Rochon have been investing in residential and commercial real estate ventures for more than the past decade.

The media often quotes Dan Rochon, and he frequently speaks about the current real estate market. The Rochon's have been featured on The Nightly News with Brian Williams, The Today Show, CNBC, The Washington Post, The Washington Examiner, WTOP News, Voted as The Best of DC Real Estate agent in the Washington City Paper Readers Poll, and more...

- Owner of the **Greetings Virginia Sales Network**
- Associate Broker in VA, Broker in MD

REAL ESTATE EVOLUTION

- Instructor at Moseley Real Estate Schools – The teacher for new agents
- Co-founder of the premier real estate website www.GreetingsVirginia.com

Greetings Virginia Sales Network with Keller Williams Realty is a full-service brokerage that helps clients in the Washington DC metro region buy and sell properties in all price ranges. We have successfully completed thousands of buying and selling transactions for our clients.

Because of their extensive experience, owners Dan and Traci Rochon are frequent speakers and are often quoted in media stories about the current real estate market in the area as well as on a national basis.

The **Greetings Virginia Sales Network** with Keller Williams Realty has been in business since 2007 and has consistently been ranked as one of the highest producing teams in the DC area.

We get stuff done. Our Team only employs, learning based, competitive people with unlimited beliefs that never give up. Our key to success is to be in business with the right people in the proper roles. Our people are committed to mastering their positions to serve our clients. We can help you buy a home, sell a home, or invest in real estate. We believe in keeping God first, then family and then business.

Our offices have locations in Falls Church and Alexandria, VA.
We will be the number one sales team in our region, and we serve clients in VA, MD, and DC. We provide solutions! We have years of experience in helping home sellers to achieve their goals and to solve their problems.

While you go through the selection process to hire the best agent, you will instinctively eliminate all the agents who do not have the same knowledge.

Dan Rochon

Made in the USA
Coppell, TX
01 March 2021